HOW TO THINK LIKE
A PHILOSOPHER

HOW TO THINK LIKE A PHILOSOPHER

Scholars, Dreamers and Sages Who Can
Teach Us How to Live

PETER CAVE

BLOOMSBURY CONTINUUM
LONDON · OXFORD · NEW YORK · NEW DELHI · SYDNEY

BLOOMSBURY CONTINUUM
Bloomsbury Publishing Plc
50 Bedford Square, London, WC1B 3DP, UK
29 Earlsfort Terrace, Dublin 2, Ireland

BLOOMSBURY, BLOOMSBURY CONTINUUM and the Diana logo are trademarks
of Bloomsbury Publishing Plc

First published in Great Britain 2023
Paperback 2024

A catalogue record for this book is available from the British Library

Library of Congress Cataloguing-in-Publication data has been applied for

ISBN: PB: 978-1-3994-0595-9; TPB: 978-1-3994-0791-5;
eBook: 978-1-3994-0592-8; ePDF: 978-1-3994-0594-2

2 4 6 8 10 9 7 5 3 1

Typeset by Deanta Global Publishing Services, Chennai, India
Printed and bound in Great Britain by CPI Group (UK) Ltd, Croydon CR0 4YY

MIX
Paper | Supporting
responsible forestry
FSC® C171272

To find out more about our authors and books visit www.bloomsbury.com
and sign up for our newsletters

In Memory

of

Andrew Harvey and Roger Coe

Praise for *How to Think Like a Philosopher*

'A very enjoyable introduction into Western philosophy. Light, conversational, entertaining and intellectually stimulating.'

Daily Philosopher

'This is an ideal guide to philosophical thinking; it does not try to reduce the views of those that it covers to bullet points, but instead engages with them in a thoughtful and witty way. Peter Cave is the perfect companion for a bright but leisurely walk through these labyrinths.'

Derek Matravers, Professor of Philosophy, The Open University,
Fellow of Churchill College, Cambridge

'Britain's wittiest philosopher.'

Raymond Tallis

'Here is an extraordinary philosophical journey taking us through a maze of thinkers. For all those seeking to understand the myriad modes of philosophical thinking—ancient and modern—this is the perfect introduction.'

Dan Cohn-Sherbok, Emeritus Professor of Judaism, University of Wales

'Peter Cave introduces the reader to thirty different thinkers. Not all are easily classified as academic philosophers: some are better thought of as sages or poets or playwrights. But each has something important to say about things that matter: rationality, science, sex, and duty, among other topics. Cave's approach is to introduce each thinker through their chosen questions. From Sappho to Wittgenstein, from Arendt to Spinoza, we are able to enter into a chosen figure's preoccupations and enjoyably think along. This is a much more effective and engaging approach than simple intellectual biography or summaries of key ideas. An absorbing and rewarding book.'

Tom Sorell, Professor of Politics and Philosophy, University of Warwick.

'Peter Cave introduces his top thirty thinkers with wit and clarity, and crams a surprising amount of judicious reflection into each of the short chapters.'

John Cottingham, Professor Emeritus of Philosophy, University of Reading

'Read this book. You may not learn to love like Sappho, cure like Avicenna, ponder like Spinoza, disguise yourself like Kierkegaard or rival any of the other fascinating eccentrics who fill the volume. But if you learn to think like Peter Cave – with freshness, humour, objectivity and penetration – you will have been amply rewarded.'

Professor Felipe Fernandez-Armesto, University of Notre Dame, author of
Out of Our Minds: What We Think and How We Came to Think It

CONTENTS

PROLOGUE

Philosophy begins in wonder.

Plato

Philosophers come in different shapes and sizes – and so does their thinking. Some write with an exuberance, with frenzy; others with meticulous care. Some with wit and charm; others with great seriousness and stolidity. Many are big, as sages, in that they offer the world a comprehensive way of looking at all things; others have a restricted focus. Some have the aim of correcting people's thinking; others seek to change people's lives. For some, indeed, their lives and philosophy intermesh; they live their philosophy.

Here, in these chapters, are significant examples of all the types, the lives, the philosophies – the *thinking* – and how that thinking may lead us to reassess how to live a human life.

Philosophers can differ over whether they deem themselves philosophers and whether they even deem certain thinking as philosophical. Through the centuries, the content of philosophy has much diminished, becoming more focused. Philosophy today is separated from the scientific disciplines; earlier they were one, albeit divided into natural philosophy and moral philosophy or, indeed, into the natural sciences and the moral sciences.

Many philosophers see philosophy as continuous with today's sciences, dealing in the most general and fundamental understanding of reality. Descartes wrote of philosophy as the Queen of the Sciences. Some, though, understand philosophical investigations as radically different from scientific ones; those philosophers view themselves as sorting out puzzles in language or making sense of how to live or treating philosophizing as itself vital to living, even as a form of deep therapy.

Introductions to philosophy usually begin with the announcement that the term is based in the ancient Greek, meaning 'lover of wisdom'. 'Lover of wisdom', though, could also be applied to certain poets, theologians, scientists, even new-age astrologers. University philosophy courses, in the English-speaking world, have a standard list, a canon, of great philosophers and topics. We always find Plato and Aristotle, Descartes and Hume and then the great Kant – and more recently Russell and Wittgenstein. The topics cover metaphysics with the mind/body problem, space and time. There is epistemology, namely understanding the nature of knowledge and truth; ethics and political philosophy; and at least a touch of the philosophy of logic and philosophy of science.

In introducing philosophical thinking, this book provides a lead-in to philosophers and to the many puzzles, disturbances and splendours in philosophy. It does more – for I have deliberately included some figures not usually deemed 'philosophers' to show that there are different ways of expressing philosophical thinking and different contexts in which that thinking may arise. Although the book centres on thirty philosophers, in quite a few cases their thinking is related to that of others. The book also weaves in some contemporary approaches that may help to illuminate the thinking of the past.

Philosophical thinking may be by way of formal arguments, but it may also be by aphorisms, provocative examples or experiments in thought. The thinkers may be recognized professors of philosophy or very distant from such a formal status, more akin to dreamers than scholars. Some are thought of as highly obscure; others are considered very clear writers. Martin Heidegger exemplifies the former; David Hume the latter.

Some are the greatest figures in traditional Western philosophy; others are little known as philosophers, but are significant literary figures. Some have had hard lives; some have not: contrast, for example, the secure life of G. E. Moore, a professor of philosophy at Cambridge, with that of Simone Weil, virtually starving herself to death in London.

In as far as the philosophers presented here have anything in common with regard to their thinking, it is that they are seeking to get at the truth, but not in the straightforward way of conducting physical experiments in a laboratory, engaging in archaeological digs or building yet bigger telescopes or colliders. They are exhibiting reality and how to live in different lights – and how well the lights enlighten can change from one day to the next.

Of course, the selection of the thirty philosophers is to some extent idiosyncratic; the chapters can provide only a flavour of the different styles of thought and theory – in part by means of a few abbreviated extracts of their writings as well as sketches of their lives.

With any philosopher, the thinking, beliefs and approaches will develop over time; so, what is provided here is but a snapshot, sometimes a medley of shots. Although the order is in the main obviously chronologically based on dates of birth, where philosophers' lives overlap, the chronology reflects more the order of philosophical influence or recognition. Perhaps I should add that most of these philosophers used the term 'man' to stand for human beings; some thoughts and quotations would sound odd or clumsy if 'person' or 'he or she' were deployed instead. The context makes what is meant clear (I hope), if gender or sex becomes a relevant distinguishing feature.

Philosophical thinking does require thinking; thinking things through. Wittgenstein – I am afraid that his name crops up a fair number of times – asks rhetorically, 'What's the good of having one philosophical discussion? It's like having one piano lesson.'

I hope that this work will tempt readers to think on, read on, rather than seeing it as one lesson. I hope that at least some of the philosophical thinking will come over as fascinating, irresistible, needing to be explored further and talked about with others. And here I risk another reference to a Wittgensteinian reflection. It is a challenge to the spirit of our times, a spirit guided by media pundits, social twitterings and commercially motivated urgings that we must have instant gratification.

The reflection is a recommendation. Wittgenstein wrote that when two philosophers meet, they should say to each other 'take your time'. That advice is timely – it can be seen as a well-deserved challenge to the *Zeitgeist*.

C. P. Cavafy's poem 'Ithaka' includes this advice:

When you start out on the way to Ithaka,
You should wish the journey long,
Full of adventure and of knowledge.

That could sound wildly grandiose for this book, but however you view your journey through these thirty philosophers and more, please, take your time.

Lao Tzu: The Way to Tao

I do not know its name. I call it Tao.

Lao Tzu

There is a tale of how in the 1960s some young people, hippies in California, for example, hear tell of a wise old woman who lives in the remotest of mountains in distant Tibet. She is as wise as wise can be and knows the meaning of life. A young man, eager to grasp the meaning of life, goes in search. He crosses continents, climbs mountains, swims lakes, leaps ravines, perspires in jungles, freezes in icy wastes – and after months and months of devoted journeying, he finds the wise old woman, living in the remotest of villages: that wise old woman who knows the meaning of life. She sits quietly, warming herself by some burning logs, her craggy face lit by flickering flames. After respectful words and knowing silences, the young man, impatient for the conclusion to his quest, blurts out, 'O wise woman, wise woman, tell me, please, what is the meaning of life?'

The wise old woman looks thoughtful; her face now half in shadow. She stretches her eyes at the distant stars, her craggy brow furrowed. The young man feels a whole universe of understanding within her gaze. Eventually comes a whispered reply: 'Life is a fountain.'

'Life is a fountain?' The young man cannot contain his anger. 'I've walked the earth. I've crossed oceans, hacked through jungles, risked body and soul – just to be told that life is a fountain?'

'You mean it's not a fountain? Well, whatever you say ...'

———

That is not a tale from Lao Tzu; it is not a tale about Lao Tzu – but it could be. It could be because Lao Tzu is identified as the author of Taoism's most famous text and that text deals with the meaning of life, offering a version of Quietism, of quietly accepting how things are – of being, indeed, unbothered by whether life is a fountain or not. In Quietist mode, the wise old woman who knows the meaning of life may just as well have said nothing. She could have showed the meaning of life by silently gazing across at the distant mountains and the setting sun.

With Lao Tzu, we experience philosophical thinking much clothed in enigma, yet for many, possessed of great depth. Before saying more about Lao Tzu the man, here is the first section from the famous Taoist (Daoist) text, *Tao Te Ching* (Daodejing), *The Way and its Powers*, the classic of *Dao* and *De*:

> The Tao that can be told is not the eternal Tao;
> The name that can be named is not the eternal name.
> Nameless, it is the origin of Heaven and Earth;
> Named, it is the mother of all things.

In reading those first lines, we may despair over their meaning, yet as we read on through the whole of the work, we encounter straightforward themes: that the greatest misfortune for human beings is not to know contentment;

that the worst calamity is the desire to acquire; that sages desire to be without desires.

———

Lao Tzu has all the makings of a sage – his name translates as 'Old Master' – though maybe he is nothing but a legend. I guess that could make him even more of a sage. He did become revered by some as a god. Who was he? Probably he was Li Er, court archivist of the Zhou Dynasty in the fourth century BC; maybe, though, he was Lao Dan, court astrologer. Some place him much earlier, as a contemporary of Confucius around the sixth or fifth century BC. Others doubt his very existence.

What, in fact, did he write? If author of the aforementioned *Tao Te Ching*, he must have been a fourth-century individual for that is now seen as the time of the work's composition. It is sometimes described as 'Laoist', a compilation, in eighty-one sections, of earlier Taoist writings, be they by an earlier Lao Tzu or by many hands.

Lao Tzu is, then, a philosopher whose very existence, activities and writings are covered by the shrouds of mystery. In understanding his work, there is the added complexity of translation and transliteration of the classical Chinese language. For ease, let us accept (or pretend) that the *Tao Te Ching* gives us the fascinating thinking of Lao Tzu.

The *Tao Te Ching* consists of thoughts so ancient, so enigmatic, presented so differently from traditional Western philosophy, that it rarely features in standard introductions to philosophy; it offers thinking that verges on religious belief and promotion of religious practices. Taoism has certainly influenced Zen Buddhism and neo-Confucianism. Taoist writings, though, can be read as deep and fascinating reflections on the nature of reality and therefore, how to conduct our lives.

Such reflections, albeit not so enigmatically presented, are fundamental philosophical fare.

What, then, is the Tao, the Way? What is the way to the Way? The Tao, in some sense, is ultimate reality; it is the way of the world, yet ineffable, beyond description, as we saw with the first lines: 'The Tao that can be told is not the eternal Tao; / The name that can be named is not the eternal name.'

When we speak of the Tao, we are not grasping the 'eternal Tao' for it cannot be named, spoken of or described, yet we are not speaking of another Tao. The seeming contradiction may lead to easy dismissal, yet philosophers often battle with contradictions in grasping reality and, of course, philosophers with a religious bent struggle over an understanding of God, sometimes concluding that no supreme transcendent being can be properly conceptualized; at best we must employ impoverished analogies.

Even hard-headed philosophical reasoning can lead to talking about what cannot be understood. In the seventeenth century, John Locke, the influential philosopher often praised as a paradigm of good sense, spoke of substance as being 'we know not what'; in the eighteenth century the great Enlightenment philosopher Immanuel Kant made reference to the unknown 'noumena', things in themselves, behind the phenomena.

We shall shortly meet some contradictions exposed by Zeno of Elea in his provocative paradoxes. Zeno and subsequent philosophers, though, go hunting for errors in the reasoning or assumptions. That contrasts with the way of Lao Tzu; he appears to wallow in contradictions. Appearances, of course, can be deceptive. It is worth keeping that mantra in mind for much of philosophy is endeavouring to distinguish what really is so from what appears to be so.

Why, though, should we be worried about contradictions – about being *contra* our *diction*? One simple answer is that they pose problems for truth and for what we should think and do. If we are told that our flight to New York sets off this evening and also that it does not set off this evening, we are at a loss. Probably Lao Tzu uses contradictions – and sometimes exaggeration – to capture attention. After all, when people say, for example, 'what will be, will be', they are unlikely to have a bland identity statement in mind, but are expressing a feeling of inevitability, of fate.

We shall soon meet Lao Tzu talking about fate, so it is worth noting that just because it is true – obviously so – that what will be, will be, it does not follow that what will be, *must* be. It does not follow that there is a hand of fate. If Samantha's falling through the ice will happen, then, yes, it will happen, but it did not have to happen; she could have stayed at home, instead of skating on the ice-covered pond.

Returning directly to Lao Tzu, he writes:

There was something undifferentiated and yet complete,
Which existed before heaven and earth.
Soundless and formless it depends on nothing and does
not change.

Looking at the world around us, there is no evidence to show that there was something undifferentiated, yet complete, but perhaps it can be shown by some impeccable reasoning. Whatever, though, could that reasoning be? It is time to recall Wittgenstein's recommendation from the Prologue: let us take our time.

Maybe Lao Tzu's mysterious observations are intended to instil a certain attitude of reverence towards the world and how to behave. Human beings do not stand apart from the natural surroundings; Nature is one unified whole. That fits with today's concern for the environment and biodiversity, but goes further. Lao Tzu's thinking can enlighten by drawing us away from obsession with 'self'. If bewitched by that obsession, our ecological concerns are solely to do with promoting whatever is needed for human survival. Without the obsession – eventually, without the self – we recognize the intrinsic value of Nature as a whole. Taoism can lead to a 'deep green' view: Nature would have value even were humanity absent.

In Spinoza (Chapter 10), reality is 'looked at' in different ways: as God, but also as Nature. Maybe for Lao Tzu, reality can be appreciated as the *eternal* Tao, unchanging, yet also as the Tao in terms of everything around us, as Nature, as changes. Maybe by grasping that twosome, Lao Tzu is able to recommend how best to conduct our lives.

> See, all things howsoever they flourish
> Return to the root from which they grew.
> This return to the root is called Quietness …

Quietism cannot be sensibly understood as a position of no action; if we are to live (or die), we act. Further into the *Tao Te Ching*, Lao Tzu is recommending that we should avoid confrontation. For example, perhaps we should quietly accept criticism, even if unjustified, quelling feelings of anger; better still, develop a disposition so that no anger arises – there is then none to quell. An opposite rendering of Quietism's passivity, though, is that of non-interference with what will otherwise happen. That could mean not stopping one's anger at what was said.

The first reading reminds me of the woman soothing her friend troubled by some adversity in her personal life. 'Be philosophical,' she advised, 'then you won't need to think about it.' The second reading coheres with the thought that one should give voice to one's emotions, 'letting them hang out'.

Lao Tzu continues his above recommendation for the conduct of life with:

> Quietness is called submission to Fate;
> What has submitted to Fate has become part of the
> always-so.
> To know the always-so is to be illumined;
> Not to know it, means to go blindly to disaster.

What, though, does that mean? If we are part of Nature and its laws, then we can do nothing but follow Nature, follow Tao. If all is fated, then how can we not submit to fate? Whatever we do has been fated, whether we adopt a passive response, quelling our emotions, or give full voice to our feelings.

A deep pervasive philosophical question is whether we have free will and, if we do, how it links to acting freely. Taoism may free us from that puzzle. If we are part of the unified whole of Nature, such that the self is an illusion, then there is no scope for anguishing about whether *I* did this or that freely. Of course, with or without the illusion, 'we' still have to decide what to do. We may also wonder what to make of our desires, given that Lao Tzu tells us:

> Simplicity, which has no name, is free of desires.
> Being free of desires it is tranquil.
> And the world will be at peace of its own accord.

That peace, according to Taoism, is undermined by society's numerous moral rules, conventions and orders concerning the conduct of life. They produce confusion, reaction and strife:

> When the great Tao declined,
> The doctrines of humanity and righteousness arose.
> When knowledge and wisdom appeared
> There emerged great hypocrisy.

What disrupts harmony with Tao is – oddly, we may feel – learning and morality. We must use the *Tao Te Ching* to learn that we should not learn. We should strive to overcome striving. The child strives to walk, to catch, to spell, to count, and eventually can do so effortlessly, without striving. 'In the pursuit of Tao, one does less each day; one does less and less until one does nothing.'

> Always eliminate desires to observe Tao's mysteries;
> Always have desires to observe its manifestations.
> These two come forth in unity but diverge in name.
> Their unity is known as an enigma.

Following on from the above, is written, 'Within this enigma is yet a deeper enigma, / The gate of all mysteries.'

Lao Tzu in the *Tao Te Ching* is teaching, is being active, telling us how to behave, yet also, enigmatically, telling people, including himself, not to do so.

A simple way of avoiding the paradoxical stances of Lao Tzu is to insist that he did not exist and, in non-existence, anything goes. A better way is to take seriously observations within Wittgenstein's *Tractatus Logico-Philosophicus*, observations such as:

6.521   The solution of the problem of life is seen in the vanishing of this problem.

The wise old woman with whom this chapter opened was blasé over what to say about the meaning of life. Lao Tzu could not express what he sought to express without contradiction. The *Tractatus* continues:

> Is not this the reason why those to whom, after long doubting, the sense of life became clear, could not then say wherein this sense consisted?

6.522   There is indeed the inexpressible. This *shows* itself; it is
the mystical.

And so, the captivating enigmatic aphorisms in Taoist writings composed well over two millennia ago touch the thinking, consciously or no, of a major Western analytical philosopher, writing around a hundred years ago. That philosopher is indeed Ludwig Wittgenstein; he was jotting down those thoughts while voluntarily serving as a soldier in the Austro-Hungarian army during the First World War.

How to think like Lao Tzu? *Best, ultimately, to say nothing, but until then, 'go with the flow', go with Tao.*

2

Sappho: Lover

Eros, looser of limbs, tosses me about, bittersweet,
overmastering creature.

Sappho

Sappho, in today's popular imagination, is famed as lesbian, but hardly as philosopher. Let us look a little at her life before assessing her credentials as a philosopher of some significance. She lived in the early sixth century BC and lived, unsurprisingly, on Lesbos, whence derived the 'lesbian' term for female same-sex erotic encounters. Tourists see the island in that lesbian light, though in the 2010s the island became associated with the tragedy of migrants' desperate flights from Middle East horrors.

Although there is little reliable information on her life – she may have been married; she may have had a daughter – undoubtedly she is the most famous poetess of Greco-Roman antiquity, receiving the accolade 'poetrymaker' in apparently the earliest use of that term. Her poetry was lyrical, designed to be sung. During ancient times, it seems not to have been her lesbianism that was of great note, but her alleged licentiousness. Because of the latter some wondered whether there were two Sapphos, one the poet, the other a prostitute. The two professions, I note, are not incompatible.

Whether two or one, Sappho, in her writings, is much devoted to love; she is not, though, normally presented as a lover of wisdom, as a philosopher. Her love focused on the erotic and on young women, though not exclusively so. Yes, she had affairs with girls, but she fell in love with Phaon, the Ferryman – and fell in love so obsessively that, according to legend, she threw herself off the Leucadian Rock to her death. Her 'lesbian' accolade, some argue, is an anachronism. In evaluating the morality of sexual relations, the ancient Greek interest may have been not so much on the participants' sex as upon who was the more active partner, and who the passive.

Despite not being hailed as a philosopher, was Sappho in fact a philosopher? Not in the sense of a writer of carefully argued treatises, presenter of deductive arguments or a sage in the manner of Lao Tzu. The great philosophers of history usually seek to present comprehensive understandings of reality, of humanity and the universe. Sappho certainly did not do that. There is, though, no objection to philosophizing about just one aspect of life or the universe. In today's academia, most philosophers specialize in just one area, be it the philosophy of language, of mind, of emotions – even of dance. Sappho's main focus – on erotic love – is fine as an object for philosophical reflection.

What of her approach; namely, that of poetry or song? That too is fine. One reason for including Sappho in this book is to show how philosophical thinking can be recognized in poetry, even in poetry not wide-ranging. Philosophical thinking can be manifested by poets who identify themselves primarily as poets rather than as philosophers. Sappho's poetry shows her reflecting on sexual love, but also on a person's identity over time – philosophical reflections, indeed.

There is one practical difficulty in dealing with Sappho as philosopher. Sadly, 'her poetry' for us consists mainly of fragments, sometimes odd words on scraps of torn papyrus

– together with brief extracts quoted by later authors. With so little work surviving, some scholars question whether Sappho existed at all, thinking of her as a poetic construct of later centuries. One twentieth-century collection of women's writings leaves a blank page for the entry titled 'Sappho'. Other collections manage to expand Sappho and her work into pages of detailed discussion, evaluating her lesbianism and how she challenged the male gaze, a challenge both to a masculine style of poetry and to masculine-dominated cultures. With that domination in mind, I note that Aristotle honoured her for her fine poetry, adding the observation 'even though a woman'.

Her life may be seen as of philosophical relevance simply because it highlights the cultural relativity of the treatment of men and women and so-called 'normal' sexual relations. It is her writings, though, deserving of focus here; and they certainly had philosophical impact. Of course, what we may find appealing in Sappho's thinking rests in part on the understanding of translators.

Socrates and Plato, without reliance on translators, praised her as the sublime poetess, 'beautiful Sappho, the tenth muse'. Plato used her language of erotic love, her descriptions of desire, to give voice to his belief that we could aspire to recognizing Beauty itself. His praise for Sappho is quite astonishing in view of his usual disparagement of poets. They are low down in the hierarchy of reincarnated souls.

What particular philosophical thinking can be gleaned from Sappho's fragments? A term of hers that has sparked reflection is *bittersweet* (γλυκύπικρον; *glukupikron*). In a fragment (130) we encounter:

Once again limb-loosening Love makes me tremble, the bittersweet irresistible creature.

The 'bittersweet' reference offers a quick summary of the conflicting feelings that arise simultaneously when moved by passionate love. There is the sweetness of being drawn to the beloved, yet also the helplessness and desperation, as if invaded by an alien desire. 'When I desire you, a part of me is gone,' writes Sappho.

That bittersweet conflict at a particular time is distinct from love-driven conflicts that arise over time. Love and desire, however sweet now, may bring bitterness later on, be it through loss, jealousy or other desires taking control. However much we may delight in a love affair, we may be aware that later on, we shall regret the involvements or suffer from the loss of the beloved. Love exposes us to risk. Sappho's 'bittersweet', though, is bringing out how, contrary to any idea of rationality as the greatest value, conflicting feelings of erotic love are part of what it is to be human; for many, it is being human at its very best.

Sappho's language exposes love's madness; experiences run across all our senses. In one fragment (31), Sappho refers to a man who 'seems equal to the gods' and who is fascinated by a girl opposite him; she is 'speaking sweetly and laughing delightfully'. The poem is written as if Sappho is addressing the girl, and articulates how the sight and sound of the girl

> makes my heart flutter in my breast;
> for when I look at you even for a short time,
> it is no longer possible for me to speak
>
> but it is as if my tongue is broken
> and immediately a subtle fire has run over my skin,
> I cannot see anything with my eyes,
> and my ears are buzzing …

There are various speculations by commentators. Was Sappho jealous of the man? Was she showing how her love for the girl far exceeded any interest in a man, even one akin to the gods?

Those questions aside, Sappho's language brings to the fore the extensive effects of erotic love on the senses, on what we see, on our hearing, on tingling of the skin, on becoming tongue-tied. She continues:

> a cold sweat comes over me, trembling
> seizes me all over, I am paler
> than grass, and I seem nearly
> to have died.

There can be the sense of panic and desperation – all so human. We may well grasp why Sappho flung herself off the rock. Such frenzy in life certainly shows that the judgement 'man is a rational animal' does not always apply. Indeed, were rationality constantly to the fore, always triumphant, would not much that is valuable in life be lost?

Throughout history there have been numerous scandals, showing how sexual desire can dominate lives. Schopenhauer – we meet him much later – draws attention to how erotic desire 'does not hesitate to interfere with the negotiations of statesmen and the investigations of the learned. It knows how to slip its love-notes and ringlets into ministerial portfolios and philosophical manuscripts.' Sappho vividly shows how we are often rocked by such desires and how those desires should not be dismissed as unworthy, but should be praised.

The philosophical question arises of quite what is the object of sexual desire? Sappho describes how she is affected by the girl. She hears the sweet laughter, maybe adores the smile – and so forth – and so, would any girl with those qualities 'do' for her? If you want a glass of Chablis, it usually matters not at all whether it is this glass or that glass, if from the same bottle. The erotic love for someone, though, is aimed at that particular individual. The object of sexual desire – an obscure object, true – involves a particular individual. Of course, there are related questions about the meaning of wanting to 'possess' the other and be 'possessed', questions touched on when we reach Jean-Paul Sartre (Chapter 24).

———————

Earlier there was mention of how love places us at risk. It is a hazard for we may be at the mercy of the changes in the other and the other's desires. In Fr 94, Sappho describes the loss being experienced by the other woman in the words of that woman:

'I'm not pretending; I wish I were dead.'

And then Sappho describes the scene:

She was leaving me in tears,
and over and over she said to me:
'Sappho, it hurts; what's happened to us is just so bad;
it isn't my choice, I swear it, to leave like this.'

Sappho answers: 'Go and be happy; remember me', reminding the girl of all the good things enjoyed, 'for at my side, many the crowns of violets and roses and many the garlands woven from flowers you have cast round your delicate neck'.

Despite awareness of possible losses and vulnerabilities such as the above, love still leads to (it seems) voluntary commitments. In Thomas Hardy's 1895 novel, *Jude the Obscure*, we have:

And so the two swore that at every time of their lives, until death took them, they would assuredly believe, feel, and desire exactly as they had believed, felt and desired during the preceding weeks. What was as remarkable as the undertaking itself was the fact that nobody seemed at all surprised at what they swore.

The undertaking is remarkable indeed and, even though aware of the risks, people wittingly make commitments in terms of continuing to love each other 'whatever happens'. That is a projection of the self – and of the other person – into the future, even a dim and distant future.

Of course, we are all well aware of the loss of youth, of smooth skin, of hair. The mirror exposes us to wrinkles, memory to forgetfulness and knees to weariness. Some Sappho fragments show her contemplating the inevitability of ageing and mortality. In Anne Carson's version, Sappho speaks of how 'my skin once soft is now taken by old age / my hair turns white from black. / And my heart is weighed down and my knees do not lift / that once were light to dance as fauns.'

While Sappho laments the difficulties and losses associated with growing old, she also reflects on ageing in the context of more general ruminations on the relationship between permanence and change in human life and in all of nature. Soon after Sappho, arrive the 'pre-Socratic' philosophers intrigued by such matters. Parmenides insisted that in reality nothing changes; Heraclitus, by contrast, maintained that 'everything is in flux' – everything changes.

Sappho also has us facing death. She writes of how 'you will lie there when you die, and there will be no memory of you ever, nor desire for you in the future: for you do not have a share of the roses of Pieria ...' (55) – that is, your art, even as a famous poet, may not transcend to that of immortality. Elsewhere, though, she does speak of how 'someone will remember us in the future' (147). What, though, constitutes my 'self' such that it can be remembered?

Commentators have drawn much more from Sappho, despite the raggedness of the surviving writings. Some emphasize how she draws attention to the loss of boundaries. Through ageing and death, for example, Sappho suggests that a woman's beauty may be rediscovered in the natural surroundings of scents, flowers and song. Here again, as with Lao Tzu, contemporary passions for human beings as part of Nature exist in writings of antiquity.

Perhaps because of her sex or the lesbianism or the eroticism – probably combined with some voyeurism – Sappho has provided a continuing fascination over the centuries. In recent decades, her glorification of the erotic has received much attention, in part because of the development of feminist and gender-fluidity movements. Her thinking is seen as breaking down the boundaries of sexual stereotypes. She was also associated with the posing of riddles; that, from a philosophical perspective, can be viewed as showing once again the conflicts to which our rationality gives rise when seeking sharp boundaries. In fact, some argue that her association with riddles also leads into gender matters, for such riddles would often be presented by courtesans to their male 'clients'.

Overall, Sappho's poetry may be an incantation to the gods – to something beyond – and it is worth noting how often in orgasmic pleasure, there are cries of 'Oh, god', as if being transported out of this world. That 'out of this world' thought leads us to Plato.

Plato expressly applies Sappho's uplifting descriptions of erotic arousal to – curiously – people making progress in their philosophical understanding of reality, of beauty and truth. Sappho's work, then, as well as being philosophical, has been a stimulus for the proper understanding of the philosophical quest as ascent – at least according to Plato.

How to think like Sappho? *Embrace the Muses, the erotic and irrational.*

3

Zeno of Elea: Tortoise Backer *and* Parmenidean Helper

All is one.

Parmenides

Philosophers conduct thought experiments. In armchairs, they dream up scenarios that are perfectly possible, apply some seemingly good reasoning, yet reach outrageous conclusions, offensive to common sense. Zeno of Elea was an originator and master of certain thought experiments, though maybe without the armchair. His experiments were so striking that they are now well known as 'Zeno's paradoxes'; they are much examined. He tells, for example, of a race between Achilles and a tortoise.

Achilles is renowned as the fastest runner in ancient Athens. The tortoise is a regular slow-moving creature, yet able to head in the appropriate direction towards a winning line, without stopping. For ease, let us call him 'Mr T'. Achilles, ever an Athenian gentleman, gives Mr T a head start, well, many heads; suppose Mr T has a starting position one hundred feet ahead of Achilles. Let us pretend that Achilles runs ten times faster than Mr T. There is no contradiction in any of that. Here, then, is Zeno's reasoning; it is simple, yet leads to a startling conclusion.

Before Achilles can win the race, he must overtake Mr T. Before he can overtake Mr T, he must reach Mr T's current position. He therefore needs first to get to Mr T's starting location, one hundred feet ahead. By the time he does that, Mr T will have 'run' to a position ten feet ahead; so, Achilles must now reach that new position, by which time, Mr T will have managed to have gone one foot further on; and by the time that position is attained by Achilles, Mr T will be 0.1 foot ahead ... And so the race continues, seemingly endlessly. Mr T is always ahead; Achilles always has another distance to run.

That is, I quip, philosophy for the downtrodden: happy is Mr T for, it seems, Achilles can never catch him up, let alone overtake him. True, the distances ahead are diminishing – 0.1; 0.01; 0.001; and so on – but they never vanish to zero. For Zeno, that thought experiment has shown at the very least that we are in a conceptual confusion in our common-sense belief about how the spatial world is divisible. Philosophers ever since have tried to overcome that confusion. Before we look more closely, Zeno's thinking needs some context.

Zeno lived during the mid-fifth century BC and spent most of his time in Elea, a city in the then Greek-speaking part of southern Italy. He may well have visited Athens; Socrates may have heard him lecture. Plato and Aristotle certainly tried to deal with his paradoxes. In fact, we have Aristotle to thank for judging Zeno's paradoxes so important that they deserved to be preserved. We must not, by the way, conflate this Zeno with another eminent Zeno, namely, Zeno of Citium, founder of Stoicism (noted in Chapter 7).

To grasp the role of Zeno's paradoxes, we turn to Parmenides, born c.515 BC in Elea. His philosophical work has been a major influence on Western philosophy and, unsurprisingly, he became known as the founder of Eleatic Philosophy. Zeno is thought of as a member of that group and not solely because of locational residence.

All that we have of Parmenides' thinking are parts of his great metaphysical poem *The Way of Truth*. Its enigmatic prologue tells of the philosopher, the poet, on a mystical journey, beyond the realm of day and night, being welcomed by a goddess. The philosopher must learn from her all things, 'both the unshaken heart of well-rounded truth, and the opinions of mortals in which there is no true reliance'. Although the journey is possessed of a mystical air, the goddess's intention is to display the truth, as established by reason. That truth is radically different from everyday opinion. Here, she entices:

> Come now, and I will tell you the only ways of inquiry that are to be thought of:
>
> The one, that a thing is and that it is impossible for it not to be, is the path of Persuasion (for she attends upon Truth).
>
> The other, that a thing is not and that there is a requirement that it should not be; this I declare is an altogether indiscernible track – for you can neither know what is not (that cannot be done) nor point it out.

The Way of Truth relies on a simple assumption: regarding whatever we are investigating, 'either it exists or it does not exist'. Those are the two options. The second option is dismissed; after all, there is nothing to investigate if 'it' does not exist. The path of truth must, then, address only what is. In everyday life, we fail to take on board that simple point for, says the goddess, we look with aimless eyes and our hearing is filled with noise.

Once we are clear that we are able to address only what exists, reason shows us that what exists must be imperishable, uncreated, changeless, perfect (apparently, even well rounded), for, were it not, there would need to be reference to what does not exist – at different times and in different places – but that would be placing us on the 'altogether indiscernible track'.

Parmenides offers us a 'monism': reality consists of one fundamental thing or type of thing. His monism is extreme for the one reality is a single eternal undifferentiated whole. Such a monism may remind us of Lao Tzu's mysterious claims about the eternal Tao; it also returns us to Zeno's paradoxes for they have been understood as supporting the Parmenidean understanding of reality or, at the very least, showing that if we think about reality in the everyday way, we meet with contradictions.

Paradoxes feature heavily in philosophy, but quite what is a paradox? The word derives from the Greek – 'para' and 'doxa' – 'above, beyond, belief'; but that fails to capture fully the nature of philosophical paradoxes. After all, some people find it beyond belief that wealthy countries such as the United Kingdom and the United States have so many citizens who are homeless and hungry. In 1616 a certain John Bullokar offered as a paradox the affirmation that 'the earth doth mooue round, and the heauens stand still'.

As seen with Zeno's Achilles and Tortoise paradox, we start off with what seems to be obviously true and yet, after some simple reasoning, conclude with something that seems manifestly false. Here is another famous philosophical paradox, also derived from Greek antiquity. We may reasonably accept that any statement is either true or false, but that hits the Liar Paradox. 'I am lying' – if true, then it is false; if false, then true. That paradox derives from Epimenides, a Cretan, also of the sixth century BC. It needs to be tidied – after all, maybe some claims are neither true nor false – but once tidied up into, for example, 'This proposition expressed is not true', we confront a lingering paradox that still causes trouble. Let us, though, return to Zeno.

In the Achilles and Tortoise paradox, Zeno had deployed a picturesque and memorable tale to open our eyes to a confusion in our thinking that is usually hidden. We can strip away the animation and the fun of the tortoise and concentrate solely on any physical movement – as Zeno does in other paradoxes. You aim to cycle across San Francisco's Golden Gate Bridge; before you can reach the other side, you get halfway across, then you must traverse half of the remaining half and then half of that remainder, and so on: half, then a quarter, then an eighth, then a sixteenth – the series is endless. However hard you cycle, you can never reach the end; there is always another half-distance to go.

In those examples, distances are being run or cycled, but Zeno does not believe any of that happens in reality for via another paradox he shows how we can never get started in a movement. Before I can reach the window at the other end of the room, I need to get halfway; but before I can get halfway, I need to get a quarter way, but before – and so on. Here there is no distance that we can rightly say is the first distance to be crossed for there is always a prior half-distance. Of course, there is nothing essential about the fractions being 'halves'.

Bertrand Russell once commented that the point of philosophy is to start with something so simple as not to seem worth stating, and to end with something so paradoxical that no one will believe it. Whether that in fact is the point is open to doubt, but certainly many non-philosophers may well believe that it is, given the outcome of a lot of philosophizing.

Similar puzzles, I add, arise over persistence through time and space without any motion. For you to exist over the coming hour, you must exist for the first half-hour, then an additional quarter, then a further eighth and so forth. Once again, there is an endless series. Consider any extended object. This book is so many inches wide; its width, then, is constituted by an endless number of ever-decreasing widths. As we look at it from the left to the right, there's half the width, then a quarter, then an eighth – and so on.

Zeno's paradoxes arise because when considering any distance, it seems that 'in thought' we can divide again and again in ever-decreasing spans – and those divisions are endless. We confront smaller and smaller distances to cross, but they are still distances, however small. Dividing a distance again and again does not suddenly create no distance at all. As well as supporting Parmenides in his insistence that reality must be an indivisible unity, Zeno may also then be challenging Pythagoras (yes, of Pythagoras's Theorem fame) and his application of mathematical concepts to reality.

Whatever is quite going on in Zeno's thinking, we may be at a loss over how he handles a fundamental problem with his stance. If we are suffering illusion – if we are on the Way of Falsehood, so to speak – in perceiving the world around us as divisible, containing movement, what are we to make of our experiences, our thoughts and the sequences of sounds, of words, in Zeno's paradox lectures, that chop and change, come and go? Are those changes also somehow illusory? Is it an illusion that we are having changing illusions? Are those illusions not 'really' changing? Such questions exemplify a good move in many philosophical discussions for it is often useful to ask how a philosophical position plays upon itself. We met that feature of the 'self-referential' with the Liar Paradox above, where 'This proposition is not true' turns upon itself, creating the conceptual chaos.

Zeno, of course, propounds his arguments and, maybe with some Zenoic arrogance, concludes that reality is not as most people take it to be. Motion, divisibility, change, are illusions. Philosophers in their philosophical thinking, though, even if seduced by Zeno's arguments, would usually conclude, maybe with some humility, not that there is something radically wrong in our common-sense understanding of reality, but that there must be something wrong in the arguments.

A temptation is to point to mathematical ignorance as the cause of Zeno's paradoxical trouble. Mathematicians and philosophers of a mathematical bent happily talk of how an infinite or endless arithmetical series can converge to a limit. For example, the series half plus a quarter plus an eighth – and so on – converge and the resultant sum is one. In response, we may still ask how it is, if it be so, that an end can be reached by means of following an *endless* series. To converge is not to reach.

Philosophical thinking can have the determination of a Zeno to show up reality for what it is and to show us up for getting it all so wrong. Others 'save appearances' by way of establishing that the concept of infinity, when properly understood, can be applied to the physical world, usefully so without paradox. Another way of philosophical thinking, though, is to challenge the assumption that a concept with problem-free application over there must also have problem-free application over here.

Consider the game of chess: there are no part moves; there is no place for halves or quarters of moves. To insist that because there are moves in chess there must therefore be part chess moves is to misunderstand the nature of chess moves. It is to treat the moves as if they were bread rolls, where we can have half a roll. In fact, games of chess, with moves, can be played with no movements of pieces at all, but as written lists of sequences of pieces on different squares. What is and what is not possible with regard to the moves of a chess game do not carry over to what is and what is not possible in the world of movements of pieces of bread or wood, be they shaped as chess pieces or not.

Zeno may respond by noting that, in contrast to the inapplicability of mathematical division to chess moves, it seems that mathematics can be properly applied to physical movements with useful results – train timetables do not (usually) contain fantasy arrival times – and yet we suffer the paradoxes. That rests, though, on the 'properly' in the response. After all, computer simulations can accurately and properly model weather changes, including rain; but that the simulation and the computer, when modelling such, remain dry does not show that rain is dry. Mathematicians' talk of parallel lines meeting at infinity does not show that there is a place in the universe where they meet. And while a 'summed' infinite series of abstract runs may consist of ever-diminishing lengths, that does not prove that an Achilles in hobnailed boots in the real world could 'run' distances any smaller than say a few feet.

The challenges of Zeno's paradoxes and Parmenides' *The Way of Truth* remain serious and wonderful examples of philosophical thinking. They provide provocations with which philosophers must deal and live through – and they are exciting ones at that.

How to think like Zeno? *Embrace paradoxes – ever ready to reject common-sense understandings of reality.*

4

Gadfly: aka 'Socrates'

The unexamined life is not worth living.
Socrates

Student encounters with philosophy in the Western tradition very quickly and early on are with Socrates and the enquiry loosely known as 'Socratic dialectic'. Philosophical thinking is at its best when in debate, in the to-ing and fro-ing of questioning, delving, proposing, rejecting – being in dialogue with others – in the quest for the truth about the nature of, for example, knowledge, courage, justice, even of truth.

It is because Socrates went out of his way to question the Athenian 'great and the good' about such matters that he received the accolade of 'gadfly', a horsefly, a botfly. He also received a death sentence. Here he is, standing before a jury in the Athenian Court:

> If you kill me you will not easily find another like me, who, if I may use such a ludicrous figure of speech, am a sort of gadfly, given to the State by God; and the State is like a great and noble steed who is tardy in his motions owing to his very size, and requires to be stirred into life.

He was charged with corrupting the youth and worshipping false gods. In reality, it was for his gadfly stirrings, for his Socratic questioning.

> I am that gadfly which God has given and all day long and
> in all places I am always fastening upon you, arousing and
> persuading and reproaching you.

Although Socrates is such a highly important and influential
figure in philosophy, he is no mainstream philosopher. He
was, if you like, the forerunner of philosophers. The Greek
term for philosophy was first coined by Plato, the follower
of Socrates. We could say something similar about Jesus. He
was not a Christian, but his life and teachings gave rise to
Christianity.

Socrates wrote nothing, but we have one of his followers
to thank, namely, the aforementioned Plato, one of the very
greatest philosophers, for recording Socrates' philosophical
thinking in all its glorious expression. At some point the
voice of Socrates in Plato's earlier writings transforms from
authentic Socrates to Plato himself in the middle and later
dialogues. Virtually all of Plato's writings portray Socrates in
dialogue with well-positioned Athenians – the politicians,
the wealthy, the know-it-alls, all those, in fact, who claim
to 'know'.

In the dialogues, Socrates as gadfly 'stings' others into
reflecting more deeply about their so-called knowledge.
The dialogues are often named after a key participant: we
shall shortly hear of Meno, for example, in the dialogue
Meno. Socrates in fact was not just a gadfly; he was
sometimes portrayed as a torpedo-ray that electrifies his
opponents or as a venomous snake, striking at the heart of
dubious beliefs, or as a stingray with a numbing effect on
others because of his display of their inconsistencies. The
typical outcome of a dialogue is that he has revealed to
his opponents that, after all, they did not know what they
thought they knew.

The gadfly image provides us with a central component of much philosophical thinking – namely, to challenge, question and engage in free speech. Openness of debate, perhaps because it stings, can always come under attack; we encounter that today, even in liberal democracies, where speakers, for example, may be barred from debates, meet with 'no-platforming', a 'cancel culture', or may silence themselves, fearing their speech be deemed 'hate speech'.

Our Gadfly, Plato tells us, also viewed his activity as akin to that of a midwife, giving birth to latent knowledge; that birth had required us to think clearly and honestly. The midwife is a highly powerful and apt metaphor: philosophers, in the main, conduct their philosophizing by reasoning rather than by empirical research. Empirical research can be scientific experiments involving explosive risks in chemical laboratories or archaeological digs leading to dirty hands and limb breakages, or may require hugely expensive particle accelerators at CERN. Philosophizing, ideally with a glass of wine or two, in dialogue with others, avoids those risks, though it may lead to condemnation if one says out loud things that others object to hearing. It also runs the risk – well, the near certainty – of disturbing our casual, convenient and comfortable so-called knowledge.

Philosophical thinking, maybe surprisingly, can show us a lot about the world – and our lives within – without any direct engagement with empirical research. That is a fascinating feature of philosophy, of how our concepts have developed through language and how the language embodies much empirical information (even misinformation) about the world. Mind you, some maintain doubts about the value of philosophers and their reasoning. Aristophanes, the dramatist, offered a picture of Socrates as existing with his head in the clouds, out of touch with reality. That portrayal, though, is unfair. For example, when questioning Meno, a political and military figure, Socrates stung him into consideration of knowledge and true belief. Do they differ? How do they differ? Having opened Meno's mind to the topic, Socrates tells of the fine statues sculpted by Daedalus. The statues, so the myth went, were so lifelike that they needed to be tied down.

If you have one of his statues untethered, it is not worth much; it gives you the slip like a runaway slave. A tethered specimen, though, is very valuable for the statues are magnificent creations.

Seeing Meno's bewilderment, Socrates explains:

True beliefs are a fine thing and do all sorts of good as long as they stay in their place; but they will not stay long. They run away from a man's mind, so they are not worth much until you tether them by working out the reason.

The dialogue opens Meno's eyes to the fact that to possess knowledge, we typically need some sort of justification, evidence or reasons, for what we believe. Without the justification, even if we have possession of the truth, we are exposed to silver tongues that may lead us astray or to social media bombardments to get us to believe something else. Of course, more needs to be said, for we could unwittingly be tethered to false beliefs through indoctrination; the tethering, then, ought not to be so strong that we close our eyes to any counter-evidence to what we believe.

As a result of Gadfly's stinging proclivities, Socrates' opponents, as Meno above, often lapsed into confusion and inconsistencies. Socrates became judged the wisest man of Athens. 'Why ever do they think that I'm the wisest?' he wondered. He came to realize that he was the wisest because he knew that he didn't know. Being pedantic, I need to add that he needed to add 'apart from that piece of knowledge'. Not being pedantic, I add that that feature of Socrates' understanding of himself is worth serious reflection; it merits application to ourselves.

Who knows whether Socrates was being ironic in his claim to ignorance, but for all of us there is value in stepping back and recognizing, maybe gloomily, that we can often be wrong and not know what we think we know. Philosophical thinking requires some humility and humility is a value to be derived from Socrates – as also is irony. I should add the more optimistic thought that sometimes we may wrongly think that we do not know things when we in fact do know. In both cases, there is value in reflecting, thinking further, and even trying things out. You may be convinced that you have forgotten how to speak Greek and how to swim, yet once back in the land of tavernas, you find yourself conversing pretty well, and once in the water, swim you do.

———————————

This chapter opened with Socrates defending himself at his trial. Were he alive now, replicating his activities in Athens, the police could be threatening arrest. After all, he could well be speaking out on controversial matters, perhaps causing offence to certain minority or even majority groups. Newspaper headlines could be calling for him to be hanged or at least imprisoned with 'keys thrown away', though that would be for activities other than the gadfly stinging. As was not unusual in ancient Greece, Socrates' activities included romantic love for certain teenage boys, 'beardless youths', a love that was not confined to guiding a boy's intellectual development into adulthood. Socrates, though, certainly argued for, and aspired to, the elevation of romantic love into an intellectual love of beauty and truth, these days vaguely known as 'Platonic love'.

By the way, the great nineteenth-century translator and scholar of Plato – Benjamin Jowett at Balliol College, Oxford – took a dim view of those students drawn to Socrates' interest in love's physical aspects. Jowett maintained a purification agenda; he tried to stop his students from analysing Plato's writings about Socrates and the beardless youths. Today's schools and universities revise their programmes to exclude works that may offend or upset some students or that may express views or use language no longer acceptable. Mark Twain's *Huckleberry Finn* comes to mind. Those revisions, censorships, do not bode well; they draw near to the Athenians condemning Socrates to death and, as we shall see, to Spinoza having his works banned and to Bertrand Russell being sacked when in New York.

At the trial, Socrates manifested no remorse, sought no excuse for his actions. In his speech to the jury – reported by Plato in the work *Apology*, though paradoxically with no apology – Socrates argued that the city of Athens should be praising him for his challenges. True, Socrates was not much burdened by the humility mentioned earlier, of knowing only that he did not know.

It was a show trial. It was inevitable that he would be found guilty and sentenced to death – to drink hemlock, a poison – but it was not inevitable that the sentence would be carried out. Socrates could easily have escaped from Athens – he had wealthy friends – and the authorities probably would have been pleased with that outcome. Socrates, being Socrates, though, was determined not to take flight; and Plato's dialogue *Crito* has Socrates explaining why.

Socrates argued that he should obey the law, even when, as in this case, he could show that what he was doing, his so-called law-breaking, was beneficial to Athens. The reasons that Socrates gave for obedience are presented, in Plato's fine dramatist hands, as Socrates imagining the Laws speaking to him.

The Laws point out that Socrates' relationship to them is akin to that of a child to his parents and one should obey and respect one's parents. Socrates had benefited from education and the security of the State. Furthermore, he had been free to leave, yet had voluntarily remained; thus, he effectively had accepted the Laws. Those considerations, even today, are relevant to whether and when civil disobedience is justified. For Socrates, the consequences of escape would have been his acting unjustly. Socrates, being Socrates, could see that clearly – and for him to act unjustly would be to self-harm. Here we meet the provocative and fascinating belief that what is in one's best interests coincides with what justice demands.

———————

We encounter the end of Socrates' life in Plato's dialogue *Phaedo*. Some have argued that Socrates' death was a suicide for, as said, he could have escaped, but instead he voluntarily took the hemlock.

Socrates likened himself to a swan; yes, he was keen on metaphorical descriptions. All his life had been a swan-song. Without any philosophizing during life on earth, one's soul could pass into the body of a donkey, a hawk, a wasp, an ant and so forth. Socrates' idea seems to be that, on earthly death, his soul could continue, without the worldly distractions of food and drink – and young men's bodies, we could add. That tied in with his understanding of genuine knowledge, of the eternal truths of mathematics and goodness: that knowledge is a form of recollection from our existence prior to this earthly life. In a way, his death was a cure. It freed him from distractions of the flesh, allowing him access to an eternal reality – well, assuming he avoided being landed in the body of a donkey or hawk – and so on.

The hemlock's numbing slowly moved up his body. His last words, addressed to Crito, are reputed to have been:

Crito, we owe a cock – a rooster – to Asclepius; pay it and do not neglect it.

Asclepius has usually been taken as the God of healing, though some believe he was an historical figure with healing powers. Socrates' last words can be seen as alluding to his beliefs: that the soul is immortal, that, with death, he is being healed, freed from this earthly existence. Of course, it could also be possessed of an ambiguity, dovetailing with the Socratic irony. Does this healing god deserve to be paid, when his patient is about to die?

Plato closes his account of Socrates' death, of the 'end of our friend', saying that of all the men he has known, 'he was the wisest and justest and best.'

To value Socrates, his life and philosophy, there is no need to buy into the belief that we each possess an immortal soul. Apart from the significance of gadfly questioning – and, I should argue, apart from the value of irony – Socrates shows us the importance and fascination of not gliding through life without reflection. His most fundamental thought is that the unexamined life is not worth living; it derives from the Delphic oracle 'Know thyself'. Allow me to add that, at times, we may well feel it is better not to examine our lives too closely. There are, as ever, degrees and degrees of examination; there are times and places – even for deep philosophical reflection about one's life …

———

How to think philosophically with Socrates? – *Enter into honest, questioning dialogue, taking arguments to wherever they lead.*

5

Plato: Charioteer, Magnificent Footnote Inspirer

'Nobody Does It Better'

*All who actually engage in philosophy aright are
practising nothing other than dying
and being dead.*
Attributed to Socrates by Plato

'Platus', in Greek, means 'broad' and Plato of the fourth
century BC was indeed broad as in broad-shouldered, though
also broad in intellect, broad in vision and broad in seeking
the best for society. Plato expanded our appreciation of so
many perplexities and possible answers and approaches to
life and the universe. 'Nobody does it better.' Well, some
back Aristotle over Plato, but for deploying philosophy to
lift our eyes to wonders beyond this world, Plato has no
competition.

Plato is first encountered as presenter of Socrates. The
excellence, provocation and fine arguments and metaphors
within Plato's thirty-three dialogues led to the twentieth-
century observation by Arthur Whitehead, mathematician and
philosopher, that the whole of Western philosophy, since Plato,
is but a 'footnote to Plato'. While Plato was hugely stimulated
and influenced by Socrates, it is pretty clear that most of the

Socratic dialogues express Plato's development and distinctive and astonishing thinking.

Plato valued rational enquiry as the means for grasping how to live well; his writings present the image of our thinking possessed of the aspiration properly to grasp the Good, the Beautiful, the Truth. For Socrates and for Plato, thinking is at its best when in dialogue with others. True, one can try to dialogue with oneself, but that is typically not as effective.

In the early twenty-first century, a British regulatory body would visit universities – to check their standards, research levels, quality of teaching, value for money and so forth. It was rumoured that, at one meeting, Bernard Williams, as a senior Oxbridge professorial philosopher, suave, highly respected, highly intelligent, was asked by some keen investigators to tell them the latest methods of good teaching practice in philosophy. We can imagine Williams looking thoughtful before reputedly saying, with a wry smile, 'Well, we work mainly with the Socratic method.'

'Very interesting,' came the reply from the keen investigators.

'And how recently has that been developed?'

'Oh, about two thousand years ago,' came the answer.

There is a vast wealth of material in Plato for discussion, but let us first focus on his presentation as a way into some of his substantial beliefs. Why did Plato present all his philosophical thinking as dialogues? As already touched upon, Plato (as with Socrates) held that the philosophical quest needed to be by oral discussion, face-to-face to-ing and fro-ing. That moves us to a fresh question: why, then, did Plato write at all?

Perhaps Plato viewed his dialogue format as a stimulus to readers to seek out dialogue with others; perhaps the particular dialogues were also intended as useful reminders of what was discussed. Yes, they are a poor second-best to the real thing of face-to-face discussion, but the second-best may motivate us to head for the best. And that best was how the teaching at certain traditional universities worked – with one-to-one tutorials or supervisions where a student or two directly presented and debated with a tutor. Well before the Covid-19 pandemic, though, much of the teaching of philosophy and other humanities had become lectures to theatre-size audiences, with students taking notes, feeling no need to do their own thinking.

Philosophy in the 'written' form cannot orientate to the particular reader and answer the particular misunderstandings, appreciate the needs, questions and worries; further, authors themselves cannot learn from the readership. The oral is better because speakers can take into account the context, the looks of bafflement or of surprise in those around them. The written word lacks that flexibility; it lacks the cut and thrust of personal engagement.

Plato's *Phaedrus* explicitly raises such matters of philosophical thinking, presentation and engagement. It is a curious dialogue, switching abruptly from the topic of love to that of rhetoric. Shortly we shall see how both topics are vital to Plato's urgings over how to think philosophically and live well.

In the discussion of love, the dialogue offers us two winged horses with a charioteer; it is to illustrate the tripartite division of the soul. The horses are flying to the 'ideals' – in this context, regarding love for a youth. The black horse is dominated by physical sexual motivation: he can be violent in his desire to have his way with the boy. The black horse is compelled as if a slave to his desires; that is, he is simply motivated by what he wants. Harnessed to the black horse is a white horse, a creature with a sense of propriety, honour and obedience to the law.

No need for us particularly to dwell on loves and lusts to recognize internal conflicts, as on display with the metaphor of those two horses. There are many readily recognized everyday examples: we succumb to an extra glass of wine when we know that we ought not; we may fail to control our rage, when control, as we well know, would be better in the circumstances.

Let us not, though, forget the charioteer in this picturesque division of the soul. He is presented as the natural ruler within the person, within the soul, seeking wisdom, truth, knowledge, motivated by having managed a glimpse of the true ideal; he can correct the ways of the two horses. Yes, even the white horse's sense of obedience to the law needs to be corrected.

Thus we have Plato's tripartite division of the soul, a way of thinking of a person's mind, one that, indeed, influenced Sigmund Freud. The tripartite division, though, is not making use of a distinction between the conscious and unconscious. It also is not bringing to light three faculties of the mind that may conflict: the black horse representing desire/appetite; the white horse, duty; the charioteer, reason. After all, the black horse tries to persuade; the white horse reasons about duties; the charioteer desires truth. Plato is arguing that to live well, we need to identity with the charioteer for he is motivated by what is best for the unity of the soul, of the person as a whole. The two horses distort; they err over what is best.

Can we make much sense of the tripartite division? My comments above suggest that the 'I' forms another actor, needing to choose whether to identify with one of the horses or the charioteer. I am meant, though, to be the charioteer – yet apparently not in control, when the horses determine what to do. Am I not then identifying with one of the horses? Plato's tripartite division is not easy to think through, especially as it is intended to help our understanding of the ideal outcome: the unity of the soul.

The ideal unity of the soul is used to point us to the ideal unity, the well-running, of the city state, as argued for in Plato's most famous and greatest dialogue *Republic*. In that dialogue we meet numerous metaphors: in the Republic, the ideal State, we need the rulers to be as if 'guard dogs', the Guardians of the State, to guard against the wolves, the mob and the Sophists (please see below).

In *Republic*, Plato shows (these days uncontroversially so) that justice in the State requires women and men to be treated equally in most ways; women should take the same positions, education and so forth, alongside the men. Still controversial, though, is Plato's argument that justice requires giving up the family unit. Families distort, undermine justice, for parents give preferences to their own children. The community needs to hold the children in common, treating them impartially. Thus we see how Plato's philosophical thinking can give rise to radical ideas for how best to live well, once we secure a grip on, here for example, justice. To expand on living well, we need to pop back to *Phaedrus*.

Socrates is walking alongside the River Ilissus with Phaedrus; he pays attention to things around him: the river, the greenery, the sky. The doctor, the rhetorician, can have days off – the philosopher, in contrast, is always attending in his quest for understanding. Plato's Socrates is not here manifesting some 'green' credentials for he comments, 'Landscapes and trees, you see, have nothing to teach me; only people in the city.' Much, though, is made of the sounds of the cicadas, of those clear-winged singing insects; they have something to teach us – albeit by way of a curious myth, a very curious myth.

The cicadas were once men, but when the Muses came onto the scene, singing their beautiful songs, the men were so taken by the sounds that they forgot food and drink. They started to sing themselves and sang themselves to death, apparently being transformed, by way of later generations, into the cicadas we hear singing today.

Although the myth is bizarre – and it is worth taking on board how bizarre tales in philosophers' thinking may stimulate us to grasp matters afresh – it has a valuable moral. The moral is that in philosophy, as in life, we can be lazily relaxed in both body and mind; and that endangers our well-being. The men were taken in by song, ending up as nothing but singing insects.

Laziness of mind, argues Plato, is a threat to proper philosophizing. Such laziness leads to the treatment of philosophizing as the deployment of tricks to win arguments and learning how to reel off pat summaries or spot logical fallacies. That laziness sees wisdom as a matter of showing off with clever talk, smart replies. The lazy approach promotes the superficial. It is to be condemned. Be it through laziness or careful attention to focus groups, politicians in their speeches and interviews are typically adept at displaying the superficial in the form of platitudes, disingenuous replies or saying whatever they think will go down well.

Returning to *Republic*, we meet its most famous allegory: the Allegory of the Cave. It is designed to show how we need to resist accepting appearances as constituting reality. Until we seriously philosophize, we are enmeshed in the superficial, in appearances. We are akin to prisoners in a cave, gazing at shadows of physical items on parade. In everyday life, we are unwittingly confined to appearances. The shadows are less real than the physical items, but the physical items themselves are less real than – than what?

Philosophizing, for Plato, is a striving to leave the cave, to attend to the realities. That contrasts with the activities, the rhetoric, of the Sophists, mentioned above; they will argue a case for a fee (regardless of the truth of the matter) or will even doubt whether there is any objective truth. Protagoras was the most prominent fifth-century sophist; he happily argued that he could always make a weaker argument appear the stronger. 'The measure of all things is man,' he insisted. That is often taken as an extreme relativist position that there are no objective truths. If it is, we then have the philosophical dance of how it stands to itself; recall the Liar in Chapter 3. If 'all truths are relative' is presented as an objective truth, then it refutes itself; if it is presented as just a relative truth, relative to Protagoras's thinking, then why should I bother to pay attention?

For Plato, rhetoric, when properly understood and enacted – and not deployed for sophistical effect – must have the aim of truth, of looking into the soul for what is good. Plato's attitude towards the Sophists is worth bearing in mind when we meet today's use of 'sophisticated'. I resist urging us to reflect on the role of barristers and attorneys, with their deployment of sophisticated silver tongues, when representing certain defendants.

We are encountering Plato's arguments that reality consists of abstract Forms or Ideas. When, for example, we grasp that two sticks are equal in length, we are grasping that they partake in the Form of Equality. Plato's dialogues later showed him aware of arguments against his Forms. He had been motivated towards Forms by the ideals of beauty, truth, justice, love, equality; but was he really committing himself to the Form or Idea of 'bed', of 'dirt', of 'hair'? In his dialogue, *Parmenides*, he argued against his theory. That is another reason why Plato is a great philosopher; he did not stick by a theory regardless.

In the *Symposium*, Plato describes the ascent to the Form or Idea of Beauty – the ideal, as we may think of it – using some descriptions from Sappho (as noted in Chapter 2). The steps have value: for example, there is the attraction of a young man (recall Socrates and bearded youths), recognition of his beauty, being drawn to him, attending to him, being in love with him and so forth. Plato's imagination, curiosity, intellectual power, leads to a contemplation of the ideal, of a Beauty that is everlasting, neither growing and decaying nor waxing and waning. It is a Beauty that is not fair from one point of view, yet foul in another, fair at one time, yet not at another. Plato, thus, is often seen as the pre-eminent philosopher who sees beyond this earthly shabby world.

There is a touch of insanity in lovers, as if their love were 'meant' to be, overriding everything else, and there is that touch in philosophers, suggests Plato. Lovers may throw all else to the wind – they may give up family and friends – and that too is what the committed philosopher does. Even that is not so simple. Plato's Guardians, the philosophers, see the light, the ideals, the reality, the Forms, outside the cave, yet Plato has them returning to the cave, to the everyday world to rule over the city, the Republic, ensuring justice.

Plato casts our eyes to the heavens, to ideals, to eternities, to the Forms. He wants us to appreciate that there is more to life and reality than that suggested by our everyday living. However attractive and appealing is the picture that he paints, we need, in practice, to come down to earth; that downward direction is very much in play with certain philosophical thinkers – and so, next is Aristotle.

———

How to think philosophically with Plato? – *Lift eyes to eternities, to Forms of Beauty, Truth, the Good.*

6

Aristotle: Earth-Bound, Walking

All men by nature desire to know.

Aristotle

In the early sixteenth century, Raphael painted *The School of Athens*, a fresco that covers one of the walls of the Stanze di Raffaello in the Vatican City, Rome. Represented is a temporal tangle of philosophers associated with ancient Athens. The two central figures walking down the steps are Plato and Aristotle, Plato with an arm pointing upwards, while Aristotle's arm is outstretched directed at us and the surroundings. The painting summarizes the contrast between Plato and his pupil Aristotle. Plato aspires to a higher reality behind the ever-changing appearances of everyday life whereas Aristotle's philosophizing is grounded in the world and surrounding beliefs of common sense.

Aristotle was born in 384 BC into a wealthy family of Stagira, part of today's central Macedonia. As a young man, he journeyed to Athens to join the select few who entered Plato's Academy. He remained associated with the Academy for nearly twenty years, leaving Athens in 347 BC, travelling, engaging in scientific researches, collecting data, albeit somewhat as an amateur. It was Aristotle who set out the different scientific disciplines: astronomy, chemistry, biology, zoology, botany – the list could go on. For a few years, he even tutored the young Alexander in Macedonia, who would become Alexander the Great. They maintained a close friendship.

Back in Athens in the mid-330s BC, Aristotle set up the Lyceum, known as the Peripatetic School, for he wandered around while lecturing. His Lyceum was very different from Plato's Academy; it was open to the public for lectures. That distinction harmonizes with the difference in philosophical approach. Aristotle, unlike Plato, would first establish the reputable common-sense beliefs about a topic and relevant evidence, and then work through them, tidying them up, ridding them of any inconsistencies, the aim being to secure the truth and right explanations. His approach is that of an empiricist: look at the data 'out there'.

Aristotle was devoted to Plato, respected him as a person, philosopher and teacher. That he developed a philosophy fundamentally opposed to Plato's does not undermine that devotion and respect. When investigating the nature of goodness, Aristotle knew that it may be unwelcome. It challenged 'our friends who introduced the Forms – but piety bids us to honour the truth before our friends – and all the more so, given that we are philosophers'.

Aristotle's surviving writings are vast – and they form only a small proportion of his total output. None has the literary elegance of Plato's. They read as a mishmash of treatises as lecture notes, topics suddenly changing, repetitions and additions made. Although in his scientific researches, his resultant speculations were often mistaken – he was just starting out – in metaphysics, epistemology and ethics his thinking has held, and continues to hold, immense sway. St Thomas Aquinas, the great thirteenth-century Dominican friar, philosopher and theologian, deemed him 'The Philosopher' and gave Christianity an Aristotelian understanding.

The very term 'metaphysics' gained currency through Aristotle's work – well, through a cataloguer at the great Library of Alexandria in the third century BC. The cataloguer had come across Aristotle's *Physics*; he then found another bundle of writings without a title, so he headed it, so to speak, as *Meta* the *Physics*, that is, 'after-physics'. Happily, that bundle *Metaphysics* was devoted to the nature of 'being', of 'being qua being', of going beyond physics.

In *Metaphysics* and a related work, *Categories*, Aristotle investigates different categories of being. Apart from obvious ambiguities (for example, 'bank' and 'bank'), if the same word is used, then we may casually assume that the same meaning is in play. Aristotle drew attention to 'healthy'. We speak of healthy people, a healthy environment, healthy foods, healthy hair. Those uses are related, but the healthy environment is not healthy in the way in which a person is; rather, the healthy environment may contribute to people's health.

Aristotle investigates how the being of a human being is radically different from the being of a horse or golden ring or pallid colour. Items such as human beings, horses and golden rings, are deemed 'primary substances' that possess qualities, features, properties. A pallid colour does not have being in that way.

Although Socrates *is* pale, he may become florid, while remaining Socrates. In contrast, Socrates *is* a man; and (recent transgender arguments aside) anything that is not a man would not be Socrates. Socrates could not turn into a porcupine or peach, while remaining Socrates. Aristotle would have dismissed as nonsense Franz Kafka's *Metamorphosis* tale of Gregor Samsa finding himself inhabiting the body of an insect. Aristotle carefully sets us on the investigatory road of identity and change – with a degree of common sense.

The Gregor Samsa tale harmonizes with the belief of many religious people; namely, that I am a mind or soul or substance that can exist with a changed body or no body at all. Both Socrates and Plato accepted at least the possibility of that existence. We shall find trouble enough with that belief, when meeting Descartes. Aristotle's understanding is very different. He holds that Socrates' mind or soul is the form of some biological matter – Socrates' body, as we may think of it – just as a sphere may be the form of this block of wood or that piece of gold. The biological matter of Socrates can change to some degree (hair falls out; skin wrinkles), yet his identity remains intact because of the form; he is still Socrates. I am guessing that Aristotle would reject the thought that an insect's biological matter could be 'informed' as a man and as Socrates in particular. Although he is arguing against minds existing separately from matter, he is also rejecting a simple materialism, for example that of the atomists – whom we shall next be meeting through Epicurus.

The problem of identity was illustrated by a tale, a 'thought experiment', about the Ship of Theseus, Theseus being the mythical founder of Athens. The tale was reported by Plutarch in the first century AD. The Ship is gradually repaired over the years, with new timbers, new ropes, sails and so forth – until at some point, no original materials are present. Is it the same ship as before? Materially it is totally different, but its function is the same. 'It's just a matter of words; we have different criteria of identity in play here' may be the response. That response, though, is not so convincing when we have changes to a human body, brain transfers and the like: 'Will it still be *me*?' seems to be a substantial and more pressing 'personal identity' question, especially if the resultant individual is to be tortured.

Aristotelian metaphysical investigations included the tricky relationship between particulars and universals. Lovers of Forms – at one stage, Plato, the originator – would argue that there is a universal abstract Form Pallor in which Socrates participates as do many other people. Aristotle has none of it. More accurately, he brings the Form down to earth: pallor is 'said of' and 'present in' Socrates, accidentally. We still have the mystery of how 'it' (?) is present in others as well. Talk of universals takes us into questions of particulars resembling each other and what constitutes resemblance.

With human beings now to the fore, let us flee the metaphysics and turn to Aristotle's *Nicomachean Ethics*. The 'Ethics' of the title can mislead for the Greek term '*êthika*' focuses on a person's character; the frequent occurrence of the term 'virtue' found in English translations is of Aristotle's '*aretê*' and that means 'goodness' in the sense of 'excellence'. It would be odd to describe an axe as virtuous, yet Aristotle would deem it possessed of '*aretê*' if it possessed a sharp blade and was excellent for chopping.

Starting from common opinion, Aristotle asks what we human beings all ultimately seek for our lives. The translated answer is 'happiness', but translation again can trip us up. The Greek term is *eudaimonia* and that has more the idea of flourishing whereas 'happiness' may direct us to sensations of pleasure.

To flourish as a human being, according to Aristotle, is to have excellences regarding certain character traits. We may, of course, ask: do all human beings seek such flourishing? Some may opt for 'contented pig' status, more of which is in Chapter 16. Further, some – notably Immanuel Kant (Chapter 14) – argue that moral duties take priority over happiness; and they are not to be cashed out in terms of happiness. The Aristotelian approach, though, has the immediate appeal of asking what will make *me* happy; that contrasts with moral demands to perform one's duties or take everyone into account. Surprisingly though, once working through in Aristotelian mode what will make me, us, happy, we realize an outcome not radically different from typical moral stances.

Aristotle sought to transform our souls for the good – and that aim is found throughout ancient philosophy, albeit with different conclusions. Many twentieth-century philosophers lacked the courage or conceit to tell us how we ought to behave; rather, philosophers could only analyse the use of moral language (please see Chapter 29). Many philosophers today, though, adopt an updated Aristotelianism – neo-Aristotelianism. That 'neo' draws us away from Aristotle's ready acceptance of slavery and exclusion of women from his concerns. Neo-Aristotelianism – perhaps because it is such a mouthful – soon became Virtue Theory, now transformed into Virtue Ethics. The latter pulls away from ethics being seen as adherence to theory or a set of principles.

What will make us happy, make us flourish? Aristotle's emphasis is on virtues, on character traits, but that is not thereby recommending Christianity's faith, hope and charity; it is not understanding virtue as opposed to the vices chased by police vice squads. Aristotle works through different character traits, our common-sense views on them, to bring out those best to engender flourishing. His thinking is a naturalism: what we naturally hold as worthwhile.

With some notable exceptions – certain recent politicians spring to mind – people typically value honesty. Honesty does not guarantee a flourishing life, but it is likely to help. Sometimes it may need to be tempered by kindness; sometimes it is better for someone not to learn the truth. To flourish, we also need friendship; friends may help us through difficulties, but that usefulness should not be the motive. If people knew that you only became friends for what you could get out of them, things would not go well. We need to become disposed to doing things, on occasion, for the sake of others – and not out of self-interest.

The flourishing life requires development of a variety of character traits; it also requires intelligence and wisdom. 'The man who fears everything and does not stand his ground is a coward'; he hardly is flourishing. The man who goes to meet every danger is rash or foolish; again, that is scarcely a way to flourishing. The virtues, such as courage, generosity, temperance, are destroyed by excess and defect. Further, one act of courage, as a one-off, does not establish the individual as courageous. Indeed, the virtues, returning to Socrates, form a unity: honesty may require the courage to stand up and tell the truth and courage may require the wisdom to know when to do the standing – and so forth.

Aristotle's thinking here is orientated around 'function'. For flute-players, the good resides in the function of flute-playing well, so, argues Aristotle, we need to find what is the distinctive function of man. He argues that it is intellectual activity; as a result, performing that function well is the highest good – the end in view.

There are various assumptions and moves in Aristotle's argument that merit challenge; for example, the fundamental assumption that man has a function. In Chapter 24, we shall see Sartre heartily challenging away.

Aristotle investigates different types of causes and his preferred explanations assume that natural changes are working to an end or 'telos'; it is as if something in the future draws forward the actions of humans and animals and, indeed, trees and planets. It has become plain that successful scientific explanation, so far, is not teleological. Rather, science applies the abstractions of mathematics to understand how nature works – and that is more in line with Plato's thinking.

Although Aristotle's approach to explanation in natural science has not fared well, he has been applauded for his work on logic, the science of valid argument. He was the first to formalize a group of arguments; he gave us the 'syllogism'. In its basic form, it has two premises, using 'all', 'some', 'none' and a conclusion. Solely from the form, one can tell whether an argument is valid, that is, whether the conclusion follows from the premisses. Here is a simple form, where the letters A, B, C can be replaced by appropriate general terms:

All As are Bs;
All Bs are Cs;
Therefore, All As are Cs.

There are any number of instances: all cats are mammals; all mammals are animals; therefore, all cats are animals. A valid form is not sufficient to show that the conclusion is true. All pigs are winged-creatures; all winged-creatures can fly; therefore, all pigs can fly.

Here is an example of an invalid form. Some As are Bs; some Bs are Cs; therefore, some As are Cs. That conclusion does not follow. Some cats are friendly creatures; some friendly creatures are llamas; therefore, some cats are llamas. Clearly, an invalid argument.

Care is needed. Although not a syllogism, we may accept that the following is valid. Cats are mammals, Jemima is a cat, therefore Jemima is a mammal, but we ought not to conclude that that form of argument ensures validity. If we did, we should need to accept: cats are numerous, Jemima is a cat, therefore Jemima is numerous.

It needed the logicians Gottlob Frege and Bertrand Russell, over two thousand years later, to show the limitations of Aristotle's approach. An example to illustrate the complexity and one that it is appropriate upon which to close (using a lyric from the 1940s film *Ship Ahoy*) is:

All the nice girls love a sailor.

That may mean that there is one lucky sailor or even that each nice girl loves all and any sailors. It is most likely to mean that regarding any nice girl, there is some particular sailor or other loved by her.

Bringing the above type of complexity back to Aristotle's ethics, Aristotle seems to move from 'Everyone wants a state of happiness' to 'There is one state of happiness that everyone wants.' Of course, that may be challenged; perhaps people have radically different ideas of what constitutes happiness. Apparently, some traditional Chinese thought over the centuries has happiness (*lè*) understood as satisfactions found in long-term commitments to, for example, family traditions, listening to music, appreciating the universe – even inducing good men to serve in political office. Aristotle, ever the empirical philosopher, would examine such ideas, seeing how well they fitted the evidence, and would assess whether his understanding of happiness needed further investigation or revision.

―――――

How to think like Aristotle? *With feet firmly ground-bound, investigate all around, with curiosity and wonder.*

7

Epicurus: Gardener, Curing the Soul,
Ably Assisted by Lucretius

When death is there, we are not;
when we are there, death is not.

Epicurus

There is a tale that when the then monarch first saw the newly completed St Paul's Cathedral in the City of London, from the royal lips came the outburst that it was 'amusing, awful and artificial'. Today that would sound pretty disparaging, but the words then meant, in the early eighteenth century, that it was pleasing to gaze upon, deserving of awe, and full of skilful artifice. Words change their meaning. So do the subject of tales; the regal observation above has been attributed to various monarchs: James, William and Anne.

Today, to describe certain people as 'epicures' is to note their particular pleasure in fine foods and drink. More generally, today's popular understanding of Epicurus's philosophy – Epicureanism – in as far as there is any popular understanding, is that it is a philosophy that prizes pleasure. Epicurus is casually associated with the slogan 'Eat, drink and be merry, for tomorrow we die.'

Hedonists maintain that the ultimate value is pleasure and certainly it is correct to say that Epicurus was a hedonist. Whenever engaged in philosophical thinking, though, we need to learn what the philosopher means by the central terms – in this case, 'pleasure' – as we needed awareness of the historical linguistic context to grasp the meaning of the royalty observation above. People today may well understand Epicurean pleasures as sensual gustatory delights and, with hedonism more generally in mind, enhancements of the pleasures of eroticisms, fun and games, bound or unbound. Matters are not that straightforward.

Let us set Epicurus in context. He was Athenian, born in 341 BC, though he settled in Athens only in his mid-thirties, remaining there to his death in 270 BC. Prior to that, he studied philosophy in Colophon (now in Turkey), lectured, moved to Lesbos, gained followers, and then to Athens where he founded a school. It became known as the Garden, the name being indicative of the land he had purchased. Our knowledge of his theories depends on three letters from him and some collections of sayings and observations, preserved by another writer, Diogenes Laërtius.

In his understanding of the world around him, Epicurus was an atomist, building on theories two centuries earlier of Leucippus and Democritus. Let us resist embroilment in the atoms and the nature of their intermeshings and swervings, save to note Epicurus's out-and-out commitment to the atomists' materialism. The soul, the mind, is constituted by atoms, albeit finer ones distributed among the cruder atoms of the human body. Death occurs when the atoms disperse, going their separate ways, the collection broken up. Death of the human body is also the death of the soul, the mind. That receives central emphasis in Epicurus's thinking, for Epicurus is offering a therapy, a way of having a pleasurable life – and that requires freedom from superstition and fear of what may happen in an afterlife.

The Epicurean aim is to cure the soul. To effect the cure, what is needed, says Epicurus, is not 'the pretence but the real pursuit of philosophy' just as 'we do not need the semblance of health but rather true health'. That explicit medical gloss to the value of philosophical thinking harmonizes with other ancient Greek and Roman philosophers, such as the Stoics and even the Skeptics, though the cures do, of course, differ.

Epicurus seeks to show us the truth about human life, death and gods; and, if he succeeds, we shall realize: 'nothing to fear'. The therapy should work, once we properly understand his arguments, though maybe it also works, even more so, if we can memorize and repeat the conclusions. Epicurus's philosophical project of helping people to secure psychic health, as we may see it, harmonizes with this reputation for being humane and helpful in other ways.

'Pleasure is the beginning and end of the blessed life,' writes Epicurus. Infants setting off, seeking pleasure, we may reply, is no secure basis for what we as adults should value. Infancy to one side, Epicurus assumes that what is right and wrong should be understood in terms of our feelings – and he assumes that we all recognize that pleasures are the sole feelings that are valued as good. Of course, we still need reason, good reasoning, to work out how best to live to maximize pleasures. We may also reflect that Epicurus clearly places value on securing the truth about the value of pleasure.

If we accept the Epicurean line above, we may yet be critical of Epicurus when we gather what he understands by pleasure. Pleasure, for him, seems to be nothing but the absence of pain. There may well be qualifications to this; perhaps he does recognize positive pleasures, but would argue that to pursue them runs the risk of pains – and they are not worth the risk. Risk avoidance fits with his emphasis on pleasure as imperturbability (*ataraxia*). Thus, his Epicureanism differs from today's popular notion.

> When, therefore, we maintain that pleasure is the end, we do not mean the pleasures of profligates and those that consist in sensuality, as is supposed by some who are either ignorant or disagree with us or do not understand, but freedom from pain in the body and from trouble in the mind.

Epicurus's philosophical thinking is to lead us to a trouble-free mind, yet if we are concerned with the truth, we should surely be open to other therapeutic philosophies; for example, the third-century-BC Chrysippus, known as the second founder of Stoicism (second, after Zeno of Citium), would urge us to use our own reasoning and see that we should follow Nature. Or Skeptics, following Pyrrho's line, would explain how the best way to live undisturbed is to suspend all beliefs. Whether they are right or wrong, encountering such arguments would disturb; so, should we shelter in the Garden, away from all opposing arguments?

To return directly to Epicurus, he needs to discriminate between desires, urging that some be overcome. Many desires, for example, are neither natural nor necessary; they derive from bad opinions. The desire for fame is an example. Some desires may well be natural or may naturally develop, but are not at all necessary. The desire for luxury food and drink is an example.

> It is not continuous drinkings and revellings, nor the satisfaction of lusts, nor the enjoyment of fish and other luxuries of the wealthy table, which produce a pleasant life, but sober reasoning, searching out the motives for all choice and avoidance, and banishing mere opinions, to which are due the greatest disturbance of the spirit.

The sober reasoning, though, only has value in that it leads us to see that the life of pleasure, that is, one with no pain, with only the most minimal of disturbances, is a life that is content with very little. Epicurus was indeed content with very little. The thought seems to be that if you are on a meagre simple diet, a small delicacy is as good as a feast. Further, you have not needed to suffer the pains of labour, hope and disappointment in searching for luxuries. Epicurus, it appears, would have no problem with luxuries, if they did not risk pains. Indeed, he writes:

> If the things that produce the pleasures of profligate people also dissolved fears about heavenly things and about death and pains and if, moreover, they taught the limit of appetites, we would have nothing to reproach them for.

Epicurus speculates that it is probably because we are insecure in our lives that we seek wealth, power and fame to shield us from risks, not realizing that they add to the pains.

One particular source of pain is fear of death. Religions and superstitions can make us feel bleak and anxious about a possible afterlife; they may lead us into obsessive behaviour. Thus we have the mantra at the beginning of this chapter that sums up Epicurus's position. That position and arguments for it are found in detail in a great philosophical poem *On the Nature of the Universe*, written by Lucretius, a Roman, writing in the first century BC, and follower of Epicurus:

> Look back at the eternity that passed before we were born, and mark how utterly it counts to us as nothing. This is a mirror that Nature holds up to us, in which we may see the time that shall be after we are dead. Is there anything terrifying in the sight – anything depressing – anything that is not more restful than the soundest sleep?

The similarity of the non-existence prior to birth and the non-existence after death needs challenging. A key difference is that we have no difficulty at all in making sense of how we could carry on living for longer than we in fact shall: 'it will still be me, with my memories, continuing into the future'; contrastingly, there is difficulty in making sense of 'it would still have been me, had I been born two centuries earlier'.

Here is another argument by Lucretius, directly expanding on this chapter's mantra.

> If the future holds travail and anguish in store, the self must be in existence, when that time comes, in order to experience it. But from this fate we are redeemed by death, which denies existence to the self that might have suffered these tribulations. Rest assured, therefore, that we have nothing to fear in death. One who no longer is cannot suffer, or differ in any way from one who has never been born, when once this mortal life has been usurped by death the immortal.

Let us recall the Epicurean commitment to materialism and hence to the belief that death is annihilation. Of course, some people may be in pain precisely because they are not convinced by arguments for that belief's truth or they cannot persuade themselves of its truth.

Accepting death as annihilation, we may yet wonder whether the argument works: is it true that an event can be good or bad for individuals only if they exist as subjects of experiences at the time of the event? If so, then, yes, nothing bad after my death can be bad 'for me'; and so, maybe it would be irrational to fear being dead. Even if that is so, we may still fear dying because of the pains usually involved in dying and the possible distress to others. Further, even if the dying is easy, we may still fear death for it deprives us of future years of life. That deprivation is a loss of further pleasures of life, even if those pleasures are nothing more than those of tranquillity and maybe small delicacies of food.

We thus have questions here to do with the relevance of the length of a human life. The highly important Cambridge philosopher and atheist Frank Plumpton Ramsey died at the age of twenty-six; John Keats died at the age of twenty-five. Did they not lose out on something that (say) Jean Sibelius and Thomas Hobbes did not – for Sibelius died at the age of ninety-one and Hobbes at the age of eighty-six? We may compare a person's actual life – say, one that ends at the age of thirty because of an accident – with his possible life, one that could have continued to age ninety. There may be greater pleasure in that longer life.

If we think of the maximum possible human lifespan as being two hundred years, then Ramsey, dying aged twenty-six, missed out on more years than did Hobbes, dying at age eighty-six. Indeed, oddly – even, it seems, contradicting his own arguments – although Lucretius tells us not to fear death, he does appear to recognize that death may occur too soon and that we may have suffered leakages of pleasure.

> Why do you weep and wail over death? If the life you have lived till now has been a pleasant thing – if all its blessings have not leaked away like water poured into a cracked pot and run to waste unrelished – why then, you silly creature, do you not retire from life's banquet as a guest who has his fill of life?

We may note how Lucretius with his Roman banquets may not be all that enamoured with the simple meals of Epicurus. His banquets do not quite fit with Epicurus's simplicity.

Let us end with some humane thoughts of Epicurus. He places a high value on friendship. 'Friendship goes dancing round the world, announcing to all of us to wake up to happiness.' He even goes as far as insisting that a wise man would feel the torture of a friend no less than his own, and would die for a friend rather than betray him, for otherwise his own life would be confounded. Those worthy thoughts do not sit well with the Epicurean requirement of freedom from anxiety; having friends could well add to our worries.

On his last day, Epicurus spoke of the day as blessed. He was no doubt aware of his basic beliefs about life, his Four-Fold Remedy (*tetrapharmakos*): God presents no fears, death no worries; what is good is easily obtained, what is bad is easily endured.

———————

How to think like Epicurus? *Provide therapy for troubled souls, ideally in a garden.*

8

Avicenna: Flying Man, Unifier

No doubt, there is existence.

Avicenna

Here is a philosopher describing how he worked. Born c. 970, he is perceived as the greatest metaphysician of the first millennium:

> At night I would return home, set out a lamp before me, and devote myself to reading and writing. Whenever sleep overcame me or I became conscious of weakening, I would turn aside to drink a cup of wine, so that my strength would return ... Thus I mastered the logical, natural, and mathematical sciences...

Here is indeed a philosopher at work. While for many, the cup of wine is a necessity, it is not, of course, sufficient for good philosophical thinking. Abū 'Alī al-Husayn ibn Sīnā is the philosopher here. He is typically designated, in the Western world, by the Latin name 'Avicenna'. He has been hugely influential within Islamic philosophy and also within Jewish and Latin Christian traditions.

Born near Bukhara in Central Asia, Avicenna grew up in no backwater. Bukhara, being on the Silk Road, was a significant town, with lots of comings and goings. His family was part of the political elite and, as a young man, he had access to the palace library of the ruler. It was well stocked with Arabic translations of the Greek philosophers as well as Islamic works.

Avicenna was precocious. Allegedly, by the age of ten he knew the Qur'ān by heart. In adulthood, he was courtier to various Persian rulers, travelling with them as physician and adviser. During that time, he reworked Aristotle's philosophy, harmonizing it with the Islamic faith. It was Avicenna's reworkings of Aristotle with which subsequent Arab philosophers dealt.

As well as a philosopher and theologian, Avicenna was well known as a physician. His major work, the *Canon*, for many centuries was the definitive medical textbook covering all manner of accidents, diseases and psychological upsets. There is the tale of a Persian prince who refused to eat and who was convinced he was a cow. Qua cow, he would moo, demanding to be killed so that his flesh could be the basis for a good stew for the court. Avicenna, pretending to be the butcher, ready with knife to slaughter, suddenly stopped, declaring that the cow was too lean and needed to be fattened first. The prince understood, mooed some more, and started eating. As he gained strength, his bovine delusion departed.

Medical matters apart, Avicenna's philosophy ... well, that 'apart' implies a separation, but separation is not in the spirit of Avicenna's thinking. He sought a unified understanding of everything and his great work, *The Cure*, twenty-two large volumes, covers logic (with rhetoric and poetics), physics (including nature, the heavens, mineralogy, meteorology, botany, zoology), mathematics (including music and astronomy), metaphysics as well as practical philosophy, with politics, household management, medicine and ethics.

Avicenna was a polymath, eager to investigate all topics, as was Aristotle, but unlike Aristotle, his thinking was aimed, as already implied, at a unification of all knowledge. At a general level, he combined the thinking of the Arabic developments of Aristotelianism and Neoplatonism (*falsafa*) with Islamic doctrine (*kalām*). Today, scientists speak of a theory of everything, a unified theory that explains all aspects of the physical world. We may question what sense can be made of such an 'explanation', but Avicenna went well beyond that idea of current scientists. His theory of everything was truly to cover everything, encompassing God, the soul, the world around us – and indeed cases and cures of bodily ailments.

In the typical mainstream university philosophy of Britain and the United States, save as an option, Avicenna and other influential Arabic philosophers rarely receive mention. If touching on theology, pride of place goes to St Thomas Aquinas, the Dominican friar, who, as mentioned in Chapter 6 on Aristotle, rendered Christianity to an Aristotelian reading much as Avicenna was doing two centuries earlier with his Aristotelian approach to Islam.

As God is central to Avicenna's philosophy and, of course, to Islam, let us explore Avicenna's thinking in that arena. Here is the starting point: Avicenna is baffled by existence. To make sense of it, he argues, we need to grasp how it is necessary – otherwise, why should there be existence? Of course, we may wonder how that 'necessity' rids us of mystery; we could request quelling of a new bafflement: why is it necessary, if it is, that there be any necessary being? Still, let us enter further into Avicenna's thinking via his argument that became known as the *burhān al-ṣiddiqīn*, the 'demonstration of the truthful'.

The argument's conclusion is that a necessary being exists and, furthermore, that being has the central qualities typically attributed to God by the monotheistic Abrahamic religions of Judaism, Christianity and Islam. Avicenna's argument, in fact, possesses features later found in Aquinas's reasoning and the reasoning of major seventeenth-century European philosophers; for example, it is similar to Leibniz's Contingency Argument for the divine existence.

Avicenna accepts from the very beginning that things do indeed exist. Some sceptics may ask: can we really be sure that anything exists? The quick reply is that even if the existence of things is an illusion, the illusion exists. There is also Avicenna's Flying Man thought experiment for establishing a basic personal existence; some see Avicenna as anticipating Descartes with his 'I think, therefore I am.'

The Flying Man – sometimes Suspended Man, Floating Man – is supposedly a grown man

hovering in a void such that he is sightless and feels nothing. His limbs are separated so that they do not contact one another. There is no sound or smell. This individual is in a state of total sensory deprivation. He has just been created, so he has no memories of prior sensory experience.

Avicenna asked what a person in that situation could and would know. If you think that all knowledge derives from sensation, the answer would be 'nothing'. Avicenna insisted that, in such a condition, the individual would yet be aware of his own existence. The example is meant to demonstrate that possession of body has nothing to do with what is essential to a human being. If it did, it would be impossible for the Flying Man to grasp himself, his existence.

The thought experiment has been much discussed, not least with regard to the exact conditions set. We should certainly ask whether such a state of sensory deprivation is possible and whether, in such a state, a remaining self-awareness is possible. Those objections to one side, the illustration is useful in understanding Avicenna's philosophizing for it draws attention to one of his key distinctions, namely between what is essentially or necessarily the case and what is contingently so. A person may be single, supercilious and sensual, but they are not essential for someone to be a person, whereas maybe some degree of self-awareness is essential. That necessary/contingent distinction runs throughout philosophical thinking. Let us see how Avicenna uses it in his alleged proof of God as a being that necessarily or essentially exists.

Items that have causes cannot be necessary beings, solely with regard to their natures, for their existence would depend upon the existence of other things, namely their causes. To exist 'contingently' means to be capable either of existing or not existing – and the existence or non-existence depends on whether or not there has been a cause for that existence. Look around us: everything we see is contingent. Yes, the items exist, but they might not have existed; and they would not have existed had the relevant causes been absent or different. In contrast with contingent existence, to exist 'necessarily' is to exist in a way that rules out non-existence; the item's nature guarantees its existence. Of course, some things are guaranteed, by their nature, not to exist; a round square, for example.

Avicenna speaks of how contingent items need to be 'preponderated' to exist or not exist, that is whether, so to speak, the scales are tipped this way or that way, tipping the items into existence or not. Contingent existent things *in themselves* neither must exist nor must fail to exist, but become 'necessary through another', through an external cause, through the scales tipping in their favour.

Do we have any good reason to believe that there are any necessary existents? We noted above how Avicenna believes that there is one necessary existent and, as may be guessed, he insists that he has a good reason for that belief. Consider the aggregate of all contingent things. By definition, there is nothing contingent outside the collection of *all* such things. What then is the cause of that total aggregate? What tipped the scales such that the aggregate exists rather than not? That aggregate could not have come from nothing. There must then be a necessary being, a being that must exist in itself, upon which the aggregate's existence depends.

We may and should challenge Avicenna's reasoning here. Even though each individual item of the aggregate is contingent, it does not follow that the whole aggregate is contingent. Maybe a collection sufficiently numerous gives rise to necessity. After all, speaking figuratively, one swallow does not make a spring, but maybe a vast number do; and speaking financially, my sale of shares in Company X does not lead to Company X's collapse, but lots of sales may. There are tipping points.

Even if there is no way in which a sufficiently large aggregate of contingent items becomes necessary, it does not follow that there must be a necessary being in which to ground the aggregate of all contingent items – unless an assumption is made. The assumption is that there must be a cause for every contingent being to exist. Leibniz, as we shall see in Chapter 11, holds to a similar assumption, the Principle of Sufficient Reason. Why hold to that assumption? Maybe it is just a 'brute fact' that a sequence or sequences of contingent items exist. Of course, certain people may be inclined to make the assumption because they already believe that God as a necessary being must exist; but that puts the so-called cart before the so-called horse.

To enter further into thinking as Avicenna thinks, let us assume that his argument for the existence of a necessary being works. Avicenna now needs additional arguments to show that the necessary being he has proved to exist is identical with God as understood by Islam and, indeed, by all the Abrahamic religions.

According to those religions, there is but a single god – God. May there not, though, be distinct aggregates of contingent items pointing to distinct necessary beings? Avicenna justifies the answer 'no' on the basis that there would be nothing to distinguish the necessary beings in themselves. For there to be a distinction, something 'outside' must have caused that distinction, but a necessary existent does not depend in any way on anything outside.

There remain further puzzles: for example, what sense can be made of God as the necessary being who 'created' the aggregate of contingent items, the universe? Acts of creation occur in time, so did time exist separately from God? If, though, time is in some way an attribute of God, we then have the puzzle of how a creation occurred in time or, if that puzzle is overcome, why God created the universe at a particular time rather than another.

Avicenna understands God as unchanging and eternally sustaining the universe; so, we ought not to think of God as setting things going at a beginning. Yet if God is unchanging, how can He know about the temporal changes that occur among contingent items? Maybe He can grasp unchanging universal laws of nature, maybe they are attributes of His being, but it is difficult to see how He has knowledge of particulars. He could know, through essences or definitions, that all men are mortal, but not of the doings of that particular man, Socrates, on this day rather than that.

That latest puzzle leads us into the most significant conflict that Avicenna has with traditional belief in Islam and indeed with the typical belief of other faiths. He is committed to necessitarianism: properly understood, everything that happens happens necessarily so. That necessity does not sit well with much religious belief, if applied to God and human beings.

The argument for God's existence rested on the existence of contingent things, those contingent things lacked necessity 'in themselves'. Once we grasp that they have been caused by a necessary being, then we should see that their existence and everything about them necessarily follows. Well, we should see that unless we can make sense of God, the necessary being, as having contingent causal attributes. That latter idea, though, would require causes outside of God that tip the scales in favour of God creating this item rather than that, now rather than then.

On the necessitarian view, it follows that we, the creatures created, lack free will, if free will is to be understood as incompatible with such necessity. Further, it seems that God lacks freedom to choose or to will; to that extent, He lacks genuine agency. To hold to that position is an apostasy from the traditional Islamic perspective.

Of course, there remain many other areas of Islamic belief that need to be squared with Avicenna's necessary being as possessed of the attributes of God: His goodness, intelligence and care for creation – or, more accurately, care for, it seems, only certain creatures.

Kalām in Islam is the rational theology derived from the Qur'ān. There is a tendency to see *kalām* as just a matter of bringing reason to bear on what has been 'revealed' as opposed to philosophical reasoning that may challenge apparent revelations, but, throughout the thinking of Avicenna and certain others, there was no such sharp opposition. Avicenna's approach does, however, lead him to accept that to some extent God is beyond human understanding, but not so 'beyond' that we know nothing about Him.

Avicenna's thinking was certainly successful, if success is understood solely in terms of the extent to which his work was and is influential – and not merely in Islam. It is difficult to know how his thinking is to be assessed, though, if we take seriously his much-quoted aphorism:

The more brilliant the lightning, the quicker it disappears.

There is no disappearance of the search for answers to Avicenna's fundamental question of why there is existence, of why anything at all exists, be the search along lines scientific, philosophical or theological. Curiously, the question is not asked: were nothing to exist, ought there not then to be the question of why is there nothing rather than something?

How to think like Avicenna? *Be determined to explain existence – and all things – through a unified theory.*

9

Descartes: With Princess, With Queen

I think, therefore I am.

Descartes

Where philosophy is concerned, anyone with a slight familiarity – even many with no familiarity – may find themselves occasionally announcing sagely, 'I think, therefore I am'; they may even offer the Latin original as '*cogito, ergo sum*', even '*je pense, j'existe*', muttering something about a French philosopher, Monsieur Descartes, and his famous 'cogito'.

By pure reasoning, Descartes drew fascinating, wide-ranging and influential conclusions from that simple cogito certainty, the most startling being that when we use the word 'I' we refer to the soul; and the soul is the mind, is the self, is a substance totally distinct from the body and from all material things. Although we happen to be connected to our particular human body, with the luxuriant hair, fine physique and coquettish smile or – all right, in my case – with the declining eyesight, greying beard and sighs of weariness, we could exist disembodiedly.

Descartes does not stop there.

Amazingly, from the cogito, he also concludes that God, as traditionally understood, does exist; furthermore, each one of us will continue to exist after bodily death – though there is a caveat. I am a soul, a simple substance, without parts; so, I cannot be destroyed by being broken up as a wine glass could be smashed. The caveat is that God, all powerful, will annihilate me, if He chooses. Tread carefully, where God is concerned; that means, tread carefully everywhere and always.

Although many analytic philosophers find Descartes' conclusion bizarre – they insist that he must have gone wrong in his reasoning – let us remember that millions, maybe billions, of people, probably many readers, embrace his conclusion, with varying degrees of certainty, be it by faith, scriptural commitment or reasoning.

Descartes' philosophy aims to create a well-ordered mind, a tranquillity, overcoming the mind's illnesses. God is no deceiver, but we, mere human beings, are liable to make mistakes, become disturbed, unless we reason carefully and pay attention to what is possible. There are pleasures in contemplating the truth; there can be contentment, once we realize that we have a psychological freedom to overcome any distresses.

Descartes has become known as the Father of Modern Philosophy. Although writing in the 1600s, the 'modern' indicates how different is his approach compared with the European philosophers before him. Descartes saw himself as starting afresh in understanding humanity and the world; and that meant not kowtowing to the Church or, indeed, to his schoolmasters' teachings of pre-Christian philosophers, notably Aristotle. His *Meditation I* tells of how now he has sufficient maturity, leisure and freedom from care to think clearly.

Some years ago I was struck by the large number of falsehoods that I had accepted as true in my childhood, and by the highly doubtful nature of the whole edifice that I had subsequently based on them. I realized that it was necessary, once in the course of my life, to demolish everything completely and start again right from the foundations if I wanted to establish anything at all in the sciences that was stable and likely to last.

Descartes' work of meditations was distinctive not only in the seeming fresh start, but also in orientation as pretended autobiography. Readers were urged to follow in their own 'first person' way and think through the matters with their own 'fresh starts', over months, rather than a quick read. To increase wider accessibility, going beyond that afforded to classical scholars, the text, originally in Latin, was soon translated into French. Descartes commented: 'Common sense is the best distributed commodity in the world, for every man is convinced that he is well supplied with it.' Descartes displayed a sense of humour.

Descartes determined that he would doubt everything as far as he could. After all, he had often made mistakes, sometimes through poor eyesight, through dreaming or tiredness. It was even possible – logically possible; no contradiction in the supposition – that a malignant demon, an evil genius, existed, deceiving him into thinking there was a world around him – a world of oceans and oysters, brains and biscuits – when in fact it was all illusion. Maybe the universe, including his body, his brain, was just treacle and he experienced a litany of false impressions courtesy of the evil genius.

The metaphor he deployed was that of a basket containing some good apples, but also some rotting ones. To avoid the rot spreading, it is wise to throw out all the apples and put back only the good ones. Similarly, in adopting his Method of Doubt, we should discard all those beliefs with even the slightest uncertainty and keep only those that are indubitably true. There are problems with the apple analogy; after all, we need some beliefs – perhaps they form the basket? – to assess other beliefs. A better analogy, put forward by Otto Neurath of the Vienna Circle (Chapter 13), is: 'We are like sailors who must rebuild their ship on the open sea, never able to dismantle it in dry-dock and reconstruct it there out of the best materials.' We have to rely on some of our beliefs to assess others, discarding some, retaining others – and then maybe reviewing those initially held firm.

Returning to Descartes' approach, whatever the mistakes or deceptions encountered, realized Descartes, he would have to exist to undergo them. 'I think – I am having experiences; I am perhaps being deceived – therefore I am.' In fact, it does not follow that Descartes could not doubt all that. After all, ply him with sufficient cognac and maybe he could doubt his existence. When we think of possibilities and impossibilities we have to be careful, and the care needs to extend to distinguishing between the psychological and the logical. We may make mistakes in believing something is impossible; we may also make mistakes in thinking something is possible, when logically it is not.

Descartes' famous doubting with the 'cogito' conclusion was not original. St Augustine, spanning the third and fourth centuries, had made similar observations – as some pointed out, to Descartes' irritation. Descartes, though, used the 'cogito' to ground his insistence that the mind really is distinct from the body. The mind lacks size or place in space, but essentially has thought. Things are the other way round for the body.

The reasoning to establish that essentially he, Descartes, was an immaterial substance has often been challenged, as was Avicenna's similar thinking with his Flying Man. Surely, it is possible for Descartes to fail to notice that his thinking just is identical with certain neurological changes; after all, people may fail to realize that Clark Kent really is Superman. Kent and Superman, though, are attired differently, whereas can we really make sense of neurological changes as somehow dressed up as our mental experiences? For Descartes, the nature of the mind is transparent to us – with no sign of neurology.

Descartes' *Meditations* deployed his Method of Doubt, his Systematic Doubt, to overcome doubt. To his satisfaction, once he had established his existence he could then examine his ideas and – hey presto – those ideas led him to conclude that God must exist and, unlike any supposed evil genius, is no deceiver.

One argument for the existence of God that Descartes propounds (he has three) rests on the idea of God as a being with all the perfections, to be understood as with maximum reality, independent of everything else. Now, existence, he claims, is a perfection; hence, God has existence, hence He must exist.

That argument, a few paragraphs in *Meditation V*, relies on reasoning alone. It is open to many objections, not least the unclarity regarding quite what is meant by 'perfections'. One key point to recognize, when philosophizing, is that whatever features something has of which we have an idea, we cannot thereby conclude that anything exists with those features. I may have the idea of a Super-Unicorn, a beast just like a regular unicorn save for its possession of necessary existence. My having that idea, though, does not show that there is in fact a Super-Unicorn. Let me hasten to add: that quick objection does not rule out digging deeper into Descartes' argument, a version of the Ontological Argument for the existence of God, an argument famously associated with the eleventh-century St Anselm of Canterbury – and an argument, once revised and revamped, still with some adherents.

Descartes' metaphysical position about mind and body is known as Cartesian Dualism. Each mind, each 'I', is an immaterial substance that can exist independently of the material world understood as one substance extended in space. I happen to be directly linked to a part or modification of the material substance, to this human body, this biological blob, such that I may feel thirsty, cross my legs, run to catch the train and so forth. Cartesian Dualism is also Cartesian Interactionism. What we think of as a person on this 'mortal coil' is, roughly, a mind and a body interacting with each other. I am, though, essentially my mind.

Is a human being in fact that twosome? Descartes was in correspondence with Elisabeth, Princess of Bohemia – such philosopher/royalty interactions were not all that unusual in those days – and she gave Descartes a run for his money. She rightly emphasized that I and my body form a unity; a person surely is not made up of a mind that just happens to be linked to a body in the way in which people may feel linked to their boxing gloves, mobile phones or wine glass.

Descartes recognized that unity; he accepted that he was not solely as a 'pilot in a ship', but far more intimately linked to his body. He squirmed, though, with unsatisfactory explanations of the unity, sometimes saying that the mind operated solely through the pineal gland, 'the seat of the soul', in the centre of the brain, sometimes saying that it was united to the whole of the body. Wisely, the Princess would not let him off the hook; she kept pressing home the unity requirement. Finally, in a fit of exasperation, Descartes announced that, in effect, a person's mind and body form a third real thing, another 'substantial unity'. But how? – continued the Princess.

The mind/body interaction puzzle led one influential Cartesian, Nicolas Malebranche, to offer 'occasionalism' as a solution. A human mind, immaterial, not in space, cannot move bodies, arms and legs, but omnipotent God, even though immaterial, can do anything. Hence, on the occasions when I want to walk, typically God intervenes and moves my legs for me. Unfortunately, God is thus landed with responsibility for all our wicked deeds.

———————

With Descartes' commitment to souls for human beings, where does that leave non-human animals? The answer is 'not in a great place'. Descartes has had a bad press over non-human animals. It had been circulated that he deliberately pinned down the live pet dog of Helena, a servant girl and mother of his daughter, to cut it open and explore its organs. There is no good evidence for that tale, but Descartes, along with many other scientists, did conduct vivisection, that is, experiments on live animals. Was that because Descartes lacked compassion for animal suffering?

Descartes certainly wrote that non-human animals have physical movements similar to ours when we are in pain, but are 'not in pain in the strict sense'. If experiences necessarily require a mind, a soul – and if animals are lacking in that regard – then they are incapable of suffering. They may squeal and yelp, but squeaky toys do that. For Descartes, it seems, there is a radical discontinuity between human beings and non-human animals.

If we are to treat physical behaviour as no reasonable guide to inner experiences, we hit the problem of 'Other Minds'; how can I tell that the human beings around me have experiences and thoughts? Surely, I ought not to generalize irresponsibly from an example of one: 'Consciousness, reasoning, is tied to this (my) living human body' – that is my one example – 'therefore there must be similar consciousnesses tied to all those other living human bodies.'

If Descartes' approach is right, then we are mistaken in having feelings of sympathy for other animals; but why put the reasoning that way round? We see a goat bleating, struggling, trapped in some barbwire cutting into its flesh; we do not wonder whether the goat is really in pain – no more so than when seeing a human being (not on stage) struggling and crying out. From that evidence, maybe we should conclude that Descartes' reasoning must be mistaken. Of course, we can lose a grip over where to stop in our sympathies. I doubt if many people think of the local mosquito, carrying malaria or not, as undergoing pains – or pleasures.

Descartes' apparent understanding of human bodies and non-human animals as pieces of machinery led some opponents to argue that secretly he was an out-and-out materialist and no true believer in souls at all. Some have argued that Descartes was a spy. Descartes certainly had form for what he owned up to. His 'search after truth' did not always extend to putting that truth before the public. In 1633, he was about to publish *Le Monde ou le Traite de la Lumière* (*The World or Treatise on Light*), a work that included arguments to show that the earth orbited the sun. He held back upon hearing of the condemnation of Galileo for maintaining that heliocentric Copernican thesis. Those who charged Descartes as materialist even spread rumours, with sexual innuendo, that he built a beautiful blonde automaton named 'Francine', named after his illegitimate daughter, and took it round with him, even to bed.

Descartes, though, was no materialist. There is, however, no need to fall for his reliance on 'substance dualism' as the only way to be saved from the thesis that consciousness is 'nothing but' physical changes, be they mechanical, electrical, chemical or even sub-atomic. Can we really make sense of my thinking about the wine this evening, recalling the good times on Greek islands in my youth, listening to Schubert or imagining what I shall be doing next year, as 'nothing but' some electrical impulses? I am tempted to quip: I think not – and yet I exist.

Have I forgotten about the Queen in this chapter's title? Not at all. We are about to meet Queen Christina of Sweden.

Descartes as philosopher and mathematician became famous, infamous even, and Queen Christina requested his services as tutor. She was learned and keen to transform Stockholm into the 'Athens of the North'. Descartes was reluctant to accept, but knowing that he should not refuse a royal request, he obeyed and went off to Stockholm. To his horror, the Queen expected him to give tutorials at 5 am. Descartes, though, was used to remaining in bed at least until noon. The early tutorials, in a particularly harsh Stockholm winter, led to his pneumonia. He was dead within months. His theories – and rumours – lived and live on.

———————

How to think like Descartes? *Search for truth and thus discover the soul and its immortality – and find pleasure enough in that.*

10

Spinoza: God-Intoxicated Atheist

Think least of death.

Spinoza

It is quite an achievement for a philosopher both to be praised by some as a virtuous God-intoxicated thinker and simultaneously to be praised by others as a fine atheist. There were, of course, yet others who condemned him for being a damnable atheist and others still who condemned him for being so obsessively God-intoxicated.

Here we meet Spinoza, whose thinking led him to be treated in two radically different ways. He achieved those mixed and extremely different responses not because he was two-faced or radically unclear or changed his mind, but because, unappreciated by many of his readers, he drew attention to how our understanding of the universe can legitimately be maintained from at least two distinct perspectives. In fact, the universe, for Spinoza, has an infinite number of ways of being, though we mere humans can handle only the two. The curved glass from one side is convex; from the other side, it is concave. Spinoza described the different ways of approaching all that existed – of *Deus sive Natura*, of God or Nature, as he termed it. Others gave us different ways of seeing Spinoza.

Baruch – Bento, Benedict, Benedictus – Spinoza (de Espinosa) is encountered with a variety of names, but 'Blessed Person' was a common meaning. He was born in Amsterdam of Jewish immigrants from Portugal. Portuguese was their mother tongue. Our Spinoza was given the Jewish name, 'Baruch'; but was called at home by the Portuguese 'Bento'.

Spinoza was, it seems, born to be a natural Jewish philosopher, thinking deeply about the nature of God. He concluded, though, contrary to Judaism, that God could not be conceived as separate from the natural world around us, or, indeed, the whole universe. The result was ...? Well, in later centuries, Spinoza's understanding of God and Nature ('Nature' meaning the universe) was much admired by Goethe, Novalis, Einstein and many others. For example, Einstein, when asked whether he believed in God, replied, 'I believe in Spinoza's God.' During Spinoza's lifetime, though ... well ... We are about to see how philosophical thinking can sometimes get us into trouble – if we say what we think. Recall Socrates.

On 27 July 1656, at the age of twenty-three, Spinoza suffered a real curse – courtesy of his Amsterdam synagogue, the Talmud Torah congregation. He was excommunicated.

Cursed be he by day and cursed be he by night; cursed be he when he lies down and cursed be he when he rises up. Cursed be he when he goes out and cursed be he when he comes in. The Lord will not spare him, but then the anger of the Lord and his jealousy shall smoke against that man, and all the curses that are written in this book shall lie upon him, and the Lord shall blot out his name from under heaven. And the Lord shall separate him unto evil out of all the tribes of Israel, according to all the curses of the covenant that are written in this book of the law.

This effectively ordered other Jews to keep away from him. At the time, Spinoza was trying to continue his father's trading business, but, unsurprisingly, business dried up. Spinoza eventually made a living by grinding lenses to a high and much-admired specification by scientists of his day – scientists with whom he frequently corresponded; for example, those of London's Royal Society.

Things did not improve in the way he was treated – for he remained true to his beliefs and was hence classified by many as a heretic. Leibniz – we meet him shortly – corresponded with him and visited him in November 1676 in the Hague, but later, when he heard of more condemnations of Spinoza, he, ever the diplomat, downplayed their meetings: 'Oh, I bumped into him in passing' was the feeling he sought to give.

The honesty, sincerity and intelligence of Spinoza's attempt to make sense of the world – of God – is clear in his major work, *Ethics*, written in Latin. It covers the whole understanding of reality (not solely ethical matters); it was published after his death. As was to be expected, it was banned, though friends made and circulated clandestine copies, editions and translations. The work was added to the Catholic Index of prohibited books and a copy placed in the Vatican. Ironically the Catholic censors unwittingly aided scholarly understandings of Spinoza, though not until 2010 when that copy was rediscovered.

Spinoza's *Ethics* was in fact titled *Ethics, Demonstrated in Geometrical Order* (*Ethica, ordine geometrico demonstrata*); the work was distinctive for a philosophical treatise, being set out in the manner of Euclid's *Elements*, with numbered definitions, propositions, cross-references, proofs and 'QED's. Here is a flavour of the beginning of Part One, 'Concerning God'; that part in total consists of eight definitions, seven axioms and thirty-six propositions:

Definitions

I. By that which is *self-caused*, I mean that of which the essence involves existence, or that of which the nature is only conceivable as existent.

II. A thing is called *finite after its kind*, when it can be limited by another thing of the same nature [...]

III. By *substance*, I mean that which is in itself, and is conceived through itself: in other words, that of which a conception can be formed independently of any other conception [...]

Axioms

I. Everything which exists, exists either in itself or in something else.

II. That which cannot be conceived through anything else must be conceived through itself [...]

Propositions

Prop. I. *Substance is by nature prior to its modifications.*

Proof. – This is clear from Def. iii and v.

Prop. II. *Two substances, whose attributes are different, have nothing in common.*

Proof. – Also evident from Def. iii. For each must exist in itself, and be conceived through itself; in other words, the conception of one does not imply the conception of the other [...]

The structure of the book is not quite as severe as this extract makes it seem, for in fact Spinoza is often driven to providing long explanations of what he means, with notes and appendices.

Spinoza's God is neither the Jewish God of Abraham, nor the Christian God in some mysterious way identified with Christ, nor, for that matter, Allah – as typically understood. Spinoza's God has no jealousies, rewards and concerns. Reality, the one substance, is God or Nature.

Spinoza is typically seen as holding to a version of pantheism; more scholarly reflection points to a position of panentheism whereby Nature – we – are 'in' God, but God is greater still. Thus, Spinoza can be read as operating within the religious tradition whereby 'all things are in God and move in God' (Acts 17: 28) and rigorously working out what logically follows, using the concept of substance. With emphasis on 'God' we identify the active generative aspect of Nature; with emphasis on 'Nature', the things thus generated. Talk of God's purposes, intentions, decisions, if taken seriously, is engagement with fairies. To understand the world, we need to attend to the chains of causes and effects. To end up speaking of God's will or God's design is, wrote Spinoza, with contempt, the 'sanctuary of ignorance'.

Let us note here how a concept can dominate our philosophical thinking of the world. Here, it is the concept of substance; we found Aristotle working with it centuries earlier. A substance is independent of other things for its existence. Once that independence is strengthened, to something completely independent of every other thing, dependent on nothing else, we find ourselves concluding that there can be only one substance. Were anything else to exist, independently of that substance, it would limit that substance; so, all things must in some way be dependent on the one substance, on God. Descartes had accepted that; when he spoke of minds and matter as substances, he had *created* substances in mind, ones totally independent of everything else except God.

We may wonder why even to entertain the idea that a correct understanding of the world requires application of the 'substance' concept. Perhaps it derives from acceptance of a coherent concept of God and then, in Spinoza's case, working through the consequences with honest intellectual rigour. As a result, what we think of as separate objects, of peas, porcupines and people, are in fact modifications of that one substance; they are akin to waves on the ocean. The modifications exist, mysteriously so, under both the attribute of extension and the attribute of thought. Spinoza thus 'solved' Descartes' mind/body interaction problem: my mind and my body are one and the same mode, but under different attributes. It remains controversial how that is to be understood. Analogies are often given: one example is how the same thought may be expressed in both German and French.

As all seemingly distinct items are modes of the one substance, for Spinoza there is no fundamental separation between human beings and other animals – horses, insects, fishes – for he speaks of all acting, as far as they can, according to their nature. The emotions and feelings of animals only differ from those of human beings to the extent that their natures differ. 'Horse and man are alike carried away by the desire of procreation; but the desire of the former is equine, the desire of the latter is human.'

True understanding, argues Spinoza, cannot be confined to our little sphere of concerns; it needs to be an understanding of the whole, God or Nature, with its infinite number of infinite attributes or ways of being. Even if we accept the applicability of 'substance' and how items are but modes of that one substance, we still have the questions of how to understand the relationship between modes and, in particular, between conscious states and the physical, the mystery mentioned earlier.

Given that substance has the attributes of the physical and of the psychological, it seems as if we should think of psychological events as running in parallel with all the physical events. May not the physical world of causes and effects be manifested as the psychological world of reasons and conclusions?

On an easier level, we find Spinoza recommending how the State should be organized. That is an important topic within his 1670 *Tractatus Theologico-Politicus*. He had it published anonymously, seemingly from Hamburg, in the hope it would be read without immediate condemnation as being by the dreadful Spinoza. The ruse failed – and he received more condemnation, now from the political authorities, not just the Jewish community.

In the work, Spinoza argued for a secular society, for free speech, for liberty. He also gave a sustained textual analysis and criticism of the Bible, maintaining that it needed to be assessed solely as literature and history; it needed to be interpreted for moral insights and in no way treated as 'the word of God'. Spinoza's *Tractatus*, as a consequence, was deemed 'blasphemous'; a certain van Blijenburgh wrote of it as being 'full of studious abominations and an accumulation of opinions that have been forged in hell'.

Despite the 'forged in hell' condemnation, Spinoza's approach, as a philosophical thinker, to biblical studies should serve us well when encountering anything verbal, be it newspaper commentaries, politicians' speeches, medical research results – or even books on philosophy, philosophers and their thinking. In order to know what is being meant, we need to know something about the authors, their motivations, the context and the intended audience. That is healthy scholarship; and Spinoza urged it when evaluating the Torah and related scriptures, indeed, the whole of the Bible.

Returning to the metaphysics, and how to conduct our lives, Spinoza tells of a worm in the blood. The worm would consider the blood as the whole of the world, not as a mere part of a much greater reality. Spinoza's emphasis is on how a proper understanding requires an appreciation of reality under the aspect of eternity, *sub specie aeternitatis* – independently of the particular positions in the world in which we stand. People are opposed to each other in as far as they are afflicted by passions, but the dictates of reason, of seeing things objectively, bring people together. Reasoning brings a convergence between minds – their will and my will become one and the same. That is Spinoza's optimistic thought.

Logicians may argue over who makes the coffee or who first proved a theorem, but at some stage their reason is harmonious in acknowledging that certain propositions do follow from certain premises. In the grubby empirical world, we mostly lack the purity of pure reasoning, for we also have divergencies on what is for the best from our different perspectives. We need to detach ourselves from our particular position in the world – as the worm should from the blood. The detachment is through reasoning, whereby we can come to understand how individuals are acting as a result of their natures and surroundings. With that detachment, we should better cope with the world; and Spinoza certainly sought to cope. He wrote that he tried 'neither to laugh at human actions nor to mourn about them nor to detest them, but to understand them'.

———————————

Spinoza worked on himself: he was humane; he was kind. Let us overlook the report that one of his pleasures was to cast flies into cobwebs of competing spiders, laughing at the ensuing battles. Did he see their battles as showing, in the great chain of being, how all creatures are determined to self-assertion? Was it some psychological release for him, given the fortitude that he maintained when suffering all the wrongs and attacks from society? He did once comment, 'Nothing human is alien to me.'

In fact, Spinoza bore considerable injustices, poverty, condemnation, without bitterness. With that in mind, when we are outraged by someone's behaviour, may we not seek to understand how that behaviour came about? I add: and ask whether we would like to be such a person, acting in that wrongful or obnoxious way? When the answer is that we should very much *not* like to be such a person, I have recommended that we should therefore feel sorry for that individual. To date, my recommendation has received no support.

With focus on the universe as one substance, as God, as Nature, Spinoza, as said, saw human beings as mere modifications of that one substance, God or Nature. That understanding influenced many thinkers: George Eliot, of *Middlemarch* fame, did a translation of his *Ethics*; romantic poets, such as Wordsworth and Coleridge, turned to Spinoza; and Shelley, in his *Adonais*, writes:

The One remains, the many change and pass;
Heaven's light forever shines, Earth's shadows fly;
Life, like a dome of many-colour'd glass,
Stains the white radiance of Eternity ...

It is gaining an appreciation of God or Nature under the aspect of eternity, not from my own perspective, that we should grasp how to think least of death. We typically view death from our personal temporal standpoint: I think of the world continuing in time, of all these familiar things around me, yet there is no 'I'; I am absent – and that may strike me as terrifying. Step outside, though, outside of time, and there is the world under the aspect of eternity, where all ego is lost.

Although Spinoza was pious, ever keen to live the life of reason, that did not mean that he had no time for a glass of wine and some tobacco – and maybe the spectacle of fighting spiders – but he saw true happiness as recognizing our eternity through understanding God or Nature. That can, by the way, be as much by scientific empirical studies as by abstract reasoning.

———

Spinoza's vision of an eternity led Israel's first prime minister, David Ben-Gurion, in the 1950s, to lobby for removal of the curses against Spinoza – pointlessly so, for on Spinoza's death, his ultimate exclusion, according to the Orthodox, was fixed and irrevocable. That would not have troubled Spinoza and it would not have surprised him. As he said, 'All things excellent are as difficult as they are rare.'

———

How to think like Spinoza? *Seek to understand the world and others through free and rational enquiry untainted by anthropomorphic religious superstition – that is, find deepest happiness in 'God or Nature' under the aspect of eternity.*

11

Leibniz: Monad Man

This is the best of all possible worlds.
Leibniz

'Monad' is not an everyday term that slips off people's tongues. The philosophical work *Monadology* is virtually unknown outside of philosophy circles. The author, much neglected in his day, has since been assessed as one of the greatest figures in philosophy, logic and mathematics. And he is. Yes, here is Gottfried Wilhelm (von) Leibniz, born 1646, in Leipzig. His name in the big wide world is for many people encountered solely through the biscuits *Choco Leibniz* introduced in 1891 by the Bahlsen company in Hanover. No Choco Leibniz ever passed Leibniz's lips, of course, but Leibniz had been a resident of Hanover and it was not unusual to name produce after a town's 'famous son'.

Biscuits to one side, some non-philosophers would know of Leibniz through his mantra, 'This is the best of all possible worlds', though probably only via Voltaire's story *Candide*. The story mocked Leibniz's belief by taking us across a litany of sufferings, woes and despair, resulting from a catastrophe based in fact: namely, Lisbon's 1755 earthquake. Is this world really the best possible that a deity could have created? And 'best' by which criteria? Richness of ends and economy of means – and a richness in terms of maximum diversity compatible with orderliness for human life? After all, without sufficient diversity, we may suffer boredom, yet excessive diversity may lead to chaos.

Leibniz introduced the framework of possible worlds to examine what is possible and impossible. There is an infinite number of possible worlds, it seems, very similar to this actual one, the sole differences being those resulting from (say) your choosing not to read this book or this book not having been written. There is an infinite number of possible worlds, it seems, radically different from this actual one – ones, for example, where the laws of nature are different, where maybe no life at all evolved. There are, though, no possible worlds where, for example, the number nineteen is not a prime number or at this very moment I am actually both in London and not in London.

Leibniz and most philosophers think of possible worlds as just that, *possible*. Some, though, argue for their existence as being akin to the existence of this actual world and with our having counterparts in many of those other 'real', though non-actual, worlds. Thus it is that we see how philosophical thinking can spin off – and here even into directions where some cosmologists proclaim the reality, the actuality, of the multiverse; it contains this universe together with many radically different universes with different constants and laws of nature.

Leibniz held fast to – what he termed – the Principle of Sufficient Reason, the 'apex of rationality'. The Principle was at work in Avicenna's thinking, as seen in Chapter 8. Leibniz could not see how the world could exist without being grounded in the all-benevolent, all-powerful God – and so it follows that this must be the best possible world. Of course, that should remind us that, even when confronted with the immense intellectual powers of a Leibniz, we ought not to collapse and yield – we should be a Socratic gadfly, stinging

Leibniz into explaining why we must accept, for example, the Principle of Sufficient Reason. Maybe some things happen or exist without reason, as apparently believers in God find convincing; namely the existence of God. Let us say a little more about our philosopher here before turning to more of his thinking.

Leibniz was born into an academic Leipzig family. In young adulthood, declining a law professorship, he chose the practical world of diplomacy, working for barons and dukes, hoping to travel, to contact other thinkers and rise in eminence. He was invigorated by new ideas and the latest researches, be they about Eastern mysticisms or Leeuwenhoek's microscopic discoveries of items swarming with bugs: witness the wonderful title of one of Leibniz's papers: 'A Specimen of Discoveries about Marvellous Secrets of a General Nature'.

Rejecting monkish erudition that lacked the foundations of experience and activity, he devised computing machines (they worked), constructed a windmill for the Harz silver-mines (it didn't work) and invented the differential calculus (independently of Newton, despite what the English said at the time). Possessing kaleidoscopic interests, he founded the Berlin Academy, sought to reconcile Catholicism and Protestantism – the French and Germans – and encouraged Russia's Peter the Great to trade with China. Not for Leibniz to be caricatured as a philosopher, Socratic-style, with his head in the clouds.

Leibniz deployed the mantra 'Calculemus' – 'Let us calculate' – believing that once we are clear about our concepts, then reasoning, be it in philosophy, mathematics or even disputes between nations, can be grasped as a form of calculation, leading to definitive conclusions. We shall encounter that idea in philosophical thinking later on, when meeting John Stuart Mill with his utilitarianism and criticism of Jeremy Bentham's 'felicitous calculus', calculating the best means for overall happiness.

Here is an elusive gem from Leibniz: 'That which is not truly one entity is not truly one entity.' Although it sounds platitudinous, it is at Leibniz's metaphysical heart; and that heart is the monad. Leibniz conceived reality as consisting solely of distinct unities; they are the monads. The elusive gem just mentioned needs suitable stresses: what is not truly *one* entity is not truly one *entity* – where, as he wonderfully adds, a differentiation is marked solely by accentuation.

A real entity, a substance, needs unity. We recognize a flock of sheep as a collection, but the flock is not a genuine substance; it is not a unity. However much the sheep roam together sheepishly or are kept in place by a sheepdog, we can tell that they are not truly one entity. Yet a flock of sheep has more unity to it than a selection of items that I shall now pick out in my room – say, an empty bottle of wine, some coffee, books, a mouse, dust – and name it as a 'squaggle'. My squaggle has pretty minimal unity. The bottle will be thrown out and recycled; the mouse, I hope, will seek warmer climes; and the coffee will be consumed. Books and dust will accumulate.

What motivated Leibniz was the principle that anything 'really' real needs to be determinate; anything with physical size, though, can be divided again and again, endlessly – recall Zeno of Elea and his paradoxes. Commitment to Leibniz's principle ensures that what we usually take as instances of reality – arms and legs, tables and chairs, pebbles and plants – are not so. They are along the lines of the flock of sheep.

As anything extended in space is theoretically divisible without end, it cannot be real, but is mere appearance. True realities, the monads, cannot be extended. What then are monads? Leibniz turned to the mind, to the self. We experience a unity 'from within'; I cannot make sense of my *self* dividing. I am a true reality, a monad – as are you. My self, as a monad, is, for Leibniz, the paradigm of reality. The Leibnizian monad of a person is Descartes' indivisible soul or ego.

What, then, of the items around us? Are they just collections of ideas, as maintained by a certain Bishop Berkeley, that 'paradoxical Irishman' as Leibniz called him? No. Although material items cannot be composed of monads in the sense of having monads as their parts – after all, monads lack size and extension – material items have some touch of reality for they are 'grounded in' bare monads, unities that are soul-like, yet ones that lack the self-awareness of the rational souls that we are. What we think of as 'material' objects are 'well-founded phenomena', existing independently of our perceptions, but resulting in some way from the bare monads.

As with Descartes and Spinoza, we have then the obsession with grasping the world in terms of the concept of 'substance'. All three of them believe that only God is the true substance, only God is completely independent of everything else. In that sense, all three are monists. Are any of them dualists? Well, Descartes, as seen, argues that there are only two radically different types of created substance, two distinct attributes – immaterial and material – whereas Spinoza holds that the one substance has an infinite number of attributes. And while Leibniz insists that there is a plurality of created substances, they are all of the same type, namely soul-like. The labels of 'monist', 'dualist', 'pluralist' need then to be handled with considerable care.

According to Leibniz, as indicated, we should picture reality as consisting of a vast number of monads, of unities, each possessing some weak kinship to ourselves. Mysteriously, they each represent the whole universe, past, present and future. They are 'burdened with the past and pregnant with the future'. Leibniz drew that conclusion from some logical considerations;

indeed, he says that a whole new world opened before him, once he properly and logically analysed the concept of substance. That should remind us again of how philosophical thinking, indeed, any thinking, presupposes certain basic concepts, and sometimes we may rightly wonder whether those concepts are the most appropriate.

Leibniz writes of monads being 'windowless'. They do not interact; so now we have the obscurity of how they account for what seems to be cause and effect in the physical world and for my being able to decide to lift my arm. In the latter case, we are back with the mind/body interaction problem.

Leibniz's popular 'solution' is in terms of 'pre-established harmony'; it is akin to God having wound up the monads to have their perceptions, their mental states, or their representations of the world, occurring in harmony. Of course, we are returned to mysteries; and it even becomes difficult to grasp what the monads' perceptions are expressing, if only expressing each other. There are scholarly attempts to sort it all out – and also a generosity in understanding the problems with which Leibniz grappled.

One problem was the nature of causation, of the relationship between cause and effect. Descartes was suitably baffled over mind/body causation and, in Chapter 9, we saw Malebranche resorting to God for his explanation – in fact, for his explanation of the causal relationship more generally. Quite how to analyse that relationship continues to keep many philosophers in business.

For another aspect to Leibniz, here is a well-known, albeit curiously expressed, question in contemporary philosophy, 'What is it like to be a bat?' However much we learn about bats – their behaviour, their neurology, their sensory systems – is there not something that remains elusive, though we believe it exists: namely, what it is like 'from within', from the bat's perspective, to experience the world, to suffer or be satisfied, flying hither and thither? That reflection should lead us to be appalled at the tale of Descartes' alleged treatment of the dog. Leibniz, in contrast to Descartes, saw life as a continuum; he recognized the existence of degrees of similarities between humans and other animals; in reality that is a matter of similarity between monads. It is reported that after investigating a worm under a magnifying glass, he carefully returned it to its leaf. In Chapter 30, we find a related concern, in a Beckett tale, for a lobster.

Leibniz was prolific – 'an academy in himself' said Frederick the Great – yet he produced no magnum opus. His ideas, and their developments, are found in a voluminous correspondence and essays, engaging contemporaries, such as Spinoza (as already seen), Antoine Arnauld in France and John Locke in Britain. Many papers of his remain unpublished and in need of assessment. I recall an editor's footnote to one of Leibniz's papers where the editor draws attention to a further comment by Leibniz discovered on a scrap of paper. I wondered if Leibniz had thrown it away, not anticipating that centuries later researchers would be going through his waste-paper basket. A moral here is: destroy what you do not want seen.

What else should we glean from Leibniz's thinking, when musing upon our lives? Well, we must acknowledge our sense of continuity, of a unity to our experiences through time. We are monads. Leibniz also reminds us that reality may be very different from what appears to be so. Under the microscope, we see life to which our eyes are blind. Under the power of Leibniz's reasoning, we should realize that behind the appearances of evil, sufferings and disasters, there exists an all-good all-powerful god. Oops, maybe Leibniz also unwittingly shows us that even his reasoning deserves some serious scepticism.

While we may be reluctant to fall for this world as being the best of all possible worlds, in fact Leibniz's introduction of 'possible worlds' in assessing how things could have been has been exceptionally valuable in recent advances in logic and metaphysics, in, for example, the work of the American logician, Saul Kripke.

Whether we can be justified in thinking that at least some things are contingent – some things could have happened otherwise; some choices I could have made differently – is open to debate. We have already seen how Spinoza, also operating with the concept of substance and relying on rigorous reasoning, reaches conclusions very different from Leibniz's. That should alert us as follows.

However convincing the reasoning of a great philosopher, we may then encounter another great philosopher with very different reasoning. It is often not easy to assess quite what is going on between philosophers who paint different pictures of reality. We need humility; we need open minds. We need to take our time in our reflections and assessments.

Leibniz's last years were spent in Hanover, then an intellectual and cultural backwater. He was reluctantly labouring on a history of the House of Brunswick, having failed to persuade George I to appoint him Historiographer Royal and bring him to London's intellectual buzz. Leibniz died lonely and disenchanted. Only his secretary attended his funeral. His grave was unmarked.

How to think like Leibniz? *Pay attention to possible worlds and seek a reality that is determinate. Remember: this world is the best possible – so make the best of it for all and one.*

12

Bishop Berkeley, 'That Paradoxical Irishman': Immaterialist, Tar-Water Advocate

Think with the learned, and speak with the vulgar.

Berkeley

A philosophical question that sets people thinking is the following. There's a forest; a storm builds up with thunder and lightning. A tree crashes to the ground. No one is nearby to hear. Was it a silent crash? Was there thunder without the sound of thunder? Did the lightning flash – or did it light up not at all? To avoid complexities, allow me quickly to add that neither birds, badgers, buck deer, nor any other conscious creatures, were present to hear or see. For completeness, I add: nor to touch, taste or smell.

The forest illustration is not explicitly provided by this chapter's philosopher, but it is very much in his spirit; and 'spirit' is the appropriate term. He was keen on spirits; he rejected matter. He is the philosopher of immaterialism. The whole of reality consists solely of spirits – we are spirits, minds, souls – with notions or ideas and perceptions, with, that is, sensations of sight, sound, taste and so forth. Matter is a repugnancy, a contradictory notion, if understood as something that can exist independently of mind. We here meet George Berkeley. His immaterialism is often deemed 'idealism' because the perceptions are readily referred to as ideas, but not because of his ideals (though, as bishop, he doubtless had many).

A sound cannot exist unheard for a sound essentially involves an auditory experience; and experiences essentially require subjects, spirits, minds, experiencing. It is that focus on experiences – of how our contact with the world of trees, turnips and tablets of stone is through experiences – that brings us, as said, to the philosophical thinking of Berkeley, usually indeed referred to as *Bishop* Berkeley. He was not, however, appointed Bishop of Cloyne, in the Church of Ireland, until 1734 – and that was twenty years or so after his most stunning philosophical thinking hit the philosophical world.

Berkeley travelled a lot, persuaded the British government to fund a college to be founded in Bermuda (an 'earthly paradise' thought Berkeley, though he never visited), married, went to America and returned to Dublin. The funding failed to materialize (metaphorically unsurprising, given his immaterialism), but his one poem did:

> Westward the course of empire takes its way;
> The first four acts already past,
> A fifth shall close the drama with the day;
> Time's noblest offspring is the last.

His *Verses on the Prospect of Planting Arts and Learning in America* (1728) told of how, with Europe 'breeding decay', his confidence was in America (the colonies as part of the British Empire) for reason and virtue. Well, Berkeley's enthusiasm at least led to the naming of Berkeley, California, and to the University of California, Berkeley.

Once we seek to understand the world through our experiences, we can easily be led to Berkeley's seemingly bizarre conclusion. The conclusion is that everything is mind-dependent; nothing can exist outside of mind, that is, without a mind. Bizarre initially it may seem, yet on reflection it may strike us as obviously true, for our sole access to the world depends on our experiences, on sights and sounds and touch and aromas and tastes; and all of those are experiences essentially requiring conscious perceivers. Whatever can justify us in going beyond them and insisting that there must exist entities unperceived? Oops, there is something that justifies that move. Indeed, Berkeley emphasizes that his philosophical thinking is not correctly summed simply as 'to be is to be perceived'. The correct aphorism is:

To be is to be perceived – or to perceive.

Berkeley needs to accept – and he does – that even though we do not have perceptions of spirits, of minds, we know that we are more than bundles of perceptions. I am an agent: some of my perceptions I cause; some I find forced upon me – but at least, contra Malebranche, 'tis I who move my legs. Of course, if all that I have to go on are my perceptions, then Berkeley needs to provide an account of how, in some way, I infer from those perceptions the existence of other spirits, other minds, unperceived by me. Berkeley is no solipsist; he does not believe that reality consists solely of his spirit and his ideas.

On the surface, the tree that I see and touch depends for its existence on my experiences whereas my existence does not depend on the tree-like experiences. When I turn away (so to speak) from the tree, it ceases to exist – and 'pops back', if I turn again to see. Of course, all that turning amounts to sequences of perceptions, as does my body, my arms, my legs, my eyes. All that is far from common sense.

'Twas Leibniz who labelled Berkeley 'that paradoxical Irishman'; that itself is paradoxical, given that Leibniz described the material world as 'phenomena', though, for Leibniz, it was at least well-founded phenomena being grounded in Leibniz's plurality of genuine real independent substances, the bare monads. Berkeley has none of that; or is that so? As already implied, he is happy to speak of the reality of tables, trees and tablets of stones, of money, marmalade and marigolds, but they are just collections of mind-dependent ideas. Berkeley thus recommends that we ought to think with the learned, yet speak with the vulgar.

Berkeley's response to his seemingly paradoxical conclusion is not great. It is summed up in the following Ronald Knox limerick for, with one bound, Berkeley is free by invoking the greatest spirit of all:

> There once was a man who said 'God
> Must think it exceedingly odd
> If he finds that this tree
> Continues to be
> When there's no one about in the Quad.'

> Dear Sir,
> Your astonishment's odd.
> *I* am always about in the Quad.
> And that's why the tree
> Will continue to be
> Since observed by
> Yours faithfully,
> God.

The importance of the Christian religion in Berkeley's thinking is manifested in his keenly quoting the Bible that 'in God, we live and move and have our being'. We saw earlier (in Chapter

10) how Spinoza from a Jewish perspective may be understood as working with that biblical idea, yet drawing very different conclusions about reality. Once again, we should note how philosophers can cast different lights on reality, even when operating with similar concepts or starting points.

Berkeley's invocation of God is a desperate move – well, maybe not, I guess, if you are destined to become a bishop. Leibniz's phenomena were grounded in a plurality of immaterial unities, his monads. Berkeley's phenomena end up being grounded in the infinite spirit, God. Of course, if we seek to engage details, it all becomes highly confusing and confused: for example, how do my perceptions 'of a tree' relate to your perceptions 'of a tree', past, present and future, and to God's perceptions 'of a tree' – and such that in some cases we are all seeing 'the same tree'? Indeed, it is worse than that, for in his final work, *Siris*, Berkeley now writes of God's perceptions as Ideas or 'Archetypes', the most real beings, unchangeable, accessible by reason only. That hints of Plato's Forms.

Maybe Berkeley has gone wrong from the very start. Maybe he is conflating our experiences or sensations with the causes of those experiences or sensations. Yes, he is right that to one hand, the water is hot to the touch, to the other tepid, but that is accounted for by the molecular motion of the water affecting different states of sensitivity of the hands' nerve endings.

That is the line presented by John Locke, another key empiricist philosopher; he was writing in the late seventeenth century as an 'under-labourer' to the great Isaac Newton. Locke spoke of primary and secondary qualities. 'Out there' are mind-independent qualities such as size, shape, motion, impenetrability, whereas the secondary qualities, such as colour, taste, smell, sound, and warmth or cold, do rely on the perceivers' interaction with the objects possessed of the primary qualities. 'Ah', we can imagine Berkeley replying, 'You lapse into fanciful metaphysics with your talk of size and shape and motion – whatever is that motion or, for that matter, electrons, neutrons and so forth, other than useful talk for us to make predictions? All we have to go on are our experiences.'

Berkeley can be viewed as an 'instrumentalist' regarding scientific entities and physical objects thought of as distinct from our experiences. Whatever physicists and neurologists may say about molecules, fibres and the range of sub-atomic particles, they are relying on their *experiences* of scanned results in print or sentences and images flickering on computer screens. Use of scientific concepts such as 'molecules', use of common-sense concepts such as 'clouds', may be valuable for us to make good predictions, but it is a mistake to think of reality as constituted by those entities if mind-independent. For Berkeley, the regularities we experience in nature are, in a sense, as he says, 'the language of God'.

A famous reaction to Berkeley's immaterialism is that of Dr Johnson, Samuel Johnson, who insisted that he refuted Berkeley (note the use of 'refute' – a success verb, with Johnson maintaining he was right). James Boswell recalls the incident. It was in 1763; Johnson and Boswell were discussing Berkeley's 'ingenious sophistry to prove the non-existence of matter'. Boswell observed that although immaterialism was obviously false, it was impossible to refute it. That caused the strong reaction from Johnson. Boswell records, 'I never shall forget the alacrity with which Johnson answered, striking his foot with mighty force against a large stone, till he rebounded from it, "I refute it thus."'

Perhaps Johnson was appealing to the seeming agency of the stone, in its reacting to his foot, but, for Berkeley, that consisted solely of some additional experiences, nothing more, nothing less. Perhaps Johnson was merely appealing to the importance of common-sense beliefs (look out for G. E. Moore later), though that returns us to the question of the correct understanding of those beliefs. Berkeley's objection is to matter understood as mind-independent, but so long as we do not hold that mistaken belief, he is content to speak of tables and chairs, trees and treacle. He speaks with the common man. 'I side in all things with the mob.' He unites with 'the illiterate bulk of mankind that walk the high-road of plain, common sense'.

Once God is deleted from Berkeley's thinking, his approach has, at times, secured significant philosophical support, being presented as a 'phenomenalist' account of physical objects. Those objects, if correctly understood, are 'permanent possibilities of sensation', an expression from John Stuart Mill.

On the phenomenalist account, this table I am leaning on does exist, even when unperceived (untouched, unseen and so forth); but all that means is that were I, or others, to engage in certain actions 'walking back into the study' – though, remember, that walking is just a series of sensations and the study is another possibility of sensations – we should undergo again similar 'table' sensations. If, though, the existence of mind-independent objects baffles us, then surely we should also be baffled by the nature of possibilities existing and indeed by the justification for my speaking of 'we' and 'us'. I am still in need of a justification for belief in the existence of other people, otherwise I lapse into solipsism: only I and my perceptions exist. A little more on that is offered when we reach Bertrand Russell and an American lady.

———

I cannot leave the good bishop without his insistence on communicating to the public the 'salutary virtues of tar-water'. It featured heavily in his letters and in his final work, *Siris*, titled:

A Chain of Philosophical Reflexions and Inquiries concerning the Virtues of Tar-water, and divers other subjects connected together and arising one from another.

He cites evidence for its effectiveness and he carefully sets out details of how to prepare and apply, depending on the ailment in question. Tar-water is: a preservative against the smallpox, a cure for foulness of blood, ulceration of bowels, lungs, consumptive coughs – the list goes on, in detail. It is of great use in gout, fevers, gangrene, erysipelas, scurvy and hypochondriac maladies. Berkeley recommends it for seafaring persons, ladies and men of studious and sedentary lives – also for preserving trees from the biting of goats and other injuries.

Berkeley's obsession with tar-water led John Oulton Wisdom (cousin of the Cambridge philosopher John Wisdom and often confused with him) to write *The Unconscious Origin of Berkeley's Philosophy* (1953) where explanations for the obsession is given by way of an ambivalent childhood reaction to certain bodily functions and disposals.

Whatever we may think of explanations in terms of the unconscious, we should certainly warm to the thought that Berkeley deserved the accolade 'that paradoxical Irishman'. Indeed, 'paradoxical' thinking is a mark, one may think, of all philosophers, even if claiming to be of the 'common sense' variety.

How to think like Berkeley? *Focus on your experiences – and don't forget the tar-water.*

13

David Hume: The Great Infidel *or* *Le Bon David*

A wise man proportions his belief to the evidence.

Hume

Here is a philosopher, infidel or no, a philosopher of considerable influence, putting philosophical thinking in its place – and also that of the religious. I bring forth David Hume, the great eighteenth-century Scottish Enlightenment figure, a philosopher with a very good press among today's philosophers, admired for his good humour, his irony, as well as for his penetrating insights.

The *Enlightenment* identifies the times in the eighteenth century when, so the story goes, the intellectual ethos was that people should think freely for themselves, valuing reason and empirical researches, as opposed to relying on authorities, scriptures or divine revelation. We shall soon meet Kant who deployed the Latin '*sapere aude*' as 'having the courage to think for oneself'. We shall however shortly see that things are not as simple as that thumbnail sketch may convey. Enlightenment Hume, while valuing scientific enquiry, demoted reason and elevated feeling and habit.

Hume, with his Enlightenment stance, inevitably met with considerable opposition from the religious and, not so inevitably, from certain philosophers. He was condemned because of the following forthright pronouncement about thinking, any thinking, be it religious or philosophical. 'If we take in our hand any volume; of divinity or school metaphysics,' he asks:

> Does it contain any abstract reasoning concerning quantity or number? No. Does it contain any experimental reasoning concerning matter of fact and existence? No. Commit it then to the flames: for it can contain nothing but sophistry and illusion.

With Hume's methodological commitment to experiences as the source of all knowledge, he quickly finds himself in a mire of bafflement. He is honest enough to own up. Quite what can we make of our belief that physical objects exist when we lack experiences? Whatever can we make of the continuing self? After all, I have experiences seemingly of things around me, memories of what 'I' did; yet what is the 'I', the self? Although he attempted various explanations, he was dissatisfied with them all.

Philosophical thinking can often lead to bafflements; that led Wittgenstein, as we shall see, to speak of philosophy as engendering a feeling of my 'not knowing my way about'. Hume described what would happen once he closed the door of his study, shutting out those philosophical speculations and puzzlings that generated 'melancholy and delirium' within his troubled breast:

> I dine, I play a game of back-gammon, I converse, and am merry with my friends; and when after three or four hours' amusement, I wou'd return to these speculations, they appear so cold, and strain'd, and ridiculous, that I cannot find in my heart to enter into them any farther.

Yet he did enter into them further. Philosophical thinking captivates; and, in the case of Hume, he was trying to 'follow the science'. More accurately, he was impressed with how Newton had explained planetary movements. Presumably, he overlooked the difficulty of determining quite what constituted gravity. With Newton in mind, he, Hume, sought to be the Newton *of* the mind. He wanted to show how the mind operated on its impressions 'from outside' to form ideas and beliefs and so forth about the world, that is, on moral subjects. His first work title's *A Treatise of Human Nature* continues as: *Being an Attempt to Introduce the Experimental Method of Reasoning into Moral Subjects*. Hume's approach to philosophy as akin to a scientific endeavour, with metaphysics sent off to the flames, was rigorously reworked, as Logical Positivism, in the early twentieth century by those of the Vienna Circle. (Please see Chapter 29 for the Logical Positivist stance on ethics.)

On the religious front, the Great Infidel, as he became known by some, would additionally upset the Christian hierarchy by making use of a simple and appropriate mantra: 'A wise man proportions his belief to the evidence.' By the way, the accolade of the 'Great Infidel' was unjustified; Hume was possibly more of an agnostic or perhaps better described as a casual and carefree 'don't know'. Apparently, when in Paris, dining with some well-known philosophers, he was astonished and made uneasy by their outspoken and vehement atheism.

With the mantra about belief and evidence to the fore, Hume rejected reports of miracles. His thinking was very straightforward and sensible. When assessing what to believe about an alleged miracle, we should determine whether it is more likely that an extraordinary event occurred, courtesy of God – a miracle – or that reports of the event were unreliable.

On the one hand, the occurrence of the miraculous event, to be a miracle, is exceptionally, exceptionally unlikely, whether or not brought about by God or by a breakdown in what we take to be the laws of nature. On the other hand, the unreliability of reports, be it by mistake, intention or wishful thinking, especially over considerable time-spans, is well attested. One should therefore on balance reject the 'greater miracle'; that is, one should reject the veracity of the miracle reports.

We could add a caveat, for Hume made the nice quip that 'Christian religion not only was at first attended with miracles, but even at this day cannot be believed by any reasonable person without one.' All those decades ago, when I first read that sentence, I delighted in Hume's irony. What could he be understood as saying? Well: 'Oops, maybe I'm wrong; maybe there is one miracle – namely, that some people do believe in miracles.' Of course, that is not in the least extraordinary, for it is quite common to engage in wishful thinking; and some – I am unsure why – wish for an eternal afterlife and judgement.

Hume used his focus on evidence to put other godly arguments in their place, a lowly place. That there must be a divine designer of the universe has often been argued on the basis of analogy, a way of philosophical thinking. Many complicated contrivances – watches, aeroplanes, the internet – came about only through human design. The intricate workings of the universe, the interdependence of species with the environment and so forth, must therefore be indicative, by analogy, of a great divine design – so the argument goes. If we are to hold to that analogy with human beings and what they design, pointed out Hume, then we should just as readily conclude that the universe resulted from a committee of gods or perhaps it is the first 'botched job of an infant deity'. Furthermore, even if we can somehow be justified in believing that there must be a divine designer, that justification goes no way towards proving that the designer must be motivated by benevolence, by special concern for human beings, and be the inspiration behind the Torah or the Qur'ān – or who knows what.

Regarding his *Treatise*, published when he was aged twenty-seven, now recognized as a major work of philosophy, Hume wrote: 'Never literary attempt was more unfortunate. It fell dead-born from the press.' Later, some writings by Hume began to sell, partly thanks to the condemnations by Reverends and Right Reverends. 'I found', noted Hume, 'that the books were beginning to be esteemed in good company.' Later still, Hume's *Histories* became very popular, making him financially 'not only independent but opulent'.

Despite that success, Hume downplayed its significance – as indeed he downplayed the importance of humanity. He puts us in our place with the pithy observation:

The life of man is of no greater importance to the universe than that of an oyster.

That, of course, upset the Christian theologians further, for they held that God granted human beings a special place in the universe. Thus, they argued that suicide was immoral, interfering with the course of God's natural laws. Hume, ever seeking consistency, noted that if such an argument held, then it must also be immoral to duck, in order to avoid death from a falling slate in a storm.

Returning to the oyster, we should rightly question what sense can be made of taking the viewpoint of the universe, a viewpoint that we found urged, in a way, by Spinoza, and how to assess whether the life of the oyster is more – or less – important. True, we can often and rightly step back a little, to consider how well a life is going, be it ours or others. The biggest 'step back', giving the widest view that makes sense, may be understood as the one where no special preference is given to me or to my particular community. That directs us towards understanding the widest view as the most impartial view, though that is not the viewpoint of the universe. The universe has no idea of what is partial or impartial.

Morality often promotes fairness and impartiality, yet how far should that be taken? How far can it be taken? We first encountered that problem with Plato on justice (Chapter 5) and we shall delve into more queries via J. S. Mill and utilitarianism (Chapter 16). To go to an extreme, does the widest impartial view give no preference to the flourishing of human beings over that of non-human animals – of oysters?

Oysters to one side, I have not finished with Hume putting things 'in their place'. Although he made much use of reason, reason, as mentioned at this chapter's beginning, also gets cut down to size for we cannot justify how in fact we use it. Referring to past evidence to judge what will happen is an example of inductive reasoning; yet who knows how things will work out in the future? It is no use to argue that such reasoning has worked out well; yes, it has often worked out well in the past, but the future may not be like the past.

Hume's solution to the problem of induction – really, it is no solution at all – is one of acceptance, of an acceptance that we do what cannot be rationally justified. Habit, custom, is the great guide of human life, he writes. We cannot help but believe in certain uniformities in nature and act accordingly. That is a moral we should do well to accept, at least to the extent of realizing that not everything can be justified. As Wittgenstein later would emphasize: somewhere along the line, we must accept, 'this is what we do'.

Over many years, students of mine have insisted that we cannot know the future. Are they right? Do we really not know that in the next few minutes, as you read these words (if anyone is reading), this book will not transform into a wild walrus screeching out 'Born in the USA' or a band playing 'Land of Hope and Glory'?

Hume also demotes reason when morality comes into view.

> Reason is, and ought only to be the slave of the passions, and can never pretend to any other office than to serve and obey them,

he announces, adding,

> It is not contrary to reason to prefer the destruction of the whole world to the scratching of my finger.

We must rely on our passions, our feelings for each other, to ground our moral beliefs; rationality does not reveal to us at what we should aim. There is only scope for good and bad reasoning when assessing the most efficient means for achieving the aim. The aims are grounded in our humanity, in our social disposition – though, sadly, we cannot rely on everyone being possessed of humanity, of a social disposition.

Earlier, we heard of Hume's distress and philosophical melancholy. How to understand 'personal identity' was one of the major causes of his disquiet. Socrates, Descartes and others, made free use of the soul, of a mind, or a self, continuing through time, but Hume famously wrote of however much he looks 'within', he can find no such continuous entity; all he finds are sequences of fleeting experiences, fleeting perceptions. What holds them together, as a bundle, to make them 'mine' and to make this set of sequences my 'self' continuing through time? That question continues to baffle philosophers even today; thus we may have sympathy for his closing the door on his philosophical perplexities – and seeking the comfort of modest women.

In his short autobiography, written when nearing death, Hume explains, 'I was struck with a disorder of my bowels'. He, rather charmingly, describes his character and life:

> I am, or rather was (for that is the style I must now use in speaking of myself): I was, I say, a man of mild disposition, of command of temper, of an open, social, and cheerful humour, capable of attachment, but little susceptible of enmity, and of great moderation in all my passions. Even my love of literary fame, my ruling passion, never soured my temper, notwithstanding my frequent disappointments. My company was not unacceptable to the young and careless, as well as to the studious and literary; and as I took a particular pleasure in the company of modest women, I had no reason to be displeased with the reception I met with from them.

James Boswell (yes, the Boswell who told of the life of Samuel Johnson) contrived to bolster his own religious faith by visiting the Great Infidel. Boswell apparently hoped to see Hume withdrawing from his atheism and suddenly being committed to belief or hope in an afterlife provided by a divinity. Boswell's hope was not realized. Hume gave no recantation.

The tale reminds me of how the American comedian and well-known atheist, W. C. Fields, was spotted reading the Bible when close to death. Hoping that he was finally seeing the Christian light, his friends asked what he was up to, reading the Bible of all things. 'Just looking for loopholes,' was the reply.

Adam Smith, the famous Scottish economist and close friend of Hume, described how *le bon David*, right to the end, spoke with affection and tenderness:

> He had now become so very weak, that the company of his most intimate friends fatigued him; for his cheerfulness was still so great, his complaisance and social disposition were

still so entire, that when any friend was with him, he could not help talking more, and with greater exertion, than suited the weakness of his body.

Whether this lack of fear of death showed him to be the Great Infidel or *Le bon David* – well, I leave that to the reader. What it does show is that it is possible to face death and annihilation in good spirits and with good humour. Hume's philosophical thinking combined with his good-humoured disposition enabled him to do just that.

———

How to think like David Hume? *Examine the ways of the world and philosophical bafflements with good humour – and with feelings for others.*

14

Kant: Duty Calls, Categorically

Out of the crooked timber of humanity
no straight thing was ever made.

Kant

What should we make of an eminent philosopher, one of the very greatest, known for his strong sense of moral duty, with regard to the following?

When a young woman wrote privately to him, telling of her despair, her suicidal thoughts and how she found no comfort in his philosophy – she was resisting suicide only because his philosophy proclaimed it morally horrendous – he made the correspondence public, abusing her trust, and refused to see her.

When writing of sexual love, he insisted that it 'makes of the loved person an object of appetite; as soon as that appetite has been stilled, the person is cast aside as one casts away a lemon which has been sucked dry'.

When seeking to establish the immorality of suicide, he adds that masturbation is morally worse – for not only is it morally wrong but we also receive pleasure from that immorality which is delivered neither by suicides nor unsuccessful attempts at suicide.

Yes, this is Immanuel Kant, treated both within and without philosophy as the great Enlightenment philosopher of the eighteenth century. He is placed in the heavenly firmament, the greatest stars, of Western philosophy – with Plato and Aristotle. The young woman mentioned has no place among the stars. She is Maria von Herbert, hardly known at all. Nine years after her correspondence with Kant she took her life; she was in her early thirties. In dealings with Herbert, Kant failed to live up to his standards; I guess that he showed himself to be human in accordance with his aphorism heading this chapter.

Kant lived all his life in the small Prussian town of Königsberg. For decades, as a professor of philosophy, he was largely unnoted outside of the town. Transformation occurred in the early 1780s, as he entered his sixties; that age has provided aspiring hope for many philosophers, though one that gradually diminishes. In 1781, he published his *Critique of Pure Reason* and, with the revision in 1787, he never looked back, seeing himself as having effected a Copernican revolution in philosophy. That *Critique*, two subsequent critiques, *of Practical Reason*; *of Judgement*, and further works, made his name and fame. Possibly those critiques and maybe those of Karl Marx have generated the fashion among some students to speak of even their smallest essays as 'critiques', though not yet as Copernican revolutions.

In order to explain the celestial motions, argued Copernicus, the earth could not be a fixed point; its motion contributed to the appearances of the heavenly bodies. In a similar fashion, in order to explain how we have experiences of objects, we need to recognize the contribution of the mind, the perceiving subject. There are certain necessary preconditions – the shape, so to speak, of consciousness – that physical objects, to be experienced, must satisfy. The mind's framework determines how we treat our sensations as being of external objects. Kant's summary is: thoughts without content are empty, intuitions without conceptions blind.

With the mind's structure, a necessary structure, we can grasp the experienced world around us, the starry heavens above, as open to scientific investigation with necessary laws of nature. That is one of a duo that impressed Kant.

Two things fill the mind with ever new and increasing admiration and awe, the more often and steadily we reflect upon them: the starry heavens above me and the moral law within me.

That moral law within is telling us how we ought to live. A little reflection may therefore make us question the Copernican credentials of Kant's revolution, though not the revolution. Copernicus displaced earth's central role in the physical universe; Kant gives humanity's mind the fundamental role in determining what constitutes both the objects that we experience and, through our reasoning, the nature of morality.

The *Critique of Pure Reason* was condemned by some because it 'unsettles the powers of understanding, spoils good principles and poisons the source of human happiness'. Reputedly, it drove some students mad. In Jena, two young men duelled because of an argument over its meaning. Who knows quite why so much fuss…

At the time, the *Critique* was read as within the sceptical tradition, along the lines of Berkeley and Hume. Kant wrote, though, of how Hume awoke him from his dogmatic slumbers. Hume's philosophical thinking, grounded in our perceptions as experiences, led to his bafflement about the self and the physical world. Kant overcame that bafflement by combining Hume's insights with those of philosophers, such as Leibniz, where reason was the great guide. Kant brought together elements both of empiricism and of metaphysics, showing, he thought, that, contrary to Hume, metaphysics was possible.

To make sense of the world around us, of the mouse running under the desk, of the empty wine bottle being the same bottle that was full earlier in the day, we presuppose a structure of unity, identity, causation – and indeed of space and time. Kant investigates that presupposition under the label of 'Transcendental Idealism', explaining, for example, how our understanding necessarily depends upon twelve pure concepts.

Kant was keen on labels and divisions and, ever since, there has been a major philosophical industry devoted to arguing over exactly what Kant meant. Happily, it is accepted that we can say nothing about any underlying reality, the 'noumenon', thing in itself. Of course, we may even question whether we can make sense of what we can say nothing about; recall Tao.

Kant's greatness is not confined to his metaphysics; it extends to his thinking about the grounding of morality. That thinking is more accessible and can be related to how he conducted his life. Although he did believe in God, he rejected the typical proofs and had no time for justifying morality as grounded in God's commands.

Kant is usually presented as possessed of an austere, steady and principled reputation, a bachelor gentleman of habit and firm discipline. The tale is that the good people of Königsberg would set their watches by him – and that on only one occasion did that reliance fail. Kant was reading Rousseau's *Emile* and became so engrossed that he forgot his afternoon walk. The story is unlikely to be true for *Emile* was published in 1762 and even as late as 1764 Kant had not yet acquired his disciplined austerity. That austerity is a caricature – well, it is until he realized that he must buckle down and do some deeper philosophical thinking.

Kant, prior to that buckling, was the elegant Magister, possessed of an irregular life. He played cards, attended theatres, very much a man about town. He followed fashion, enjoyed dining, the company of women, displaying his wit, his erudition. Out and about in Königsberg, he would often wear a finely powdered wig, silk stockings and would go walking with his hat perched upon the golden knob of his wooden staff.

All that changed, it seems, when he worked through the nature of morality, arriving at his great moral principle, the Categorical Imperative – a 'deontology' of duties.

Hypothetical imperatives announce what ought to be done, *if* ... For example, if you desire wealth, become a lawyer. Those iffy conditions are based on biological contingencies such as desires, but Kant thought morality should not be so iffy. Reason shows us that, always and everywhere, $2 + 2 = 4$; that arithmetical truth holds universally, even on Pluto, whatever your desires. Kant thus is drawn to deploying a universalizing test to check out what is morally permissible. The test is the aforementioned Categorical Imperative. Kant gives three versions, here as Formula of Universal Law:

> Act only on that maxim through which you can at the same time will that it should become a universal law.

The requirement is logical consistency. Suppose we wonder whether it is permissible deliberately to make a promise knowing full well we have no intention of keeping that promise. If we universalize the maxim, willing that everyone acted in the same way, a contradiction arises. Under such a supposition, the institution of promising would break down: no promises would ever be accepted. Hence, making lying promises is not morally permitted.

Were we to will that people commit suicide whenever they wanted, that would 'contradict nature' – well, so Kant announces, though it is difficult to see how. Certainly, there would be no logical contradiction, unless in some way

Nature builds in a logical demand to keep on living. Whether poor Maria von Herbert saw through Kant's reasoning and disregarded it or committed suicide, heavy with moral guilt – who knows?

Kant's reasoning deserves challenge or explanation at every step. For example, we cannot consistently will the universal law that everyone is only a seller of women's hats for there would then be no buyers. Surely the trade of milliner is not morally disreputable.

Kant as the austere Kant comes about because he argues that moral deeds to be moral must be motivated by duty. Having the right feelings, being disposed to act out of kindness, courage or compassion – important in Aristotelian Virtue Ethics (Chapter 6) – seem not to carry moral weight for Kant, though no doubt they are desirable on other grounds. Woe to those people who help beggars because they are moved by compassion; they are failing to act from the duty that morality demands. Being compassionate or mean-natured is a matter of biological luck. Our moral worth should not rest on luck. Curiously, Kant seems committed to the idea that no luck is involved in our having sufficient reasoning power to grasp the moral imperatives and sufficient will-power to do our duty. His metaphysics mysteriously allows for freedom of the will; will and reason apparently stand outside the causal chains involving physical objects.

The Categorical Imperative is also delivered in a way that comes down to the following: we must always respect people as rational agents; we should never treat another person solely as a means to our ends. That would be his objection, it seems, to people enjoying each other as sexual objects, without procreation and love in view; and probably he would see something contradictory even in people genuinely freely engaged in sex work. To treat other human beings merely as means to our ends would lead us into contradiction for we should have to accept that others also possess the right to mistreat us solely as means.

The question hence arises whether poor Maria was being used solely as a means by Kant, when he made her plight public. Obviously, we frequently do use people – medical staff, shop assistants, philosophy authors – but, it is argued, not *solely* as a means. That is established because they have voluntarily taken on those roles. Of course, some greyness now arises. How free are people in taking jobs, if the alternative is starvation? Are people without means really acting freely in working in the sex trade – or in the abattoir – if such occupations disgust them, yet they are the only employments available?

———

Humanity's crooked timber is also on view, according to many, in our (mis)treatment of non-human animals, a treatment that harmonizes with the Kantian thinking. He writes:

> When [man] first said to the sheep, 'the pelt which you wear was given to you by nature not for your own use, but for mine' and took it from the sheep to wear it himself, he became aware of a prerogative which ... he enjoyed over all the animals; and he now no longer regarded them as fellow creatures, but as means and instruments to be used at will for the attainment of whatever ends he pleased.

Kant's morality speaks of rights and duties; it is grounded in rationality and is confined to the world of rational agents. Kantian morality rests on reciprocal relationships, but non-human animals cannot reciprocate. It is a nonsense to blame sheep for failing to keep promises or wolves for chasing after sheep or, indeed, human beings. Kant does find room for some indirect duties: we ought not to mistreat other animals for fun; if we do, we may fall into bad habits and mistreat human beings.

We should resist the Kantian confinement of morality to rational agents and reciprocation. We should surely accept that morality extends to any beings that can suffer. That thought was pithily expressed later by Jeremy Bentham and supported by John Stuart Mill as part of their utilitarianism; there, morality is grounded solely in consequences for all creatures regarding happiness – for their pleasures and absence of pains.

Kant's emphasis on reason and principles leads to some other odd stances. We have already encountered one, namely that to perform what morality requires, we must be motivated by our moral duty, by a good will, not by our emotions, for our emotional dispositions are matters of biological luck. To erase all elements of moral luck, Kant is led to deal solely with intentions, motives, the will, rather than consequences, accomplishments, achievements:

> Even if it should happen that, by a particularly unfortunate fate or by the niggardly provision of a step-motherly nature, the good will should be wholly lacking in power to accomplish its purpose, and if even the greatest effort should not avail it to achieve anything of its end, and if there remained only the good will (not as a mere wish but as the summoning of all the means in our power), it would sparkle like a jewel in its own right, as something with its full worth in itself.

Another odd outcome can arise when certain duties conflict. It may be unfair on Kant, but in one short essay, we have, as I term it, 'The Axe-man Cometh'. In 'On a Supposed Right to Lie Because of Love of Humanity' (1797), responding to a paper by Benjamin Constant, Kant addresses the question of whether we ought to lie to a would-be murderer about his intended victim's whereabouts.

Kant argues that so long as we adhere strictly to what we sincerely believe to be true, we cannot be blamed. Suppose you believe the intended victim to be indoors, so you tell the would-be murderous axe-man that she has left. Well, argues Kant, the victim may in fact have slipped out unbeknownst to you and, by sheer misfortune, the murderer bumps into her and 'executes his purpose'. You would then, with justice, be accused of causing the woman's death. Such possible consequences are outside of your control; morality concerns that over which you have control – in this case, keeping to the Categorical Imperative by telling what you believe to be the truth.

––––––––––

A little before his death – very ill, almost blind – Kant, the story has been told, rose when his doctor entered, waiting for the doctor to be seated before following suit. He was pleased to note of himself: 'The sense of humanity has not abandoned me.'

On 11 February 1804, Kant's last words were '*Es is gut*' – 'It is good' – after having some wine and water mixed. Those last words have been read as 'This is the best of all possible worlds', but they could simply have meant 'It is enough', be it of the wine or of life. Kant died the next day.

––––––––––

Let us not end on that sombre note. Kant told jokes and even sought to analyse them. There are four discussed in his *Critique of Judgement*. Here is one.

An Indian at an Englishman's table in Surat saw a bottle of ale opened, and all the beer turned into froth and flowing out. The repeated exclamations of the Indian showed his great astonishment. 'Well, what is so wonderful in that?' asked the Englishman. 'Oh, I'm not surprised myself,' said the Indian, 'at its getting out, but at how you ever managed to get it all in.' At this we laugh, and it gives us hearty pleasure ...

Well, I can picture the not so austere Kant laughing, saying 'At this we laugh' with a heavy Prussian accent.

———

How to think like Kant? *Respect others and yourself – and never abandon your humanity.*

15

Schopenhauer: Pessimism With Flute

The two enemies of human happiness
are pain and boredom.

Schopenhauer

To the extent that philosophers are known in the popular world cloaked in their philosophy, one philosopher immediately comes to mind. His cloak is that of pessimism. Some see that position as outrageous; we should always think positively. Others treat the description as an accolade, recognizing the inevitable sufferings in our existence. Friedrich Nietzsche (we meet him shortly) knew of the accolade, but sceptically challenged its application to Schopenhauer – by asking a question:

a pessimist, a repudiator of God and of the world, who MAKES A HALT at morality – who assents to morality, and plays the flute to 'injure no one' (*laede-neminem*) morals, what? Is that really – a pessimist?

Of course, we have not heard the quality of our philosopher as flautist; perhaps his playing justified feeling a certain despair at the world – indeed, morality is, at heart, compassion.

The philosopher known as the 'Philosopher of Pessimism' is indeed Arthur Schopenhauer. He was born in Danzig, now

Gdansk, Poland, in 1788, into a business-orientated family, his father being a successful ship-owning merchant. In connection with the business, Arthur, as child and youth, visited Germany, France and England, becoming fluent, it seems, in those languages. Although his father had him destined to continue the family business, Arthur gave that up after a few years, his scholarly talents leading him to studies in medicine and philosophy and subsequently into lecturing.

His lecturing did not go down well, not least because, when at the University of Berlin, he foolishly timetabled his lectures to clash with the amazingly popular lectures of Hegel. Later in life, his philosophical work became recognized and he won a prestigious prize for an essay on freedom.

Schopenhauer was a metaphysician in the old style. That is, he sought to present the underlying grand principle behind the universe. He wrote:

> To repeat the whole nature of the world abstractly, universally, and distinctly in concepts, and thus to store up, as it were, a reflected image of it in permanent concepts always at the command of reason; this and nothing else is philosophy.

His major work is *The World as Will and Representation*, published in 1818, a little before his thirty-first birthday. The work was a rejection of the philosophies of Kant and Hegel where reason and rationality are presented as key to the nature of reality. To think in the way of Schopenhauer, we need to recognize the fundamental drive within all of us: the *Will*. The unknown noumenon of which Kant wrote was the Will, understood by Schopenhauer as completely lacking in reason or rational aims. We have, in some way, direct inner acquaintance with the Will.

What is distinctive in Schopenhauer's thinking here is how he understands the Will as a great undifferentiated impersonal force that grounds not only all our drives, instincts, desires and reasons, but also everything around us; what we think of as distinct physical objects are manifestations of Will.

The everyday idea of an irrational will within human actions, beliefs and feelings, fits in a vague way with the importance given in recent decades to psychoanalysis, irrationality in art, and explanations of human behaviour. John Maynard Keynes, for example, in opposing models for successfully understanding financial markets in terms of the behaviour of rational agents, spoke of 'animal spirits', the irrationalities, in people's economic decision making. Schopenhauer, though, with his presentation of the Will, as impersonal, underlying everything, leads us more to the Tao of Chapter 1. He did, indeed, dip into ancient writings such as those of Hinduism and Buddhism.

There is obscurity in Schopenhauer's understanding of the metaphysics of human life. We are, it seems, aware of the Will 'from within' in our actions and aware of it 'from without' through our perceptions. In some mysterious way, my action of running is a manifestation of the Will – of which I am aware through my inner feelings and also through my perceptions, the representations, the sight, of my legs moving.

In even greater obscurity, human beings coming onto the scene give rise to the fragmentation of Will, of the differentiation of objects around us, and hence to conflict. Once addressing that conflict, we are in the understandable world of tensions between people. Schopenhauer writes, with regard to society:

A number of porcupines huddled together for warmth on a cold day in winter; but, as they began to prick one another with their quills, they were obliged to disperse. However the cold drove them together again, when just the same thing happened. At last, after many turns of huddling and dispersing, they discovered that they would be best off by remaining at a little distance from one another.

Schopenhauer understands that we porcupines are driven together through the needs of society. We come together and then are mutually repelled by the many prickly and disagreeable qualities of our natures and particularities. A moderate distance is achieved through codes of politeness and fine manners; transgressors are told to keep their distance. Allow me to add a quip here, a quip with a feeling of underlying truth. There is one thing that the wealthy are keen for the poor to keep: it is their distance.

Whatever we are to make of Schopenhauer's Will, his writings are attuned to what we often feel. Although he did not speak explicitly of his pessimism, he did speak of the suffering involved in our existence, in our being alive, and the suffering within our deepest nature, instincts and desires. He was, indeed, the first major philosopher since Plato to attend explicitly to the huge importance of sexual desire in our lives; Plato though saw that desire as leading to Beauty, whereas for Schopenhauer it was pernicious – further, the importance we give to sex was comical. We find Schopenhauer's line of thought brought to the fore in Samuel Beckett (Chapter 30).

Schopenhauer's own life displayed the dominance of the sexual instinct, for, in contrast to the quality of his flute-playing, the quality of him as womanizer was well attested. The sex drive is the strongest expression of the Will. In a marriage, he argued, the man is a cuckold for the first part and then a whoremonger for the second. I have no knowledge of the extent of his empirical researches to reach that generalization. 'Tetragamy' would be the solution, he argued: that is, a man (I assume) marrying for a fourth time. It is a moot point why he thought that one should stop at four.

Not for Schopenhauer any idea that 'love' between individuals could be ethereal without the lurking presence of sex. Sexual desire, he argues, disturbs the most earnest of occupations, deranging even the greatest intellects for a time.

That was noted in Chapter 2 with Sappho. He asks why there is so much crowding, blustering, anguish and want regarding such an essentially trifling matter as sexual relations? Why do they play so important a part in life, creating 'disturbance and confusion' in the otherwise well-regulated life of mankind?

He has an answer: the ultimate aim of all love affairs, be they tragic or comic, is really more important than all other aims for it decides nothing less than the composition of the next generation. 'The *dramatis personæ* who shall appear when we are withdrawn are here determined, both as regards their existence and their nature, by these frivolous love affairs.' Indeed, he notes:

> We begin in the madness of carnal desire and the transport of voluptuousness; we end in the dissolution of all our parts and the musty stench of corpses.

Schopenhauer was, of course, writing a long time before there were reliable unobtrusive means of birth control; the change that 'the pill' brought about in sexual relations is so easily forgotten, now being in distant history. Let me challenge talk of the essential 'aims' of the sexual impulse. We should pack away silly stories telling us that when a heterosexual couple engage in sex, if their conscious aim is not procreation, then there must be that aim at an unconscious level, the level of Will. Why ever believe that? – though Schopenhauer apparently did.

There is an area of human life about which Schopenhauer spoke freely, though today much care is needed, for he was drawing attention to important differences between the wants and character of the sexes. He writes – dangerously, were it to be written today:

> Women are directly adapted to act as the nurses and educators of our early childhood, for the simple reason that

they themselves are childish, foolish, and short-sighted – in
a word, are big children all their lives …

Unsurprisingly, he gets it in the neck. Quite what is the
evidence that he wants us to assess? And what is his reasoning?
We can rightly reject Schopenhauer's particular assessments
of the sexes, while also rightly accepting that, obviously, there
are differences between the sexes. The moral concern for the
flourishing lives of women and men should not lead us to insist
that typically there are no 'on average' female–male differences
relevant to differences in flourishing. After all, biological
differences account for the difference in child-bearing potential
and have some impact on the differences, on average, in health
and longevity; so, it would be surprising if they generated no
differences at all in emotions, interests and other psychological
features.

Schopenhauer was a misogynist, at least in as far as he
portrayed women with certain qualities that he disparaged. The
misogynist charge has also been pressed upon him because he
was once found guilty of harming a seamstress; he had pushed
her downstairs because of her noisy chatter – he hated noise (I
concur over that) – yet showed little concern for the harm he
had inflicted. He was ordered to pay her a monthly sum. On her
death, he merely recorded: 'The old woman dies, the burden is
lifted.' Mind you, he would probably have reacted in a similar
way had the noisy chatter emanated from men. In response to
that, we could reflect that perhaps he viewed the conversation
as mere 'chatter' because it occurred between women.

Let us return more directly to his pessimism. All human
beings – all creatures, maybe – strive to achieve outcomes;
sometimes we achieve them, sometimes not. Throughout our
lives, either we want something that we lack, for we are striving
to attain the desired outcome, or we have got what we wanted.
Either way, we suffer. We suffer either through the lack of what

we want or through boredom, that is from the lack of want, now having secured what was wanted. To want is a suffering; the lack of want is a suffering.

True, a multitude of different wants may criss-cross; we may be temporarily satisfied (or not) at different times, but a mishmash of 'lack' sufferings combined with a mishmash of 'boredom' sufferings does not detract from the suffering and boredom overall. Boredom is a great evil, according to Schopenhauer, bringing about gambling, drinking, a mania for travelling – maybe, I add, writing more philosophy papers? Possibly that suggests some sense in my senseless quip that it would be better to be pebbles on a shady beach, with the ocean waves washing over us.

Worries over the disvalue of life are also revealed by persistent questions of the 'What's the point?' ilk. Many of us feel that we are on a treadmill, of sleep, waking, work, resting, sleep, maybe with the odd spasm of pleasure in between. Even the lucky ones may at times reflect, with some emptiness, on the point of it all. Many people see the point in their lives as their children or grandchildren, but that is, what I term, 'passing the point-of-it buck'; for what is the ultimate point? Using a reference from Albert Camus, writing in the twentieth century, we may feel for Sisyphus of the ancient Greek myth. He was condemned by the gods to roll a boulder up a hill to the top, eternally so, for the boulder always rolls back down. Another Greek myth, the Ixion myth, affords a similar image, Ixion being chained to a fiery wheel, spinning to eternity. Schopenhauer, who mused upon such images, offered an escape.

What is Schopenhauer's escape? It comes as a surprise that the Philosopher of Pessimism does not recommend suicide. Suicide he sees as defeat, for it is succumbing to the Will; it gives us the illusion that we are in control. Albert Camus saw the human condition with its pains, struggles and pointlessness, as one of absurdity. It required defiance: more will, a stronger will.

Schopenhauer's answer, by contrast, seems to be to eliminate the illusion of one's own particular will; and that may be achieved by losing oneself in the arts, especially in music. Of course, one may wonder whether that 'losing of oneself' is not a somewhat similar solution to that of suicide; it is, though, presumably less messy and less upsetting for others – and certainly less final.

With Schopenhauer's understanding of Will as the reality underlying everything, including our bodies and what we take to be our 'selves', our death in a sense is not the end of us. That cannot, of course, be any comfort to those who seek personal immortality; and it is no comfort to us who are content in our ultimate demise but discontented in the thought that billions of others – of the whole range of sentient life – will continue to suffer, until one day all life is extinguished. We are back to the image of pebbles on the seashore, with ocean waves washing over them.

The chorus in Sophocles' *Oedipus at Colonus* proclaims: the happiest (the most blessed) are those 'not to have been born'. Schopenhauer's pessimism may warm us to that thought, a thought we also find in Samuel Beckett. Unable to undo having been born, at best we can engage the world as melody for, in Schopenhauer's enigmatic words, 'music is the melody whose text is the world'.

How to think like Schopenhauer? *Ridicule – disparage and deride – rationality; lose sufferings – lose self – in music.*

16

John Stuart Mill: Utility Man, With Harriet, Soul-Mate

'Tis better to be a dissatisfied Socrates
than a satisfied pig.

J. S. Mill

Any familiarity today with this philosopher's thinking has the philosopher's name associated with utilitarianism and liberty. J. S. Mill, to distinguish him from his father, John Mill, was a great Victorian, highly influential, a reformer and challenger of religious privileges, as were both his father and Jeremy Bentham, his 'secular' godfather. His philosophical thinking led to political action, be it delivering pamphlets in support of contraception (illegal at the time) or arguing for equal rights for women (ridiculed at the time). He was elected as a Member of Parliament, called for women to have the vote (receiving more ridicule), even complaining about the mistreatment of horses.

This great Victorian was educated at home by his father, being taught Greek from the age of three, Latin at the age of eight. Although he is best remembered for his ethical and political philosophy, he wrote far more widely, and was influential regarding logic, metaphysics, the philosophy of science and political economy. His *A System of Logic* (1843) became a set university text and shows his way of philosophical thinking by means of careful analysis; that care is found later in Bertrand Russell, Mill's secular godchild.

Mill's philosophy was imbued with British empiricism, understanding our knowledge as derived through our experiences. Consider reasoning. We have seen how Aristotle developed logic and how Spinoza sought sound deductive arguments, where conclusions have to follow, 'logically follow', from true premises. When introduced to Aristotelian syllogisms, students are often given: all men are mortal; Socrates is a man; therefore, Socrates is mortal. In fact, Aristotle's syllogistic forms do not include singular propositions, such as 'Socrates is mortal', as premises. It seems to have been Mill who first introduced the 'Socrates' example, bringing it some fame; but he used it as an example to challenge the value of deductive reasoning.

How does it challenge? Well, in seeking to prove that Socrates is mortal, we asserted as first premiss that *all* men are mortal, which, as Socrates is a man, presupposes that he is mortal. Our first premiss already includes what we are seeking to prove. The deduction involves a *petitio principii*; it begs the question. The Latin is used, I guess, to convey authority.

How can that first premiss – or any unrestricted universal claim – ever be justified? We rely on inductive reasoning; we look at the empirical evidence from the past. Having grasped that so many millions of men have eventually died, we infer that all men die; and hence that Socrates also died. Of course, this example is somewhat tarnished, given that we in any case have independent evidence of Socrates having died.

The conclusion of a valid deductive argument, argues Mill, is guaranteed to follow from its premisses simply because that conclusion is already wrapped within the premisses. Deduction, it seems, cannot offer us any new knowledge. Things are not, though, so simple. After all, there have been many astonishing discoveries in mathematics, of 'what logically follows' from some premisses: witness the geometrical conclusions established by Euclid. Although we may agree with Mill that the conclusions are contained within the premisses of valid deductions, we should add that they are often well hidden; the deductive reasoning brings them to light.

What can justify confidence in inductive reasoning? Mill does his best; he proposes that nature is uniform. That seems to introduce circularity: is he not relying on the past to justify that proposal? Further, the proposal immediately raises the question: in what way uniform? After all, the uniformity is not such that if it rained yesterday, it is rational to conclude that it must continue to rain today.

Problems with inductive reasoning – Hume suffered with them – led the twentieth-century Karl Popper of the Poker Incident (Chapter 27) to maintain that where we have scientists seeking the 'laws of nature', they do or should forget about induction. Popper argued that scientists need to put forward universal conjectures – for example, all metals expand when heated – and then set about trying to refute them. Such a universal 'all' hypothesis could never be proven or verified, but it could be falsified, refuted. Of course, Popper's stance is not without its own puzzles: for example, a single proclaimed instance of a metal not expanding when heated may be the result of inadequate measuring or as yet unknown interferences from elsewhere or reliance on other mistaken theories.

————

Let us turn to Mill's famous thinking on morality and politics, to his utilitarianism. Utilitarianism is consequentialist: ultimately what I morally ought to do depends on the eventual outcomes and the morally desirable outcomes are those of the greatest happiness of the greatness number. Kant had explicitly opposed the serpent windings of looking into consequences to establish what morality required. The rhetorical response is: what else could determine what is right, if not, in the end, that of overall happiness?

Utilitarian thinking, at a fundamental level, is totally committed to impartiality; my good, my happiness, counts no more than anyone else's. That impartiality may yet paradoxically lead to some partiality in various ways. After all, human that we are, maximum happiness seems to require that we prioritize certain relationships of attachment; for example, those between lovers and between parents and their children. To take a totally detached attitude, having to choose between saving your child's life or someone else's, is unlikely to generate overall happiness.

Here are a couple of related examples where utilitarian impartiality requires further thought. May it not be right to sacrifice one person to save the lives of two million, two hundred or even just two, if by doing so, overall happiness is increased? Maybe happiness would be maximized if we bred some people specifically so that their organs could be used for others. Human beings do that with certain other species; many non-human animals have a terrible time because of our dining desires. At least such 'speciesism', prejudice in favour of one species over another, without rational justification, is not on utilitarianism's agenda. 'Can they suffer?' was Bentham's pithy question in setting the criteria for which creatures should be taken into account. The pains and pleasures of sentient creatures all have direct moral relevance. Trees and landscapes, for example, have moral relevance but only indirectly so, in as far as they contribute to pleasures and avoidance of suffering for human beings and other sentient animals.

The 'greatest happiness of the greatest number' principle also raises the question of which takes priority: is the primary aim to maximize happiness, even if that means fewer people than if the aim is to maximize the number of people? Should regard be given to the amount of happiness for each one? As has been pithily put, should the utilitarian aim be to make more people happy – or to make more happy people?

A related concern arises for governments when choosing economic and welfare policies. For instance, in the United States and Britain, a small number of people are radically wealthy, whereas vast numbers, in comparison, are exceptionally poor. In countries such as Norway, proportionately there are fewer impoverished, though the wealthiest are not as wealthy as in the States and Britain. Even if average happiness in the States, for example, exceeded that of Norway, we may well think Norway is to be preferred on moral grounds. In fact, countries with vast inequalities are usually assessed as overall less happy than those without such inequalities. Of course, there are disputes over how best to judge such comparisons.

As well as those number problems, there is the question of the happiness. We have met that problem with Epicurus. For Bentham, calculations, in theory, were to be done in terms of units of pleasure: if playing pushpin (a child's game) gave as much pleasure as appreciating poetry, then pushpin possessed the same moral value as poetry. Were the greatest happiness to be achieved by a society in which all people conformed to certain authoritarian laws, or lived lives of pleasurable illusions, then Benthamite utilitarians would, it seems, promote such societies.

Utilitarians are often labelled 'satisfaction theorists'. The right thing to do is to maximize happiness; that is, get your desires satisfied. One way of achieving that would be to tamper with desires, making them more easily satisfied; we may recall Epicurus. The 'satisfaction' approach and, indeed, the Benthamite approach, are not in accord with Mill's:

Socrates would rather choose to be Socrates dissatisfied than a pig satisfied. The pig probably would not, but then the pig knows only one side of the question: Socrates knows both.

Mill's 'happiness' is to be understood as a flourishing life involving curiosity, nobility, fellow feeling and much more. Mill possessed an enriched understanding of happiness, akin to the Aristotelian. In Mill's terms, it included 'higher pleasures': the appreciation of poetry is higher than Bentham's pushpin playing. By the way, 'pushpin' at the time was a euphemism for sexual intercourse; Mill would disparage the emphasis on pushpin whichever meaning was in mind.

Of course, Mill reaps the charge of elitism. To that charge, we could respond on behalf of Mill that, if Mill is elitist. then it must be because he wants paradoxically everyone to be part of the elite. He supported welfare and educational policies so that all could flourish, in realizing their true potential. We should flag a danger here: the casual talk of everyone realizing their potential, talk often proclaimed by leaders in Western democracies, overlooks how some people's potential is for the highly undesirable. Witness not just the propensity some have for rape and murder, but also the great scandals whereby corporate leaders realize their potential for ruthlessness, exploitation and maximizing self-interest.

'Look at the evidence' could be one way of summarizing Mill's philosophical thinking. To charges that utilitarian policies would lead to human organ plantations or slave classes, Mill's response would be that the evidence is that people overall would not ultimately feel happy having such policies in force – and so, those policies would not maximize happiness. To the idea that maybe happiness would be secured by the population having a drug-induced conformity, Mill would point out that as a matter of fact, human beings in order to flourish require some freedoms and autonomy. Freedoms would include the freedom to protest, to travel, and for women in public to be unveiled. Autonomy exists when you are able to realize your true desires, what is best for you. Freedom and autonomy interlink and have puzzles. The freedom to travel is not effective freedom if you lack the fare. Autonomy is not genuine if your desires result from marketing manipulations.

Mill famously promoted the Liberty Principle (also known as the Harm Principle). It has many problems of detail, but it is worthy as a guiding approach. He actively argues that a society would be worse off, if it dwarfed individuality; individuals would not be better off, if turned into robots. Mill's promotion of liberty need not then be understood as contradicting his utilitarianism. Flourishing lives are not robotic lives.

Mill's life displayed another element relevant to his utilitarianism for, when aged twenty, he was in a mental malady, asking himself: 'Suppose that all your objects in life were realized; that all the changes in institutions and opinions which you are looking forward to, could be instantly effected: would this be a great joy and happiness to you?' Mill's answer was 'no'. 'The end had ceased to charm.'

He broke free from the crisis when he recognized that happiness embraced feeling, not just active goal seeking. This was courtesy, in large measure, of Wordsworth's poetry and walks in the Lake District, appreciating nature. 'Ask yourself whether you are happy, and you cease to be so.' The commendable utilitarian goal of the greatest happiness of the greatest number should not be our everyday motivation. Love, for example, is an important part of happiness. 'It was never contended by a sound orthodox utilitarian,' noted John Austin, friend of Mill, 'that the lover should kiss his mistress with an eye to the common weal.'

Mill found the deepest personal happiness through falling in love with Harriet Taylor; 'twas a pity that she was *Mrs* Harriet Taylor. It was only upon the death of Mr Taylor many years later that John Stuart and Harriet could live together in their true happiness. And they did – for seven years until Harriet's death.

Mill lived his life in accordance with his philosophy. On marriage, he documented that he rejected all the legal privileges that marriage gave husbands. He frequently expressed his indebtedness to Harriet in his writings, particularly regarding women's rights. His support for women's suffrage was considered a peculiar whim of his – how times have changed.

Sexual congress, Mill insisted, occupies an absurdly disproportionate place in human life, but it is 'superstition and barbarism of the infancy of the human race' to impose restrictions on people's private activities. In the late 1860s, venereal disease was so great among Her Majesty's sailors that the Contagious Diseases Acts were passed, allowing police to cart off suspected prostitutes for medical examinations. Mill, before an astonished Royal Commission, strongly criticized the Acts, arguing that if such examinations were right for women, then men suspected of brothel visiting should likewise be examined.

Mill was a rational empiricist. He sought and assessed the evidence. Hence, he at times changed his mind. Early on, he doubted whether capital punishment could be justified; by 1868 he was speaking in its favour, where atrocious murders were concerned. Capital punishment received utilitarian justification: it was a deterrent, yet one not as cruel as life imprisonment with hard labour. It is well to reflect on prison conditions of his times.

Another example of Mill's emphasis on thinking through the evidence concerns religious belief. Were an omnipotent God to exist, argued Mill, He must be malevolent, given the vast sufferings among both humans and other sentient beings. With evolutionary theory somewhat primitive and speculative, Mill tended to believe, albeit with only a level of probability, that there could be a finite power that ordered the world. No doubt today he would agree with the atheism of Bertrand Russell.

———

Utilitarianism is typically presented as promoting a cold calculating way of thinking. That presentation does not apply to Mill and his utilitarianism. For Mill, the man, consider the following.

From 1839, John and Harriet (then Mrs Taylor) would sometimes stay in Avignon, at the Hôtel de l'Europe. It was in that hotel, in 1858, that Harriet (then Mrs Mill) died. A few months after her death, John bought an Avignon house. He installed the furniture from the hotel room in which she died. The remaining fifteen years of John's life were much spent there, often with Harriet's daughter, Helen, who helped John continue his and Harriet's reforming work.

On 7 May 1873, Mill suddenly died at that Avignon home, a small white house. The small white house overlooked the cemetery where Harriet had been buried. From 8 May 1873, the small white house overlooked the cemetery where, next to each other, were buried both Harriet and John.

———

How to think like John Stuart Mill? *Be guided by the evidence; act always to better people's lives – and do not ignore the lives and sufferings of other sentient beings.*

17

Søren Kierkegaard: Who?

What the world needs is a new Socrates.

Kierkegaard

Take a look at any well-stocked university library, one that still values books and philosophy as a university's essential ingredients, and you will find a shelf labelled 'Kierkegaard'. Strangely, many of the works in that location will declare themselves to be by – well, Constantine Constantius, Johannes Climacus, Johannes de silentio, Anti-Climacus, Vigilius Haufniensis and many others.

Yes, they are pseudonyms of Søren Kierkegaard, yet ones that were scarcely intended to cover his tracks. Their use raises the question of whether they represent what Kierkegaard thinks. Maybe they show him playing different roles as do actors on stage. For his own beliefs perhaps we should rely solely on those works expressly labelled as by Kierkegaard, yet, given his role-playing yen, perhaps 'he' is also playing under the Kierkegaard name. Thus it is that we may become baffled by who 'he' really is who writes:

From the beginning I perceived very clearly and do still perceive that my personal reality is an embarrassment which the pseudonyms with pathetic self-assertion might wish to be rid of, the sooner the better, or to have reduced to the least possible significance, and yet again with ironic courtesy might wish to have in their company as a repellent contrast.

Thinking philosophically in the way of Kierkegaard, as the author behind differently authored works, requires recognition of a certain fluidity or worry over quite who we are, which self-declarations can be justly made and how they should be interpreted.

Kierkegaard tells of a new shop that opened in his quarter; its window displayed the sign 'Bring your washing here.' Back at home, he collected together his dirty washing and took it to the shop – only to discover that the shop was no laundry but a retail outlet for signs.

Kierkegaard writes of himself as a 'poet dialectician' and, as already seen, he is a philosopher who thinks very differently from those we have so far encountered. His focus is subjectivity: how to weave his life, its right interpretation and how to live that life. His writings, directly attributed or not, engage with anxiety, guilt, despair – and choices. Consequently, he has been judged the first existentialist. Biographers relate his anguished and bleak concerns to dark secrets in his family or his Lutheran background or the mockery he suffered because of the ridiculous appearance he cut. Many are drawn to his obsession with Regine Olsen and the mystery and guilt at his breaking off their engagement.

The Danish name 'Kierkegaard' means churchyard and he certainly encountered death. By the age of twenty-five, his parents had died as had five of his six siblings – and he thought he would live not beyond age thirty. He got as far as forty-two. To gain a flavour of his thinking, I offer some titles: *On the Concept of Irony*; *Fear and Trembling*; *Repetition*; *The Concept of Anxiety*; *Stages on Life's Way*; *Works of Love*; *The Sickness unto Death*.

Kierkegaard, as Climacus, is highly critical of those great philosophers who engaged in metaphysics, believing that 'pure thinking' would lead them to see reality *sub specie aeterni*, under the aspect of eternity. True, we can abstract when engaged in mathematics, but not when we seek to understand what it is to be human in the world around us. For that proper understanding, of the metaphysical and ethical, there is no way in which we can step outside our particular human perspective, our finite existence in this or that part of the world, at this or that time – yet does not that reflection itself manifest a 'stepping out'?

Modern philosophy, proclaimed Kierkegaard – he had Hegel especially in mind – possesses a comical presupposition; it has forgotten 'in a sort of world-historical absent-mindedness' what it means to be a human being. 'Not indeed, what it means to be a human being in general ... but what it means that you and I and he are human beings, each one for himself.'

The philosopher's attempt at a godly perspective also strikes Kierkegaard as a display of arrogance. Further, it is immoral for it blinds us to the human condition and how to live. Those philosophers, announces Kierkegaard, are builders of great castles of speculation, while actually living in a doghouse next door. Kierkegaard urges us to look at ourselves, as living agents, to grasp reality and how we, as individuals, are to live well. That is what is in his mind when he speaks of 'subjectivity as truth'. It is not to claim that truth is whatever we fancy. It is, he thinks, the way to relate my finite existence to something beyond – to, as it transpires, God.

––––––––––

Kierkegaard possessed the luxury of a reasonable level of inherited wealth; as a young man, he was something of a dandy about Copenhagen and could afford to be so. In his writings, we encounter tales and aphorisms, jokes and paradoxes, analyses and revisions of scriptural stories. A deep commitment to the Christian God is pervasive. Mind you, casual commentaries on his works often make little of that Christianity save for reference to his famous 'leap of faith' that, for them, manifests his existentialism requiring irrational leaps. I should add: or, presumably, hops, skips or jumps. But into what? Just anything?

In fact, the Danish for 'leap of faith' has not yet been found in his writings. He is, though, concerned with the problem of 'the qualitative transition from non-believing to believing', but that seems to be no matter of irrational acts of will. The transition is explored in his *Either/Or* and *Stages on Life's Way*. He presents three stages or spheres through which a human being, a developing person, passes. We may wonder whether he is presenting a piece of vague human psychology, a speculation, or a moral recommendation to aspire to contact with God.

The stages are the aesthetic, ethical and religious. The aesthetic is dominated by our desires and dispositions, certainly not by any sense of duty. It is the stage where we seek interest and excitement, eager to overcome boredom. In the *Diary of a Seducer* (part of *Either/Or*) the Seducer (who seems to be 'A', the author of the aesthetic side of the 'Either') is as much motivated by the excitement of his manipulations in seeking to seduce a girl as by the aimed-for sexual gratification. The *Diary* ends with the wonderment of whether even the girl would judge it as all just a matter of interest, overcoming boredom.

The second stage is the ethical. Here we encounter Judge William promoting the ethical commitment of work, friendship and monogamous marriage. The extent of ethics is determined, here, by social roles and conventions, by the bourgeois expectations of the Danish Golden Age. The grounding of ethics is, here, very different from Kant's universal principle of the categorical imperative and Plato's aspiration for the transcendent Good. Judge William does speak of religion, but it is of the Church, as a social institution. For Kierkegaard, that Christendom is akin to Paganism.

Author A, promoting the aesthetic stage, grounds the norms of life in the individual. Judge William grounds them within society's conventions, universal within that society. That, of course, smacks of relativism. In today's Western society, monogamous marriage no longer holds such sway. Even were such conventions genuinely universal across societies, that would not provide the grounding to life that Kierkegaard sought. In the desert, he tell us, individuals travel in large groups, being fearful of robbers and wild animals; today, individuals live in great herds and cling together *en masse* to social conventions. We need to rise above, as individuals, and enter the religious sphere.

How do we even grasp what that sphere is? Kierkegaard offers parables. He offers us Abraham who, following the 'voice of God', is prepared to sacrifice his son, Isaac. From the sphere of the ethical, Abraham is an horrendous character in even contemplating killing his own flesh-and-blood and violating the moral duty never to murder the innocent. Abraham is, using Kierkegaard's terms, engaged in a 'teleological suspension of the ethical' with his preparedness to obey God, despite violating some basic moral principles.

Other leaders in the tales of the ancients – Agamemnon, Jephthah and Brutus – have killed their offspring, but for the recognizable ethical end of society's overall good. Abraham has no such end in view. He places his trust in God's promises. He is a 'knight of faith'. His actions and beliefs are absurd, paradoxical and mad, says Kierkegaard, yet they show how our finite temporality can yet relate to God's infinite eternity. Faith is an engagement with the tension of being alone before God without the comforting support of the ethical, of doing what is morally right. Kierkegaard adds to the mystery with his comment: 'In relation to God we are always in the wrong.'

With our existentialist freedom, we may choose to stay put at any of the three stages. That points to the existentialist focus on individualism; it may bring us back to the 'leap' as a criterionless choice, a choice that lacks any rational justification. That may yet be mistaken. Although human beings are naturally in the aesthetic sphere, perhaps reasons can be given to move to the next stages, though not reasons set out as logical arguments. According to Kierkegaard, the most important truths for living cannot be communicated directly, as if we have a blank sheet of paper and can write them out with an argument, conclusion and 'QED'. No, they need effort by both author and reader, 'bringing to light, by the application of a caustic fluid, a text which is hidden under another text'. And certainly Kierkegaard, with his different authorships, provides fascinating and provocative texts that do require the effort of much musing and deeper thought.

Kierkegaard writes on irony, praises Socrates as ironic and notes how in the empty space between the trees, you may see Napoleon's face. We need to reflect on Kierkegaard's tales and paradoxes and, indeed, on the importance to him of speaking as different authors – and we may see the shape of life between the words. A much-used quotation from Kierkegaard is:

> It is perfectly true, as the philosophers say, that life must be understood backwards. But they forget the other proposition, that it must be lived forwards.

He explains how life can never really be understood in time; that is simply because at no particular moment can anyone find the necessary resting place from which to understand it

– namely, backwards. Put in simple terms, things move on – as does living.

Death, of course, needs to be addressed when philosophizing about life. We all die. It is important to appreciate that fact about ourselves through our subjectivity. Of course, death may be treated 'from the outside' as something general: All men are mortal – with the conclusion of my death.

My own dying is 'a something in general' for systematicians, for distracted people. For the late bookseller Soldin, Kierkegaard notes, dying is said to have been such a something in general: 'When he was about to get up in the morning he was not aware that he was dead.' But for me, my dying is not at all a 'something in general'.

The task is to become subjective: the idea is that 'every subject will for himself become the very opposite of such a something in general'. Kierkegaard implores us to grasp that if we separate philosophy from our individual personal lives, then it becomes but a science 'and we get the professor of philosophy' – and, today, numerous philosophy journals of technicalities and formal frameworks for teaching and research assessments. Kierkegaard feared that should the professor chance across his works, 'it would not give him pause, would not cause his conscience to smite him; no, this too would be something to hold forth on'. Nor, continued Kierkegaard, if he chanced to read that observation, would it give him pause – for it would be something more to hold forth on. Here, while holding forth, I try not to hold forth.

Kierkegaard questions the value of traditional philosophers: 'why do we have our philosophers, if not to make supernatural things trivial and commonplace?' He wants us to concentrate on ourselves as subjects. Consider the captain of a ship, needing to choose this way or that way, while being well aware that while he is undecided, the ship continues to make its usual headway. If we forget to take into account the headway, there comes an instant when 'there no longer is any question of an either/or, not because he has chosen, but because he has neglected to choose' – others have chosen for him. As Kierkegaard adds:

> to think that for an instant one can keep one's personality a blank, or that strictly speaking one can break off and bring to a halt the course of the personal life, is a delusion. The personality is already interested in the choice before one chooses, and when the choice is postponed the personality chooses unconsciously, or the choice is made by obscure powers within it.

Kierkegaard can write elusively, paradoxically, yet also provocatively. Wittgenstein thought of him as by far the most profound thinker of the nineteenth century, 'a saint'. We do not need to go that far to welcome and embrace Kierkegaard's writings, under this name or that name, as showing us that we should pay attention to our lives – as subjects, from within. He sought to bring to us the questioning of Socrates, the sincerity, the stinging of us into thinking who we are.

───────

How to think like Kierkegaard? *Remember you are this particular human being who must live a particular life of your own making ... forward.*

18

Karl Marx: Hegelian, Freedom-Fighter

Philosophers have hitherto only interpreted the world. The point is to change it.

Marx

This chapter could have been devoted to Hegel, with a postscript on Marx; instead it is mainly Marx with a prescript on Hegel. With limitations on space, choices have to be made. We have obscurity enough when we reach Heidegger, so the great obscurity of the even greater Hegel receives but a mention. This chapter gives a feeling for how Hegel's basic ideas are deployed and revised by Marx, whose work – or at least his name – is possessed of worldly impact.

Mention Karl Marx and we meet an onslaught from commentators, politicians and even those who should know better. There are shrill pronouncements on Marxism, communism or socialism, usually abusive and intermeshed with names of Stalin, Lenin or Trotsky and activities of the Soviet Union, China or Cuba. Marx's headstone in London's Highgate Cemetery is regularly defaced. To blame Marx for ills committed in his name and associated movements is, though, akin to blaming Jesus for the activities of zealous Christians keen to go to war against heretics. When, later in life, Marx heard of some positions put forward by Marxist groups, he said he was certain he was no Marxist. By the way, although I write of Marx, in many cases I should really be adding Engels, Marx's collaborator, friend and financial backer. Engels, in fact, became a promoter of Marx as a thinker as great as Hegel and Darwin, giving rise to Marxism as a major international collection of loosely related political movements.

What do we need to know about Hegel? His writings are vast in quantity, difficulty and variety of interpretations. He was a professional philosopher, eventually becoming professor at the University of Berlin, his lectures attracting large audiences. By his death in 1831, a group of philosophers, the Young Hegelians, continued his line of thinking – and Marx, when at the university, was initially drawn to that group, but moved on. He remained, though, 'a pupil of that mighty thinker', of Hegel.

Unlike earlier major philosophers, Hegel pays attention to world history and how societies, their cultural presuppositions and concepts change. The changes are not random as are numbers appearing after each spin of the roulette wheel. The changes are not to be understood simply as causes and effects in the way in which heatwaves and earthquakes cause raging fires, devastation and the loss of numerous lives. Hegel's history unfolds and the unfolding is thought of as rational, leading to an end; the end, in a sense, draws forth the development. Quite what is unfolding?

Hegel speaks of *Geist* – Mind or Spirit – as the Absolute, the end being self-realization, a unified understanding of all. Quite how individual minds relate to Geist is unclear. Some see Hegel as working in the tradition of Spinoza, grappling with the concept of God and Nature as one being, though without Spinoza's rejection of teleological explanations, explanations by way of ends. Others see him as not at all religious and not at all spiritual, but offering a framework of essential concepts that develop and are needed in our understanding of the world.

Here is one basic puzzle: if Hegel, through his reasoning, has reached that self-realization, is that the final end? Have we or it mysteriously acquired self-realization? And is the Prussian State, when he was writing, that realization by way of the most rationally arranged society?

Marx takes over the idea of history unfolding, rejects the mysteries of Geist, yet still sees that history as functioning towards an end. The unfolding is grounded in the development of human beings through their activities and changing material conditions. He writes:

In direct contrast to German philosophy which descends from heaven to earth, here we ascend from earth to heaven. That is to say, we do not set out from what men say, imagine, conceive, nor from men as narrated, thought of, imagined, conceived, in order to arrive at men in the flesh. We set out from real, active men ...

Spinoza had also insisted that philosophy should treat human beings as they are; Marx is doing that, but in contrast to Spinoza's 'are', as if timeless, for Marx human lives and interactions essentially involve change through economic conditions. Those conditions determine the thinking:

Morality, religion, metaphysics, all the rest of ideology and their corresponding forms of consciousness, thus no longer retain the semblance of independence. They have no history, no development; but men, developing their material production and their material intercourse, alter, along with this their real existence, their thinking and the products of their thinking. Life is not determined by consciousness, but consciousness by life.

Of course, there is the problem of how to treat Marx's thinking, for must it not also be nothing but a product of material intercourse? Or is there an objective vantage point for viewing what is 'really' going on? Those questions need to be kept in mind while we reflect on what Hegel and Marx think – or indeed on what any philosopher thinks. Let us recall Kierkegaard on how certain acclaimed thinkers are 'builders of great castles of speculation, while actually living in a doghouse next door'; their own thinking may be as much conditioned by material conditions as the thinking they seek to explain or disparage.

Hegel understood the move to self-realization through a dialectic whereby there is an opposition, a conflict or a contradiction, between two positions – thesis and antithesis – which is resolved in synthesis. He applies it throughout all understanding: here comes an example.

In ancient Greece, he argues, individuals and the city-state were in harmony over right and wrong, but that harmony was disrupted by Socrates and his gadfly stingings – by Socrates' dialectic as questioning, challenging. In the historical process, the *thesis* of harmony gradually gave way to the *antithesis:* the right to individual conscience, later much developed in Protestantism. The antithesis also failed – think of the French Revolution's terrors – leading to the resolution of thesis and antithesis in (luckily for Hegel?) the *synthesis* of the German society as an organic community preserving individual freedom rationally arranged within the community. Of course, once this sketchiest sketch is filled out, Hegel can be challenged over historical accuracy and explanatory value.

Marx uses Hegel's dialectic in his own theory of history; hence, we have Marx's dialectical materialism. Productive forces and relations give rise to conflict and to new economic structures, developing towards an end, towards human freedom. That freedom requires human beings not to be determined in their thinking by external forces out of their control. The forces are in fact the productive powers of human beings themselves, but the forces are seen as hostile and alien. Productive forces determine relations of production, which in turn determine the political, legal and ideological superstructure – the beliefs, the generation of rights.

With regard to that development, we may question whether Marx is making an empirical claim: have the facts of history led him to discover that development? Or was Marx offering us a conceptual scheme to frame the changes that otherwise would appear to be unconnected? Either way, he held the belief that there is an outcome, a telos, an end.

When he heard of Charles Darwin's work, he was keen to see an association between Darwin's theory of evolution and his claim of the historical development of societies through economic forces. 'Darwin's book is very important', he wrote, 'and serves me as a basis in natural science for the class struggle in history.' There is, though, a distinction between Darwin and Marx over methodology: Darwin could engage in meticulous detailed empirical research into living species and fossils; such research is far from easy when investigating historical class structures and economic conditions.

Before examining Marx's basic concepts, let us note his writing style and irony; it is far removed from the deadly dull, as portrayed by some commentators and by the appearance of dusty volumes on even dustier shelves. Here is a touch of Marx's irony – on how the criminal is useful, for he

produces the whole of the police and of criminal justice, constables, judges, hangmen, juries, etc.; and all these different lines of business, which form just as many categories of the social division of labour, develop different capacities of the human mind, create new needs and new ways of satisfying them.

Consider how Marx's writing flows when discussing the value of linen and the coat:

> Despite its buttoned-up appearance, the linen recognizes in the coat a splendid kindred soul, the soul of value ... The linen acquires a value-form different from its natural form. Its existence as value is manifested in its equality with the coat, just as the sheep-like nature of the Christian is shown in his resemblance to the Lamb of God.

Putting the complexities of Marx's understanding of commodities and value to one side, a key concept in his thinking is that of alienation, also derived from Hegel. Let us look at it first in the context of religion. Going back to Greek antiquity, there had been suggestions that God's attributes derived from those of the believers. Xenophanes, an important Presocratic philosopher of the late sixth century BC, wrote: 'If cattle and horses and lions had hands and could paint and make works of art with their hands just as people can, horses would depict the gods as horses and cattle would as cattle.' Ludwig Feuerbach, during Marx's day, spoke of human beings projecting their powers onto an abstraction, God, from which they become alienated. Here is Marx:

> Religious suffering is, at one and the same time, the expression of real suffering and a protest against real suffering. Religion is the sigh of the oppressed creature, the heart of a heartless world, and the soul of soulless conditions. It is the opium of the people.

It is worth emphasizing the 'real suffering'; the opium does not prevent that suffering. Marx, as to be expected, pays attention to the alienation resulting from the capitalism in his day. Capitalism here is understood as a mode of production in which the means of production are the private property of a ruling class – the bourgeoisie – and they employ the workers, deemed the proletariat. Marx had no problem with the private ownership of a toothbrush; it is the ownership of land and the means of production in private hands that leads to the alienation. Of course, these days, matters are muddied, with the existence of corporations with the shareholdings in workers' pension funds, but the alienation is still present. Let us see.

Capitalism demands productivity, efficiency and profit. That means, argued Marx, that the workers are to be at a bare subsistence level of living; their labour is just another commodity to be bargained over. That does not now happen, insist today's economists and politicians – well, those whose thinking is along capitalist lines. They are right in part, but not so clearly right as they like to think. In Britain and the United States, despite the vast wealth of both countries, millions of people in work remain impoverished, needing to take on poorly paid jobs, maybe with zero-hour contracts, and having to resort to food banks. And that is not mentioning those millions who, through illness or other circumstances, need to rely on social welfare typically at bare-minimum levels.

Consider further afield. Numerous workers in many poor countries suffer unsafe and squalid employment conditions, very low pay, many working almost as slaves. That arises because powerful corporations, be they of the United States, Europe, even China, seek to deliver electronics, garments and foods to their populations, with production costs as low as possible. For a practical example, consider our laptops and mobile phones: battery supply chains lead to sources in the 'Democratic' Republic of the Congo – and to the mining miseries of cobalt production. The workers are children and their parents; their tools are shovels. They live in toxic hazes, their land and water heavily polluted. The international corporations are highly profitable; the families, despite much physical scraping, scarcely scrape a living.

Those are examples of people manifestly suffering, courtesy of the corporate urgings for profit. That reflection is not confined to Marx. Even Adam Smith, the eighteenth-century economist much lauded by devotees of free markets, wrote of how the market economy can corrupt our moral sentiments, generating a 'disposition to admire, and almost to worship, the rich and the powerful, and to despise, or, at least, to neglect persons of poor and mean condition'.

Marx sees alienation, then, as spread throughout the populations even of wealthy countries. It is to do with loss of freedom, loss of governing oneself. In many, many jobs, because of the division of labour – the efficient means to maximize profits – workers are exercising routine performances, be it stacking supermarket shelves, packing items on factory production lines or answering calls, following scripts, in call centres. They are not provided with the means to develop themselves; they are not able to improve their skills at something worthwhile. Super-fast stacking is unlikely to be fulfilling; it is unlikely to be an aspiration. Those workers are alienated in that they are not 'at home' in their work. We may make use of Marx's comment, when speaking of the proletariat: a class *in* civil society that is not *of* civil society.

A second alienation is how we are dominated by the products churned out by the capitalist machinery. Yes, people can point to many useful things, but would anyone have thought of wanting, say, designer handbags, but for the corporate imperative to profit? This is where we become tarnished by luxuries; more people labour to acquire them and more people are disappointed because they lack sufficient resources. If tempted to dismiss such observations as typical Marxist envy, be reminded again of Adam Smith; he wrote disparagingly of people who walk about 'loaded with a multitude of baubles' while others ruin themselves by laying out money on such 'trinkets of frivolous utility'.

Further examples relate to corporate promotion of what counts as beauty, the need for potions to hide aging, vitamins for 'healthy' skin, shampoos to combat hair thinning – usually ineffective or unnecessary. In many cases, certain items so keenly marketed for profit are harmful – especially so in the food and drink sector and leisure sector of gambling, where corporations fight hard to prevent regulation. Thus, alienation (second type via product promotion) again arises.

The Communist Manifesto gives a third type:

> Modern bourgeois society with its relations of production, of exchange, and of property, a society that has conjured up such gigantic means of production and of exchange, is like the sorcerer, who is no longer able to control the powers of the nether world whom he has called up by his spells.

Marx talks of how we – all of us – end up as 'playthings of alien forces'. The ancient Greeks may once have thought of themselves as playthings of the gods. Now, it is market forces that seem to control us, that play with us. Witness how helpless people became because of the banking crises; witness the need, if to avoid belonging to an excluded underclass, to have internet access, mobile telephones and, for a certain age group, designer trainers.

Marx's thinking is much concerned with freedom. He distinguishes between the freedom whereby there is an absence of legal constraint on what we do (that is 'bourgeois' freedom) and 'real' freedom where people have the resources, psychological and material, to make their own choices between worthwhile options. He may be seen as wildly optimistic, thinking that one day there would be such abundance through technological advances that people could have their authentic wants satisfied; further, there would then be such a change that people would become community-minded and not alienated from their species-essence, from their common humanity. He writes of how people would be able to take advantage of opportunities 'to hunt in the morning, fish in the afternoon, rear cattle in the evening, criticize after dinner, without ever becoming hunter, fisherman, herdsman or critic'.

————

It is very easy for us – most people reading this book – to forget the sufferings of so many. It is very easy to forget that, in as far as capitalism has been given a 'human face', it is not the result of the forces of capitalism but of socially minded responses to restrain those forces. Here are some observations that Michel de Montaigne, writing in the late sixteenth century, reports by cannibals (from his essay 'On the Cannibals'):

> they said they had noticed that among us some men were overstuffed with all sorts of rich commodities while other fellows were begging at their doors, emaciated from hunger and poverty. They found it strange that these fellows in such desperate need could put up with such an injustice and did not seize the others by the throat or set fire to their houses.

Because of the irrationalities in capitalist societies, the conflicts and alienations, Marx believed capitalism's downfall was inevitable, but thereafter, who knows? He refused to write 'recipes for the cookshops of the future'.

————

Let us end with Hegel and Marx. Hegel, ever keen on paradox, tells us, 'We learn from history that we do not learn from history' – by which he means we learn too late. Hence, we have the thoughtful observation about wisdom:

The owl of Minerva begins its flight only with the coming of the dusk.

Marx, though – maybe with an early owlish flight – opens our eyes to the alienations and accompanying sufferings that arise from economic structures typically much fêted; and so, even though it is rather late, let us take to heart the considerable importance of Marx's reflection:

Perseus wore a magic cap that the monsters he hunted down might not see him. We draw the magic cap down over eyes and ears as a make-believe that there are no monsters.

How to think like Marx? *Take off the cap.*

19

Lewis Carroll: Curiouser and Curiouser

I see nobody.
The White King

Let us jump straight in to see how Charles Lutwidge Dodgson, a nineteenth-century don, delights in some philosophical thinking. It is, of course, under the *nom de plume*, 'Lewis Carroll', and occurs most famously in his two 'Alice' stories, *Alice in Wonderland* and *Through the Looking-Glass*, with their crazy fantasies, ostensibly for children. In *Looking-Glass*, we encounter the White King and Alice, facing a long winding road.

The King asks Alice whom she sees on the road. 'I see nobody,' she reports. The King sighs, 'Oh to be able to see nobody – and from this distance too.'

Later, a messenger arrives, out of breath. The King asks whom he passed on the road. 'Nobody,' he replies. The King silently and swiftly engages in a little piece of reasoning, concluding, 'So, nobody walks more slowly than you do.'

That does not go down well with the messenger who has been rushing along, maybe under a blazing sun. In sulky tones, he insists, 'Nobody walks more quickly than I do.'

The King, exasperated by the messenger's poor reasoning, proclaims, 'He can't do that – otherwise he'll be here before you.'

Lewis Carroll is at play, wittingly raising a deep puzzle about language, reality and what is not the case. Carroll knows what he is about; he was a lecturer in mathematics and clergyman of Christ Church, Oxford. Undoubtedly, he was odd – aren't we all in different ways? He was very puritanical, yet obsessed with Alice Liddell, a young daughter of Henry Liddell, ecclesiastical dean of the college. His obsession with Alice and his eagerness to photograph girls of the 'Lolita' age, nude or scantily clad as waifs, raised eyebrows at the time. He would not fare at all well these days, but happily his books have not been cast into the flames – and his two 'Alice' books continue to fascinate, both as popular children's stories and as philosophical stimuli.

Returning to 'nobody', the royal reasoning is obviously mistaken. The King treats the term 'nobody' as if it were a name, standing for a subject of a sentence – the name of somebody. The tale may seem rather trivial, but philosophers have often been haunted by how language works with negations, with what is not, as we saw with Parmenides and Zeno. Some philosophers had been led to speak of non-existent entities – unicorns, round squares, the Golden Mountain – as possessed of *being*, but not of existence. It took Gottlob Frege in the late nineteenth century and Bertrand Russell in the early twentieth (please see Chapter 21) to provide formalizations of logic and language to bring forth some clarity regarding the use of 'not' and, as mentioned in the chapter on Aristotle, 'some' and 'all'.

Matters are still not easy. Formalizing language does not guarantee eradication of underlying difficulties. Russell, when becoming acquainted with the young Ludwig Wittgenstein, reported the following. In one discussion, Wittgenstein had insisted that all existential propositions – tigers exist; unicorns do not exist – are meaningless. Russell invited him to consider the proposition 'There is no hippopotamus in this room at present' and accept it as meaningful and true. Wittgenstein would not budge in his insistence, even though Russell went through the motions of looking under all the desks, finding no such creature present.

Of course, both philosophers knew that they were not arguing about an empirical matter to be settled by looking under the desks, but about how we should understand the use of language in such contexts. What 'fact' makes it true that there are no hippos in the room? If there is such a fact, how does it relate to the facts that make it true that there are no giraffes in the room, no round squares and no Loch Ness Monster?

I recall a Cambridge seminar in the 1970s where Elizabeth Anscombe (please see Chapter 29) spoke of how there is no mystery in a wrapper of a chocolate bar describing the chocolate as 'fruit' and no mystery with a wrapper saying 'nut', no mystery indeed with one saying 'fruit and nut', but she had come across a wrapper saying 'fruit *or* nut'. Now, the puzzle is whatever fact makes the wrapper accurate in saying 'fruit *or* nut'? What fact of the chocolate makes it 'fruit or nut', as opposed to its being 'fruit' or its being 'nut'? That question becomes important in metaphysics, if trying to understand truth, assuming truth to involve some sort of correspondence with the facts.

The wonderful scenarios presented by Carroll raise questions about one's personal identity, the nature of time and the relationship between items and features, between, as we saw in Aristotle, substances, particulars and universals. Can the Cheshire Cat's smile persist even when the cat has disappeared? When the cat has lost its body, yet is still with its head (and smile), the King commands, 'Off with its head!' leading to an argument with the executioner. To behead something, there needs to be a body to cut the head off from, argues the executioner. Not at all, is the King's response; anything with a head can be beheaded.

One *Looking-Glass* tale of considerable contemporary relevance concerns Humpty Dumpty, presented as the great wall-sitting Egg. Let us refer to him as HD. HD, in conversation with Alice, announces, 'There's glory for you.' Understandably, given the context, Alice is baffled: 'I don't know what you mean by "glory".' HD smiles contemptuously and says:

> Of course you don't – till I tell you. I mean, 'there's a nice knock-down argument for you!'
>
> 'But "glory" doesn't mean "a nice knock-down argument"', objects Alice – to which HD makes the remarkable and arrogant reply:
>
> When I use a word, it means just what I choose it to mean – neither more nor less.

Alice understandably is doubtful whether we can make words mean just what we want them to mean. The great wall-sitting Egg replies: 'The question is: which is to be master – that's all.'

Of course, words can be made up – Dodgson made up the name 'Lewis Carroll', using Latin variants of his 'real' name. Very, very rarely names and descriptive terms are onomatopoeic in that their sounds have a similarity with what is named or described – for example, *woof, woof*. Occasionally, terms are used secretly as codes to hide identities, avoiding difficulties, embarrassments or prosecution for blasphemy.

Yes, HD can use 'glory' as he wants, but for him to convey his thoughts to us *and to himself* he needs somewhere along the line to use words with their regular meanings, given the context. For Alice to understand him, he needed to translate his 'glory' – and he does so into 'there's a nice knock-down argument for you'. Presumably he intended those words to possess their regular meaning. Or did he? Once we have the HD approach to word meaning, who knows? We could be sceptical and judge that the wisest response is to accept that all is nothing but meaningless babble, including that thought (see Fortuna, p.265).

Grounding language in the public world hit the philosophical headlines in the twentieth century with Wittgenstein's argument against the possibility of a 'private language'. Of course, that term also needs explanation. The question raised is how we grasp the meaning of 'sensation' words, if we are tempted to insist that no one else can have my sensations – so no one else can know what I mean when I use the words 'ache', 'pain', 'pleasure' and so forth. Today, of course, we have debates about how the words 'woman' and 'man' should be used, in view of various transgender claims. We could expand the problems to how to determine the criteria for the use of other terms where there are also consequences for the treatment of people: for example, 'democracy', 'freedom', 'antisemitism'.

———————

In addition to the *Alice* books and similar, Carroll set riddles, wrote quirky verse and developed pictorial representations (akin to Venn diagrams) for logical arguments, using bizarre examples: recall Aristotle's syllogisms.

> Babies are illogical.
> Nobody is despised who can manage a crocodile.
> Illogical persons are despised.

It may take some time to see that one can validly conclude from those three premisses that babies cannot manage crocodiles. Things get worse, for Carroll developed more complicated puzzles to do with our reasoning. Indeed, his college contemporaries probably thought of him as too clever by half – or at least by one-eighth. Here is an example of his cleverness:

> Three gentlemen, Allen, Brown and Carr, run a barber shop. One of them is always present in the shop, scissors at ready. Allen never goes out alone; he only ever goes out with Brown. So, if Allen is out, then Brown is also out. That seems

to ensure the following is false: if Allen is out, then Brown is in. But we know that one barber always remains in the shop; so, if Carr is out, then if Allen is out, Brown is in. Hence, on the hypothesis that Carr is out, we are landed with the false consequent 'then' clause, namely, 'If Allen is out, then Brown is in.' So, paradoxically, it seems that Carr can never go out.

Something has gone wrong with the reasoning, for when Allen is in, Carr is free to sally forth. The underlying problem here is how to analyse conditional propositions 'if ... then ...' when in the subjunctive form, 'if that were so, then this would be so'.

The topic may seem highly academic, but we frequently try to judge the truth, or otherwise, of such conditionals. You would like to meet Miranda again at the concert. Should you let it be known that you will be going? Were Miranda to learn you would be going, would she then also go along – or would that knowledge lead her to stay away? Which conditional is true?

A simple related example from the thought-provoking American philosopher Nelson Goodman, in the 1950s, is how to evaluate these two opposing claims, referring to the Korean War:

> Had Julius Caesar been US President, he would have used nuclear weapons.

> Had Julius Caesar been US President, he would have used bows and arrows.

Earlier we saw Anscombe's worry over which fact, if any, makes it true that the chocolate is 'fruit *or* nut'. Here, we are worrying over which facts make such counterfactual conditionals about Julius Caesar true – if there are any such facts. Or maybe to assess such counterfactuals in terms of corresponding truths is already a mistake, as F. P. Ramsey argued; we meet him with Wittgenstein (in Chapter 27) and with Beckett (in Chapter 30).

In 1895 there appeared in the distinguished philosophy journal *Mind* the article 'What the Tortoise said to Achilles'. It was by our Lewis Carroll, making a point of logic, but, as ever, in his humorous way. As we saw much earlier, in Chapter 3, Zeno had Achilles trapped into a never-ending sequence of distances to run; the problem was how to make sense of the divisibility of space and time; Carroll now makes us see that there is a puzzle of endlessness, if thinking that logical deduction needs justification.

Carroll uses a geometrical example – well, he was a mathematician – that may make things seem more complicated than they are. Allow me to simplify the example. Achilles is sitting on a boulder, writing out some simple logical deductions in his notebook:

Premiss 1: All philosophers deserve respect.
Conclusion C: Zeno deserves respect.

That conclusion does not follow from the premiss as it stands. Mr T, the tortoise, is right to expect something more for the argument to be valid – and he asks for more. Achilles is happy to oblige. He adds:

Premiss 2: Zeno is a philosopher.

'There, Mr T, you must now accept the conclusion, C, "Zeno deserves respect", if you accept both premisses as true,' says Achilles proudly.

We may agree with Achilles, but Mr T plays dumb. He scratches his shell; he is unsure. Yes, he accepts the premisses, but why accept the conclusion? Achilles, now a little tetchy, explains, 'Look: if all philosophers deserve respect and if Zeno is a philosopher, then it follows that he deserves respect.'

'Ah,' says Mr T surprisingly quickly. 'That sounds like another premiss: please add it into the argument.' Achilles naively obliges, writing in his notebook:

Premiss 3: If Premisses 1 and 2 are true, then C.

'You must now accept the conclusion,' says Achilles. 'If you do not, logic will grab you by the throat and—'

'But,' interrupts Mr T, 'I'm still not certain about all this,' his dumbness ever present.

'Look,' says Achilles, 'If Premisses 1 and 2 and 3 are true, then C must follow.'

'Ah, another premiss, I do detect,' detects Mr T. 'Please write it down as Premiss 4.'

Premiss 4: If Premisses 1 and 2 and 3 are true, then C.

Mr T still feigns uncertainty – and so Achilles foolishly announces how if Premiss 1 and 2 and 3 and 4 are true, then C. 'Ah, another premiss,' says Mr T. 'Please write it down …'

As can be seen, with Mr T's insistence, the tale continues potentially endlessly. More and more conditional premisses are added in the attempt to placate and persuade Mr T, yet however many are added, there remains an endless number still to add; and so, it seems, no conclusion can ever be shown to be validly reached. Carroll comments on how Achilles, with greater and greater despair and exasperation, fills his notebook's pages with more and more premisses.

Carroll's paper gets forgotten, then remembered, then forgotten. It is asking how we should understand the justification of logical deduction. We met that justificatory concern with regard to inductive reasoning, when dealing with David Hume's philosophical thinking. Regarding the deductive argument in question, we should simply accept that P1 and P2, therefore C, is a valid argument, full stop. Various particular arguments are valid. It is because we identify features common to different valid arguments that we are able to display valid *forms* and *rules* of argument; recall Aristotle's syllogisms (Chapter 6). It is often a mistake, though, to demand that there be some form or rule behind what we do, in order to justify what we do.

As we shall see in a wider context when meeting Wittgenstein, 'justification comes to an end', 'explanations come to an end' and 'a chain of reasons comes to an end'. Indeed, they *must* do so. And that is a most valuable reminder for anyone engaged in philosophical thinking – or any thinking at all.

———

How to think like Lewis Carroll? *Dream up silly scenarios, provoking philosophical wonderments.*

20

Nietzsche: God-Slaying Jester, Trans-Valuer

God is dead.

Nietzsche

Earlier, we met the most famous philosophical phrase known outside of philosophy, namely, Descartes' 'I think, therefore I am.' In competition could well be Nietzsche's 'God is dead' – and, maybe, as we encountered much earlier, the Socratic 'The unexamined life is not worth living.'

Friedrich Wilhelm Nietzsche, born in 1844, was no modest philosopher – or maybe he possessed a feeling for the comic and ironic. In his 'sort of' autobiography *Ecce Homo*, there are chapters 'Why I am so wise', 'Why I am so clever', 'Why I Write Such Excellent Books' – and so forth. Indeed, *Ecce Homo* means *Behold the Man*; Pontius Pilate said the words when presenting Jesus with his crown of thorns to the crowd below. In Nietzsche's philosophical thinking, much uncertainty of meaning can blaze through. In *Ecce Homo*, he notes, 'I do not want to be a saint; better to be a jester. Perhaps I am a jester.'

Nietzsche is the philosopher of aphorisms, short paragraphs, witty insults and pithy paradoxical comments: 'Some men are born posthumously.' His philosophical thinking in style should remind us of Kierkegaard's. His insistence on the subjective determination and frightening importance of 'how to live' should also remind us of Kierkegaard and why both are deemed existentialist. A fundamental difference is that Kierkegaard sought God, whereas Nietzsche mocked that search.

Nietzsche was a brilliant student; by the age of twenty-four he was a professor of classical philology at the University of Basel. Fascinated by the arts and by music in particular – he was himself a minor composer of no great merit (despite what he thought) – he would spend time with Richard Wagner, initially praising the man and his music-dramas. Eventually, though, he turned against both, possibly because with Wagner's *Parsifal* – 'a curse on the senses and spirit' – Nietzsche wrongly read Wagner as adopting Christian symbols and values. Nietzsche's work *Twilight of the Idols* has the subtitle *How to Philosophize with a Hammer*; and with the hammer, Nietzsche strikes the idols of philosophy, religion, morality – and his admiration for Wagner – and finds them hollow, needing to be smashed.

Nietzsche, constantly in ill-health, wrestled with grasping the mystery of life and the will to live. I recall a television documentary in which some (probably postmodernist) philosophers told of how he went insane because of his troubling thoughts. Now, it is true that he went insane, but not because of his troubling thoughts; it was because of his syphilis. Of course, that syphilis may have generated the troubling thoughts.

In *Thus Spake Zarathustra: A Book for Everyone and for No One* – probably Nietzsche's best-known work – he announces in upper case: GOD IS DEAD. The work is like a prose poem, an ancient scripture; Nietzsche described it as a symphony. It offers us a completely fictionalized Zarathustra who founded the (real) religion of Zoroastrianism.

The literary flow and aspirations within the work led to composer Richard Strauss's 1896 tone poem of the same name; the surging opening chords found fame through their use in Stanley Kubrick's 1968 film *2001: A Space Odyssey*. In fact, Strauss saw those chords as the sun rising on a mountain top, giving rise to the world-riddle, in line with Nietzsche's Prologue thus:

> When Zarathustra was thirty years old, he left his home and the lake of his home, and went into the mountains. There he enjoyed his spirit and solitude, and for ten years did not weary of it. But at last his heart changed – and rising one morning with the rosy dawn, he went before the sun, and spake thus unto it:
>
> Thou great star! What would be thy happiness if thou hadst not those for whom thou shinest!

During the composition of *Zarathustra*, Nietzsche published his 1882's *The Gay Science*. For avoidance of doubt, I note its other translated title, *The Joyful Wisdom*.

> Have you not heard of that madman who lit a lantern in the bright morning hours, ran to the market place, and cried incessantly: 'I seek God! I seek God!' – As many of those who did not believe in God were standing around just then, he provoked much laughter. Has he got lost? asked one …
>
> The madman jumped into their midst and pierced them with his eyes. 'Whither is God?' he cried; 'I will tell you. *We have killed him* – you and I.'

Of course, there is no way in which human beings could create God, if God is understood as all powerful. It is perfectly possible for human beings to come up with the *idea* of God, but the idea of God is not God. There is also no way in which people could kill God. There certainly is a way in which people could cease to believe in God. Nietzsche's 'God is dead' is an apt and outrageous phrase for stirring us into asking what we are to make of morality, when there is no longer (or we no longer believe in) a divine commander instructing us how to live and threatening horrors if we ignore those instructions.

Nietzsche tells us not to believe 'those who speak of otherworldly hopes', but to be 'faithful to the earth'. That does not mean living according to nature, as per the Stoics, mentioned when outlining Epicurus in Chapter 7. Nietzsche writes:

> Think of a being such as nature, prodigal beyond measure, without aims or intentions, indifferent beyond measure, without mercy or justice, at once fruitful and barren and uncertain; think of indifference itself as a power – how could you live according to such indifference? To live – is that not precisely wanting to be other than this nature?'

As a result of such observations, Nietzsche knows that he is deemed an 'immoralist'. He rejects the type of man that had hitherto been regarded as the highest: the *good*, the *kind* and the *charitable*. In his terms, he rejects the morality of decadence, or, 'to use a still cruder term, Christian morality'. He sees all that as a weakness, incompatible with a yea-saying to life.

With nature of no help, and with God no longer, 'Everything is permitted'. Or is it? That nihilistic aphorism is from Ivan, of Fyodor Dostoevsky's *The Brothers Karamazov*. Nietzsche, though, was no nihilist; he sought instead a 'transvaluation' of the Christian values. In *Zarathustra*, Nietzsche writes, again in upper case: I TEACH YOU THE SUPERMAN. That is a rather coarse translation; it became linked with the Nazis and their antisemitism. It was Nietzsche's sister who forged that link, taking control of his writings, once he was confined to the asylum. Let us retain the German, *Übermensch*.

Nietzsche sees man as the animal whose nature has not yet been fixed, a theme we find in Jean-Paul Sartre with his use of 'existence precedes essence' for man. Today's man is conceived, by Nietzsche, as a rope over an abyss, tied between a beast and a being beyond man, the *Übermensch*, a being who affirms life, who values greatness. And that brings us back to suffering.

> Have you ever said Yes to a single joy? O my friends, then you said Yes too to all woe. All things are entangled, ensnared, enamoured.

Nietzsche was upholding the adage from ancient times 'All things conspire': how can we live, knowing that a single person – beast of the field, fish of the ocean – is suffering? How can we be courageous enough to embrace life – when knowing of the suffering in the world? The *Übermensch*, instead of drowning in pity, finds greatness – though its nature, in other respects, remains a mystery. Nietzsche did predict that he would not be understood for two hundred years; we have fewer than a hundred to go then.

Whatever we are to make of the *Übermensch*, we may admire Nietzsche in his insistence that we need to give meaning to our lives and even in his dismissive attitude towards utilitarianism (he seemed to be aware of John Stuart Mill's work):

> If we possess our why of life, we can put up with almost any how. – Man does not strive after happiness; only the Englishman does that.

Of course, that raises again all the questions of how 'happiness' is to be understood. In fact, the whole of Nietzsche's thinking on reality and values raises questions and seems to embrace enigma as in: 'without music, life would be a mistake'.

Truthfulness is a core value for him, but he is nevertheless famous for insisting that we all need illusion to live well. Art is most important precisely because of its power for illusion – 'We possess art lest we perish of the truth' – and in art, he was attracted by the Dionysian element, the frenzy, irrational, as opposed to the Apollonian rational control. He asks: 'How much truth does a spirit *endure*, how much truth does it *dare*? More and more that became for me the real measure of value.'

For Nietzsche, truth depended on a perspectivalism: 'there is *only* a perspectival seeing, *only* a perspectival "knowing"; and *the more* eyes, different eyes, we bring to bear on one and the same matter, the more complete will our "objectivity" be.' Yet he also proffered elusive comments such as:

> some out of the way corner of that universe of numberless twinkling solar systems, there was a star upon which clever beasts invented knowing. That was the most arrogant and mendacious minute of 'world history', but nevertheless, it was only a minute. After nature had drawn a few breaths, the star cooled and congealed, and the clever beasts had to die.

We also have the paradox of his embrace of determinism, while emphasizing how we must choose how to live. That paradox, of course, is not confined to Nietzsche; various struggles with determinism and free choice have already been encountered through the Tao, Spinoza and Kant. Nietzsche's line is:

> if the world's wheel were to stand still for a moment and an all-knowing, calculating reason were there to make use of this pause, it could foretell the future of every creature to the remotest times, and mark out every track upon which that wheel would continue to roll. The delusion of the acting agent, the supposition of a free will, belongs to this mechanism which remains to be calculated.

'*Amor fati*: let that be my love henceforth!' That love and embrace of fate, for him, involves not waging war against what is ugly. Apparently, what is bad is *looking away* – 'I wish to be only a Yes-sayer.' Of course, his loving fate presumably is fated and if he manages to be only a 'Yes-sayer', then that too has been fated. We should, though, be wary of casual talk of things being fated, as we explored a little with the Tao in Chapter 1.

Let us close with Nietzsche's most terrifying thought: 'the eternal recurrence', 'the greatest weight'. It runs with the proposal: what if, some day or night, a demon were to steal into your loneliest loneliness and say unto you:

> This life as you now live it and have lived it, you will have to live once again and innumerable times again; and there will be nothing new in it, but every pain and every joy and every thought and sigh and everything unspeakably small or great in your life must return to you, all in the same succession and sequence – even this spider and this moonlight between the trees, and even this moment and I myself. The eternal hourglass of existence is turned over again and again, and you with it, O speck of dust!

Nietzsche then asks:

> Would you not throw yourself down and gnash your teeth and curse the demon who spoke thus? … Or how well disposed would you have to become to yourself and to life – to long for nothing more fervently than this ultimate eternal confirmation and seal?

Now, that is a challenge. One fascination about the challenge is how it can bring many of us up with a start even though it is grounded in a nonsense. The recurrence is one in which the recurrences are exactly the same: we have no sense of *déjà vu*; no awareness that this is a repeat or even the first run. What difference can the hypothesis then make to us? The eternal repetition collapses into one – this one – as far as we are concerned. Furthermore, we may wonder what would constitute a repetition of anything such that it is exactly the same, yet repeated. It seems a nonsense. Leibniz propounded the 'identity of indiscernibles'; if 'two' items or states or worlds are indiscernible, are exactly the same, then surely we do not have two, but just one.

Despite those criticisms of the very idea of the eternal recurrence, the seeming possibility of the eternal recurrence can lead us to reflect on how proud – or not – we are of our lives, our values and ways of living. Maybe anyone who can be that proud of their particular life is either engaged in self-deception or is, indeed, an instance of the *Übermensch*.

Of course, to be well disposed to one's life, to stand up for its values, need not suggest a pride in the sense of an arrogance; one could value humility. That is not, though, Nietzsche's recommendation. His most fundamental recommendation is to reflect on your life and live it in such a way that you stand up for it, declare a commitment to it – and welcome its eternal recurrence. That is the heart of Nietzsche.

———

How to think like Nietzsche? *How well disposed can you be to your life?*

Bertrand Russell: Radical, Aristocrat

The Truth is a shining goddess, always veiled,
always distant, never wholly approachable,
but worthy of all the devotion of which
the human spirit is capable.

Russell

To have a grandfather, peer of the realm, twice prime minister; to have radically minded aristocratic atheistic parents, open to romantic affairs; to have John Stuart Mill as your secular godfather; to have your parents and sister dying when you are a young child (your brother commits suicide later); and thereafter to be brought up by that former prime minister – well, that is not a typical background for a philosopher of the twentieth century, or any century. That philosopher, together with a younger colleague, changed the thinking of philosophy, at least in the English-speaking world.

The younger colleague is G. E. Moore, to whom we shall shortly turn. Here we have Bertrand Russell (1872–1970), for completeness: Bertrand Arthur William Russell, 3rd Earl Russell. He first read mathematics at Trinity College, Cambridge, then the moral sciences (as philosophy was called). He reacted against the Hegelian Idealism of the Absolute, whereby ultimate reality could not be understood as a diverse collection of mind-independent items.

Russell, stimulated by Moore's common sense, threw off all that idealist claptrap; and with his mathematical background, brought to the fore analytic philosophy, producing, with Arthur North Whitehead, the monumental ground-breaking three-volume work, *Principia Mathematica* (1910–13). They sought (but ultimately failed) to deduce mathematics from logic. Russell's thinking, though, ranged far wider than that – into all areas of philosophy – yet he also managed to fit in numerous romantic affairs, four marriages and considerable political activity.

In the public forum, his philosophical thinking led him to work for social reforms, to publish articles against religion and to promote atheism, humanism and what was then termed 'free love'. In 1957, he founded, with others, the Campaign for Nuclear Disarmament (CND) of which he was president. Mind you, some years before that campaigning, he advocated use of the 'atom bomb' against the Soviet Union. There is no need to cry 'contradiction' or 'hypocrite'; he rightly recognized that circumstances can affect what it is right to do. Of course, it does not follow that Russell was right in his assessment of those circumstances. Through Cambridge and the Bloomsbury Group, he knew the economist John Maynard Keynes, who reportedly said: 'When the facts change, I change my mind; what do you do, sir?'

A contradiction in logic, though, did cause trouble; no facts change in logic. Russell had embraced mathematics as a discipline of eternal truths and supreme beauty: 'a beauty cold and austere, like that of sculpture'. Despite (or maybe because of) his chaotic personal life, he had keenly researched within those abstract heavens, untainted by uncertainty and contradiction – until … In 1902, he discovered what has become known as

'Russell's Paradox'. It is a paradox in set theory, but it can be given a feel by a simple example. Here is mine:

> Once upon a time, the wealthy and royal would hold banquets at which jesters performed jestingly. The jesters were never invited to dine at the banquets at which they jested. One day they had the bright idea of holding a Jesters' Banquet – a banquet for all and only those jesters ineligible to join banquets at which they jested. The Jesters' Banquet would be as grand as those of the great courts and it too would need its own jester to jest. 'We must not have to jest ourselves – too much like hard work,' they agreed. Thus it was that they appointed a lad, fresh from the Cambridge 'hills' of Gog Magog, where the name itself promoted jesting. 'You shall be our Jesting Junior,' they said to the bemused lad ...
>
> The jesters are now at their Banquet. Jesting Junior is excellent, performing fine japes, jokes and jests. 'Come, Junior, come and join the banquet,' the jesters slur, somewhat intoxicated, all except Jesting Stickler. 'Our banquet is solely for jesters ineligible to join banquets at which they jest,' says Stickler firmly, 'so, Junior, cannot join us.'
>
> 'But if he cannot join us, then he is indeed jesting at a banquet which he cannot join; hence, he fulfils the conditions and so he can join us.' 'But therefore he can't!' 'But therefore he can ...'

We have a contradiction, anathema to most logicians and analytic philosophers. The Banquet involves a contradiction; so, it cannot occur – yet, paradoxically, it did.

On his discovery of the paradox, Russell passed on the bad news to Gottlob Frege, a great German logician. The bad news caused Frege to abandon his lifelong work on logic and mathematics, which had been close to completion. Frege's reaction led Russell to comment on Frege's integrity, grace and dedication to the truth.

In 1916 Russell's philosophical thinking, miles away from logical paradoxes, got him into some different troubles in London. He was fined for his writings on the war and his support for conscientious objectors. In 1918 he was sent to Brixton jail for six months; he was imprisoned for making statements 'likely to prejudice His Majesty's relations with the United States of America'. That likelihood had arisen, the authorities claimed, because he had written of how the Americans were managing to intimidate British strikers. Once Russell learnt of the appalling prison conditions, he drew on his aristocratic connections; he managed to serve his time in the 'First Division', somewhat akin to how, in certain American states, prisoners can pay for cell upgrades. For Russell, First Division status meant that he was granted an extra-large cell; it was furnished by his sister-in-law, his meals were ordered from outside, he was supplied with pen and paper. Thus, he could carry on with his writing. The particular work was his *Introduction to Mathematical Logic*, where he notes:

> In this chapter we shall consider the word *the* in the singular, and in the next chapter we shall consider the word *the* in the plural. It may be thought excessive to devote two chapters to one word, but to the philosophical mathematician it is a word of very great importance: like Browning's Grammarian with the enclitic δε, I would give the doctrine of this word if I were 'dead from the waist down' and not merely in a prison.

Russell's work on 'the' had led to his Theory of Descriptions first presented in 'On Denoting' (1905) in *Mind*. The editor had felt it was not fit for publication, but Russell had his way and some years later the theory was described by F. P. Ramsey as a paradigm of philosophy. We shall meet Ramsey again in relation to Wittgenstein.

One problem that the theory sought to solve was how we manage to express propositions about non-existent items. We encountered that problem with Parmenides and Lewis Carroll. Russell took as an example, 'the present King of France is bald'. Some philosophers, it seems, assumed that for such a proposition to have meaning, the phrase 'the present King of France' must denote something. At that time, France having become a republic, there was no existing French monarch. As Russell points out, if we enumerated the things that are bald, and then the things not bald, we should not find the present King of France in either list. Ever keen for a quip, Russell adds, 'Hegelians, who love a synthesis, will probably conclude that he wears a wig.'

Russell overcame the puzzle by analysing the proposition in such a way that 'the present King of France' is no longer a constituent. The analysis amounts to a conjunction of three propositions: 'there is something that royally rules over France; there is not more than one thing that so rules over France; and whatever so rules over France is bald'. That tripartite analysis shows 'the present King of France is bald' to be false. It is false because the first conjunct, 'there is something that royally rules over France', is false; and that is sufficient for the tripartite combination overall to be false. Others have since muddied waters, arguing that the proposition is neither true nor false; thus, the analysis is wrong. The analysis in any case requires yet more analyses – one needs to analyse out 'France' for example and that fits in with Russell's search for what he termed 'logical atoms'.

There is much, much more to the 'On Denoting' paper and here is a way into the 'more', using Russell's enjoyable tale:

I have heard of a touchy owner of a yacht to whom a guest, on first seeing it, remarked, 'I thought your yacht was larger than it is'; and the owner replied, 'No, my yacht is not larger than it is.' What the guest meant was, 'The size that I thought your yacht was is greater than the size your yacht is'; the meaning attributed to him is, 'I thought the size of your yacht was greater than the size of your yacht.'

In Russell's day, a Scottish novelist still then much read, little read today, was Sir Walter Scott, who wrote *Waverley* and numerous follow-ups. Russell, when dealing with propositions expressing people's psychological attitudes about things, gave the example: 'George IV wished to know whether Scott was the author of *Waverley*.' Russell needed an analysis such that it did not collapse into 'George IV wished to know whether Scott was Scott.' As Russell whimsically noted, an interest in the law of identity can hardly be attributed to the first gentleman of Europe.

In 1940, Russell – then short of money (as aristocrats can be; as those who have been through many marriages can be) – accepted a professorship at New York City College. Once his appointment became known, the forces of darkness, as Russell described those motivated by religious prejudices, pounced, taking the college to court. It was argued that Russell was a foreigner and needed to prove his expertise in a competitive examination. That argument was a cover for so-called moral arguments that quickly came to the fore.

On the basis of his writings, Russell was accused of being 'lecherous, salacious, libidinous, lustful, venerous, erotomaniac, aphrodisiac, atheistic, irreverent, narrow-minded, untruthful, and bereft of moral fibre'. Despite eminent philosophers vouching for his academic and moral status, Russell lost his contract; his writings, it was claimed, endangered the public health, safety and morals of the community. The appointment, the judge ruled, would have created a 'chair of indecency'.

Ten years later, Russell was receiving the Nobel Prize for Literature. Of course, it should have been for Philosophy, Logic and Social Reform – but there are no Nobel prizes in those areas. When reflecting on the New York incident, Russell observed that urban New York in 1940 was at the same stage of enlightenment as his grandfather had found in rural England in 1868, when seeking election.

Russell would warm to the Socratic thought that the unexamined life is not worth living; he would warm to the Socratic gadfly, in stirring people into questioning, thinking, reasoning, seeking the truth. A quip he would often deploy is: 'Most people would rather die than think – and that is what they do.'

Russell is right that it is wise to think things through – typically so, anyway – though, of course, thinking is never sufficient for reaching sensible outcomes; after all, the thinking, the reasoning, may be poor and the conclusions crass. Further, however good the thinking, one needs a sense of compassion, of humanity. In fighting for what he thought was right, Russell, as seen, ended up in prison in 1918 and again in 1961, then aged eighty-nine, when he was found guilty of refusing to keep the peace at a rally in London's Trafalgar Square, protesting against nuclear weapons. Over the decades, it seems, he became quite seasoned at being arrested, though not usually charged.

———

Russell's philosophical thinking would always have regard for clarity, for reason and for evidence. He used the example of a china teapot, 'Russell's Teapot', orbiting the sun, too small to be seen through the most powerful of telescopes. It would be absurd to argue that while there is 'absence of evidence' for the teapot's existence, none the less that does not establish 'evidence of absence'; and so, we should have an open mind about its existence. In contrast, Russell rightly argues that the burden of proof is on the Teapot believer. Whatever could justify postulating, say, an invisible teapot? We should deploy Ockham's Razor, derived from the methodology of the Franciscan priest and philosopher, William of Ockham: entities should not be multiplied beyond necessity.

Russell comments that, curiously, were the Teapot tale to be found in ancient scriptures, many people would be inclined to believe in it. Yes, as mentioned, Russell was an out-and-out atheist. He quipped that were he, on his death, to face God, he would justify his atheism by pointing out that God had not provided the evidence of His existence.

Three passions, Russell wrote in his autobiography, simple but overwhelmingly strong, had governed his life: the longing for love, the search for knowledge, and unbearable pity for the suffering of mankind. 'These passions,' he continued, 'like great winds, have blown me hither and thither, in a wayward course, over a great ocean of anguish, reaching to the very verge of despair.'

He added: 'Love and knowledge, so far as they were possible, led upward toward the heavens. But always pity brought me back to earth.' He concluded of his life (he died aged ninety-seven): 'I have found it worth living, and would gladly live it again if the chance were offered me.'

How to think like Russell? *Think clearly, avoid ambiguities, follow the evidence, never ignore the sufferings of others.*

22

G. E. Moore: Common-Sense Defender, Bloomsbury's Sage

Everything is what it is, and not another thing.
Joseph Butler

Now we meet a philosopher over two thousand years after Plato whose ways of philosophical thinking would appear to be in complete contrast to those that went before.

G. E. Moore was born in 1873 and went up to Trinity College, Cambridge, in 1892 to read classics. There he met Russell a couple of years older and John McTaggart Ellis McTaggart, then a young lecturer. Under their encouragement, he added the university course Moral Sciences (Philosophy) to his studies and was soon astounded by what he read. His astonishment can be seen in his response to McTaggart's thinking.

McTaggart was an Idealist in that he believed the physical world was unreal. Reality, for McTaggart, consisted of immaterial loving souls. He also declared time to be unreal. When hearing this, Moore would respond with amazement. 'Are you really telling me, Jack, that I didn't have my breakfast before I had my lunch?'

That story illustrates how Moore sought to pin down exactly what philosophers meant by their words and theories. That pinning down was achieved by bringing them down to earth, to get them carefully to relate their claims to our common-sense beliefs. I urge that as deeply important when seeking to evaluate what philosophers proclaim. Moore's question was not, of course, sufficient to silence McTaggart, but it showed that philosophical thinking needs regard for our everyday thinking, language and activities. In fact, there are different ways of analysing time; some philosophers argue that we can make sense of before/after in time – that sequence does exist in reality, independently of us – but what is an illusion is the thought that there is an objectivity to the distinction between past, present and future.

Moore became one of the leading philosophers of the early twentieth century, together with Russell and Wittgenstein. (He always published as 'G. E. Moore' for he hated the names 'George', 'Edward'.) Let us look at the opening of one of his lectures:

> I am at present, as you can all see, in a room
> and not in the open air;
> I am standing up, and not sitting or lying down;
> I have clothes on, and am not absolutely naked ...

Moore claimed to know the above with certainty – and, he insisted, so did members of the audience. He makes the good point that just because it is possible that he could have been lying down or outdoors, it does not follow that, on this occasion, he does not know that he is not lying down or outdoors. To move to an example from Russell: even if it is logically possible that the universe came into existence just five minutes ago, it does not follow that it did and it does not follow that we do not know that it did not. We ought not to dismiss the evidence that it did not by the fact that it is logically possible that all the evidence came into existence five minutes ago; it is still evidence that it did not.

There is no playing with words here. Moore insists that he is deploying their ordinary meanings. He is not relying on Bishop

Berkeley's ruse of 'speaking with the vulgar but thinking with the learned' (as we may switch the aphorism). Moore does not go on to argue that 'really' material bodies such as his clothes and, for that matter, his biological bits that are clothed, are just collections of mind-dependent ideas.

Moore occasionally came unstuck. When delivering a lecture in the States, he looked up and said that he knew for certain, 'There's a skylight in this roof.' He had hit unlucky, for after the lecture, his host took him to one side and told him that there was no window, no skylight; he had mistaken a painting that covered a portion of the dome for a skylight. In his notebooks, Moore then worried: 'I certainly thought there was a window, but did I feel sure there was? Or did I think it was certain there was?' And so on.

If you read Moore's work, you will find pages of his endeavouring to get things absolutely clear; he tries so very, very hard that we often get very, very bored or lost. That 'or' in the previous sentence is an 'inclusive "or"': that is, some may get very, very bored *and* lost. Moore wrote an article on Russell's Theory of Descriptions (met in the previous chapter): after some skirmishes, he makes clear that there is at least one defect with the Theory. Russell in his reply said words to the effect:

> it seemed to me my worst mistake was to suppose that if Scott was the *author* of *Waverley*, he must have *written Waverley* whereas he could have dictated it. From any other philosopher, I should have been dismissive, but as it was from my good friend Moore …

The friendship between Moore and Russell was somewhat fragile, up and down. Russell recalled how in a discussion, he was led to say, 'You don't like me, do you, Moore'; Moore's reply was: 'No, I don't like you' – and the discussion resumed. Moore possessed complete honesty; and philosophers in serious dialogue seek after the truth of the topic, trying not to be distracted by personalities.

Many have been astonished at Moore's influence on philosophy and his influence on the wider world – but influence, and significant influence, it then was. Some now see Moore as a simpleton, somewhat moronic in his philosophy; some are appalled by his 'confession' that none of the philosophical worries about common-sense beliefs had occurred to him, until he read philosophers.

Moore's huge influence may have resulted from his character rather than rigour of argument. That he anguished showed his sincerity and modesty, his integrity and seriousness. He was not being clever in the manner of Oxford's J. L. Austin; although Austin admired Moore, he appeared to use philosophy to show off his talents at spotting linguistic subtleties. Moore, though, battled for truth, painstakingly so. He wrestled, as did Wittgenstein, but, unlike Wittgenstein, without vanity.

Subsequent commentators have rather casually concluded that Moore must therefore have been a mild man – but that does not follow. He could fall into a rage, displaying, it seems, an innocent man's dislike for the corrupt; an example of dislike was his very low opinion of Russell's personal life of turbulent affairs. Moore's purity was likened to that of Socrates, Jesus and Dostoevsky's Prince Myshkin.

Moore's greatest influence outside of professional philosophers was on the Bloomsbury Group, though his life was very different from its other members. He was a family man, one marriage, a secure job, and sired two sons; he was unlike Russell who collected wives and unlike Keynes, cavorting and challenging sexual conventions in line with others of Bloomsbury. Moore's intellectual influence on Bloomsbury derived from his major work, his first work, *Principia Ethica*, though again it was probably his force of character, of sage-like purity and appreciation of beauty and the good, that made his words so appealing.

In *Principia*, Moore argues that there are some simple indefinable qualities such as good and beautiful. The concept 'good' cannot be equivalent to, for example, utilitarians' 'the greatest happiness of the greatest number', because we can significantly ask whether achieving such overall happiness would be good. That type of question has since raised considerable philosophical debate concerning concepts, meaning and their designations. We can significantly ask the question whether water is H_2O; and so, that shows what? That water is not essentially H_2O?

Moore's handling of the question with regard to 'good' harmonized with the *Principia*'s epigram: Joseph Butler's, 'Everything is what it is and not another thing.' The indefinable qualities such as 'good' may remind us of Plato's Forms; becoming aware of those qualities, focusing on their value, is what is important in life. Beauty and truth, love and friendship, it was said, possessed the solidity of tables and chairs for Moore. His description of two worlds gives us a feeling for his sense of the solidity of values. Here is the first world:

Let us imagine one world exceedingly beautiful. Imagine it as beautiful as you can; put into it whatever on this earth you most admire – mountains, rivers, the sea; trees, and sunsets, stars and moon. Imagine these all combined in the most exquisite proportions, so that no one thing jars against another, but each contributes to increase the beauty of the whole.

Here is the second:

And then imagine the ugliest world you can possibly conceive. Imagine it simply one heap of filth, containing everything that is most disgusting to us, for whatever reason, and the whole, as far as may be without one redeeming feature.

The only thing we may not add to either world is consciousness; there are no conscious inhabitants and no outside perceivers affected. Moore argues that it is just obvious, common sense, that it would be better for the beautiful world to exist. He concludes that beauty can exist without any awareness of it. 'Beautiful' is an objective, mind-independent quality.

We may recoil from believing that the matter could be settled so easily, but Moore's type of approach held considerable sway at the time and can still have appeal and fascination. Here is Keynes commenting on how he and other members of Bloomsbury reacted to *Principia* and its arguments for valuing friendship, love, beauty and so forth:

How did we know what states of mind were good? This was a matter of direct inspection, of direct unanalysable intuition about which it was useless and impossible to argue. In that case who was right when there was a difference of opinion?

In practice, reports Keynes, looking back, 'victory was with those who could speak with the greatest appearance of clear, undoubting conviction and could best use the accents of infallibility. Moore at this time was a master of this method.' Apparently, Moore would greet mistaken observations (those with which he disagreed) with 'Do you *really* think *that*?' – his mouth wide open, wagging his head in the negative violently. '*Oh!* He would say, goggling at you as if either you or he must be mad; and no reply was possible.'

Philosophers for centuries – and especially Kant and onwards – have wondered what is going on when we say something exists; recall Descartes' 'proof' of God's existence (Chapter 9). Is asserting an item's existence akin to asserting properties of items, for example, that these suitcases are green and heavy? Moore entered the discussion by contrasting the ease of saying how all or many or some tame tigers growl with the awkwardness of 'All tame tigers exist.' No problem in saying that some tame tigers do not growl; but can you say, with sense, that some tame tigers do not exist? Of course, our thinking would quickly then need to handle items of fiction: some cats and cockroaches do not exist; for example, Archy the cockroach and Mehitabel the alley cat (brought to fame by Don Marquis in 1916's New York's *Evening Sun*).

Once again, Moore's great care with analysis led to some valuable insights but also to many sighs of weariness at his 'ponderous, pernickety and pedantic' style. I use the triple 'p' phrase, for in a 'blind' review, I was described thus, with the added accolade of 'and clearly not a native English speaker'.

I return to Moore's character; people admired his saintly childlike innocence. Wittgenstein remarked: 'I can't understand that, unless it's also to a child's credit. For you aren't talking of the innocence a man has fought for, but of an innocence which comes from a natural absence of temptation.' Wittgenstein constantly battled to overcome vanity and arrogance.

As already implied, some philosophers, later on, viewed Moore as very much an emperor with no clothes. In a major lecture, he had claimed to overcome 'the scandal of philosophy', as Kant had deemed the lack of proof for the existence of the external world, of physical items independent of mind. Moore's proof rested on his gesturing with his hands, 'Here is a hand' – and doing the same with the other hand – concluding that the external world existed. Was he missing the point? Or was something valuable being demonstrated about the nature of proof? With that thought, we see Moore as being a philosopher for philosophers – and one who ought not to be dismissed.

Outside of philosophy, Virginia Woolf later reflected on Moore in her diary entry of 23 June 1920:

> I lay in the shallow light, which should be written dark, I think, a long time, & then Moore came & took a cold bath at 1 in the morning... He has grown grey, sunken, toothless perhaps. His eyes small, watchful, but perhaps not so piercing as of old... I dont [sic] see altogether why he was such a dominator & dictator of youth. Perhaps Cambridge is too much of a cave... of course there's his entire innocency & shrewdness, not the vestige of falsehood obscuring him anywhere.

Things move on. Emperors can have substantial clothes, yet age and culture tears them to shreds. Moore, in his later days, would sometimes be criticized at meetings for saying nothing. Was he offering himself as a great and silent sage? Not at all. Once when challenged over his silence, his reply was:

> I didn't want to be silent. I couldn't think of anything to say.

And there we have yet another valuable thing to learn from George Edward Moore.

How to think like G. E. Moore? *Bring philosophical theories down to earth – and don't feel that you must say something when you have nothing to say.*

23

Heidegger: Hyphenater

Making itself intelligible is suicide for philosophy.
Heidegger

Many philosophers are exceedingly difficult to understand. I refer, of course, to their thinking; understanding their lives is a distinct albeit also often a difficult matter. Philosophers are frequently dealing with complex concepts and perplexing ideas. They sometimes lack skills of expression, misjudge their audience or try to say too much in too few words or, for that matter, too little in far too many words. For some, the conviction is that respectable philosophy, or philosophy most likely to receive funding, must ape the sciences and aping requires technical terminology. Of course, in certain areas – formal logic – technical language is essential.

Some philosophers use elusive presentations to coax readers to dig into problems in their own way. They may deploy startling experiments in thought or frenzied outbursts. Even when philosophers determinedly deploy common terms readily grasped, they can be so focused on accuracy that their writing becomes all the more baffling: we have seen that with G. E. Moore.

In the cases above, we typically respect the philosophers and their labours. They are sincere in grappling with the problems.

With Heidegger, things are different – well, according to some. Some think of him as almost a charlatan, a pretentious spinner of new terms, of obscurity for the sake of obscurity or for the appearance of great depth and wisdom. Strive through the fog, and a few useful observations are found – but nothing much. Others revere Heidegger or at least his thought, considering him to be the greatest philosopher of the twentieth century. He certainly has had the greatest influence, or at least the most words written in examining his work. Of course, that latter achievement may partly be explained by the very impenetrability of that work.

Obscurity to one side, scepticism of Heidegger's thinking sometimes results from dislike of the man, of his support for Hitler, National Socialism and antisemitism – and his subsequent whitewashing of that support or apparent change of heart. Who knows the nature of his commitment? Probably the question only receives close attention because of his considerable influence, not solely in philosophy, but also in the social sciences and in humanities more generally. His continuing Nazi credentials are probably as uncertain as is the claim that Hitler's antisemitism, in part, derived from his reaction to Ludwig Wittgenstein. They were at the same school, with the young Jewish Ludwig manifesting far greater intelligence, wealth and conceit, than the young Adolf. That may well have encouraged the latter's antisemitism. Who knows?

Turning directly to Heidegger's thinking as expressed in his writings, philosophers in the empiricist tradition – recall David Hume committing metaphysics to the flames – have great fun, deeming many of his claims nonsense, failing even to reach the accolade of 'false', let alone 'true'. Gilbert Ryle, the one-time king of philosophy in 1940s Oxford, quipped that saying something false was almost as good as saying something true; at least in neither case is it nonsense. Mind you, Ryle did find things of value in Heidegger.

A classic example of Heidegger reaping the nonsense accolade is provided by the Vienna Circle's Rudolph Carnap with his mockery of Heidegger's 'Nothing nothings' ('*Das Nichts nichtet*'). Whatever does it mean? We may be reminded of Lewis Carroll's wordplay with 'nobody'.

When we encounter odd language, we should adopt some generosity, a principle of charity, and search for sense. With the 'nothings' case, perhaps the verb 'nothings' means that the subject has no properties or relations – there is nothing about it. If so, the claim could amount to the simple truth that there do not exist items that lack all properties, all relations, all substance. Possibly the claim amounts to the truth that there does not exist an item that is identical with an item that does not exist. With Heidegger in the frame, we may, though, doubt whether such simple uncontroversial truths were intended.

One manifestation of Heidegger's obscurity, his impenetrability, whether in German or English translation – and maybe a reason for his appeal – is his keenness to introduce new terms, often requiring hyphenation. There can be a defence. He is starting again in metaphysics; familiar terms and traditional language may carry philosophical presuppositions demanding challenge. Of course, new expressions cannot just be mumbo-jumbo, left floating unconnected to everyday language, but making them typographically distinctive may helpfully jerk us into paying attention – and Heidegger certainly does that, deploying a vast hyphenated array. 'Being-in-the-world', 'for-the-sake-of-which', 'Being-toward-death', 'Being-just-present-at-hand', 'Ek-sistence', are just a few.

Let us focus on his major work, *Being and Time* (1927). Despite its length (over 400 pages), it remained uncompleted and eventually Heidegger treated it more as a stepping stone to a work with a greater historical orientation. It centres on 'Being'. Yes, Heidegger possessed a yen for the upper case as well as for hyphenation, and the yen was not just that grounded in the German language.

What is meant by 'Being'? It is not itself an entity. Maybe in some way it is meant to be that in virtue of which entities are entities. That is obscure enough. In fact, one specific type of being is Heidegger's focus: *Dasein* –'being-there' or 'there being'. 'Dasein' seems typically to be used for what we are. The German term is retained in English translations to save us from importing our common beliefs or inbuilt prejudices about what people or human beings essentially are. Dasein, for example, is fundamentally understood as being much concerned with the question 'What is Being?', though I doubt if many people have that question in mind, even if unnoticed, whatever Heidegger announces.

Here is an example of Heideggerian thinking related to Dasein, in case readers want to experience the obscurity of thought, one of thousands.

...whenever an ontology takes for its theme entities whose character of Being is other than that of Dasein, it has its own foundation and motivation in Dasein's own ontical structure, in which a pre-ontological understanding of Being is comprised as a definite characteristic ... Therefore fundamental ontology, from which alone all other ontologies can take their rise, must be sought in the existential analytic of Dasein.

Any clearer? Well, at least there is the clarity that Dasein 'clearly' differs essentially from other entities: its mode of being is existence or ek-istence, whereas other entities are deemed to be 'presence-at-hand', sometimes 'readiness-to-hand' with 'available-ness'. I guess that comes down to the fact that in everyday life we typically encounter things that we can and do use; and we can distinguish their being from ours. In everyday life, we do not typically see them as nothing but physical objects – 'occurrentnesses' – to be investigated as physicists do. Heidegger, unusually, makes use of a simple term for them; they are 'equipment', though we should surely resist thinking of seas and sunsets and sycamore trees in the same way as thinking of string and sinks and scissors.

Heidegger's much-quoted example is a hammer in use. In use, it is not contemplated as a physical object, but as a tool for a task, though we could use it just as a weight. We may go searching for it, scramble to sort out nails, riskily hold some between our lips, while with hammer in hand we head for the broken fence, eventually hammering away, checking that fingers and thumb are well clear. We are then in a 'primordial relationship' with the hammer, nails and fence; they are 'readiness-to-hand'. We are the situation, engrossed in the hammering.

In many situations we act without awareness. Think of the numerous movements and actions we do with no consciousness of doing them: for example, when driving a car, stopping at red lights, signalling and so forth. Heidegger is not claiming that we are never conscious 'of ourselves' engaged in activities; awareness comes to the fore when things go wrong: we miss the nail; we hammer the thumb; we are suddenly aware of the child running into the road.

Heidegger's understanding of Dasein is underlined by his reaction to Kant's observation that the scandal of philosophy is its failure to prove the existence of the external world. We have seen how G. E. Moore dealt with that scandal; he displayed his hands. Heidegger displays, so to speak, the hands situated in the hammering. He tells us that the scandal of philosophy is that such proofs are expected and repeatedly attempted.

The Kantian scandal arose because of the acceptance of Descartes' stance that we are subjects confronted by objects. That presents the world 'with its skin off'. In reality, we are, though, firmly embedded in the world; and that fact is signalled by the hyphenation of 'being-in-the-world'. The hyphenation alerts us to how items are defined by Dasein's activities, their accessibility, their involvements and location, their 'readiness-to-hand' in our projects. The bed affords us resting; hammers afford us hammering; phones communication.

As well as being enmeshed with objects' functional properties, we are enmeshed with others as Dasein. It would be as much a scandal to think that we needed to prove the existence of other minds as it is to prove the existence of the external world.

Heidegger's work aligns with a focus on our 'knowing how' to do things rather than on the philosophers' obsession with the much-loved propositional knowledge, knowing *that* something is the case. Ryle, having reviewed *Being and Time*, wrote a lot on the importance of knowing how. Some twentieth-century analyses of 'knowing that something is so and so' have been offered in terms of 'knowing how' to be reliably right in transmitting information. If you want a goat, you need people who can distinguish between goats and sheep. That they can correctly announce that the creature in yonder field is a sheep is not of much use if when they see goats they declare them also to be sheep. They lack reliability in sheep/goat discriminatory talents.

In the above, I have assembled some sensible thoughts (I hope) from Heidegger, so did they require Heidegger's painfully obscure, even pretentious, presentation? Of course, perhaps the very fact that some simple points have been revealed shows that I have failed to penetrate his thinking. After all, although we use items as equipment and often do not notice what we are doing, Heidegger is trying to get deeper than that; he is trying to handle traditional philosophical puzzles of how my experiences relate to an 'external world' and to others. Let us plough on.

A key concept for Heidegger, surprisingly unhyphenated, is *care*. Unlike occurrent entities, Dasein carries meaning – things matter to us; we care about things. We have possibilities open to us, though they are, of course, limited by the surrounding conventions and social world, by family, friends, lovers, by history and by our skills and abilities. Dasein suffers 'thrownness' into the world. Its care needs to be understood by a tripartite structure of future, past and present, though inevitably Heidegger denies that that temporal division can be understood in the usual way.

Dasein's care, he says, maps onto the three temporal 'ecstases'; care has different but intermeshed orientations to the horizons of past, present and future. We find it revealed through our experiences of *anxiety*, of angst, our feelings of being threatened, though with no particular threatening object in view. Anxiety can be so oppressive that it stops us from being truly absorbed in any activity. It is the mood of lack of belonging to the world; an *uncanniness* or 'not-at-home-ness' is exposed – and overwhelms us.

Angst can be understood, claims Heidegger, as revealing to me the possibility of an 'authentic' mode of existence and temporality. For much of the time, we are inauthentic, for we 'dim down' on recognition of the not-at-home-ness; we engage, for example, in 'idle talk', small talk, gossip, dealing with the world in a superficial way. Curiosity (curiously) is also an example of inauthenticity: that contrasts with Aristotle, who, as we saw, identified curiosity as the heart of philosophy. For Heidegger, curiosity is a restless craving for novelty, for competition, distracting us from our not-at-home-ness.

To exist 'inauthentically' is also, it seems, to understand ourselves in ways drawn from non-human things in the world; it is to understand ourselves as things among other things. There is a failure in some sense to register the fundamental difference that exists between the way in which human beings are and the way in which other things are. We shall encounter that idea more clearly presented in Jean-Paul Sartre's waiter example. For Heidegger, when with inauthentic existence, I am 'absorbed' in my everyday concerns. I give the present a kind of priority in my existence; I see the future as no more than an orderly sequence of moments in time.

Whatever we can make of Heidegger's particular understanding of absorption in everyday tasks, it is surely true that we can sometimes feel unease, feel at a loss over life, express despair or have painful cries of 'what's the point?' Whether that is an essential feature of all human life, though, is surely open to doubt. Essential or not, that angst is described by Heidegger as including my awareness that I am 'beyond' my current involvements. Here we encounter more hyphenations. 'The being of Dasein means *ahead-of-itself-being-already-in … as being-amidst.*'

Once we are dealing with Dasein as projecting forward, we are bound to think of death; and, of course, Heidegger does indeed address mortality and, unsurprisingly, brings forth much obscurity. In angst I am taken out of my absorption in the world and confronted with my own death as my 'ownmost'. Because of the way in which as a human I am essentially always ahead of myself, for me to be brought vividly to confront my death is to be confronted with a loss of a present that is also equally a loss of future. 'Mortals die their death in life.'

Death, as possibility, gives Dasein nothing to be 'actualized'. It is the possibility of the impossibility of every way of comporting oneself towards anything. If I can grasp this truth and live with it, I am existing authentically.

The above on death was a mouthful; it seems just to be saying that to be authentic (better to be authentic than inauthentic?), I should recognize that at any point I may die and recognize it not as an abstraction, but that it will be *my* death. We may be put in mind of Kierkegaard here and his bookseller example (Chapter 17).

Some have seen Heidegger as much influenced by his religious conversion from Catholicism to a radical version of Lutheranism with its negative theology, a theology that maintains that God cannot be understood conceptually. Heidegger was consigning traditional metaphysics to the flames for failing to deal with Dasein, unaware, it seems, of how paradoxical that was, given his own writings would receive treatment of the flames courtesy of Logical Positivists and many analytic philosophers more generally.

In a work that was to be published only after his death, he wrote: 'Only a God could save us.' A little earlier, in his *Contributions to Philosophy (From Enowning)* he says, 'Making itself intelligible is suicide for philosophy.'

With certainty, we can surely maintain that Heidegger has not contributed to philosophy's suicide – well, not in that way.

———

How to think like Heidegger? I'm tempted to say, '*Must you?*'

True, that is rather arrogant of me; let's go with:

To grasp human reality, challenge our concepts as currently deployed – ideally by means of hyphenations.

24

Jean-Paul Sartre: Existentialist, Novelist, French

Man is a useless passion.

Sartre

Jean-Paul Sartre undoubtedly was a philosopher and wrote as a philosopher. Although for a time he repudiated the 'existentialist' label, he became deemed 'existentialist'; he is probably the best-known existentialist philosopher. His life, philosophy, politics, left-wing activisms and eroticisms, were intertwined with those of Simone de Beauvoir (forthcoming). He was probably the most famous philosopher of any philosopher within their lifetime. When, in the 1960s, Charles de Gaulle, President of France, was urged to prosecute him for civil disobedience, de Gaulle's wise reply was: you do not arrest Voltaire. Sartre enhanced France's standing, despite his disruptions.

In 1964, Sartre was awarded the Nobel Prize for Literature; for political reasons, he declined, though it remains granted to him. Bertrand Russell was earlier awarded the prize – and accepted. There is no Nobel Prize for philosophy. The literary accolade, although inappropriate for Russell, if for his poor attempts at fiction, is highly fitting for Sartre; he was a great novelist. That is fortunate, if only because his existentialism is accessible through the diary of Antoine Roquentin, the central character in Sartre's most famous novel, *Nausea*, published in 1938 as *La Nausée*. The novel was described by Iris Murdoch as more like a poem or incantation. Sartre writes, in *Words*, of how words fascinated him from childhood. In 1943, his most famous philosophical work was published, *L'être et le néant* – *Being and Nothingness* – subtitled *An Essay in Phenomenological Ontology*. Although obscure in many places, there are some memorable scenes within, polished by Sartre's literary talents.

To think like Sartre, we need to focus on the distinctiveness of human beings compared with everything else in the world. How are they different? It is their *nothingness*. Now, that sounds most odd; I guess that justifies my warning above that Sartre could be obscure. Indeed, he creates a few expressions to highlight what he means, but, although he sees himself as influenced by Heidegger, fortunately his expressions are not as dramatically irritating as those of his influencer. We do not have the obscurities surrounding Heidegger's grappling with Dasein.

A distinction made by Sartre is between being-in-itself (*être-en-soi*) and being-for-itself (*être-pour-soi*). Being-for-itself has the nothingness that, paradoxically speaking, being-in-itself lacks. That nothingness is consciousness. A human being is a being-for-itself; a corpse, a rock, a tree, are examples of the 'in itself'. The nothingness at the heart of human beings is tied to Sartre's affirmation of human freedom. One way into that is the slogan, derived from Heidegger: 'existence precedes essence'.

Paper-knives and books – they show Sartre's interests – have their essences preceding their existence. They have been designed with ends in view. Religious believers may hold that God built human beings with a function. With Aristotle, we encountered a philosopher thinking of human beings as possessed of an essential nature and function different from the nature of a horse or of a tree. Sartre has none of that. More carefully, we should read him as saying that the essence of human beings is 'no *thing*'. Of course, Sartre is not denying that we have brains, hearts and kidneys, but what is distinctive is our consciousness, a nothingness, pure reflection. Our reflection shows us that 'nothingness lies coiled in the heart of being, like a worm', though maybe not in such poetic terms.

We cannot escape that nothingness by turning to the world for safety for there we find only contingency. In *Nausea*, Antoine becomes terrified by the sheer existence of things, the mystery and absurdity of things that happen to be. Antoine records:

> So I was in the park just now. The roots of the chestnut tree were sunk in the ground just under my bench. I couldn't remember it was a root any more. The words had vanished and with them the significance of things ... I was sitting, stooping forward, head bowed, alone in front of this black, knotty mass, entirely beastly, which frightened me ... Never, until these last few days, had I understood the meaning of 'existence'.

Antoine finds that 'the root, the park gates, the bench, the sparse grass, all that had vanished'. No real diversity of things existed, 'just soft, monstrous masses, all in disorder – naked, in a frightful, obscene nakedness'. Those literary images of horror are pressing home on us how bizarre is the world around us, until our orderly conceptual scheme takes over.

————

Alienation from the physical world to one side, our consciousness, our nothingness, shows us that we are 'condemned to be free'; that means that we cannot evade responsibility for our choices. We cannot turn to anything around us for salvation. What, though, are we to make of the condemnation?

First, Sartre is not madly claiming that we are free to fly to the moon unaided, that prisoners are free to escape prison and that people with paralysed legs are free to walk. Those are lacks of practical freedom. In numerous mundane ways, day after day, we lack practical freedom in that we cannot get what we want. Second, Sartre's affirmation is of an 'absolute freedom', one manifested by our consciousness. It is the freedom whereby we can at least choose how to deal with our situations. The prisoner may choose to try to escape, to see himself as victim or as deserving of punishment; he may choose to repent – or to rebel. We may choose to see our inability to fly as a disaster or as an utter irrelevancy.

'I cannot be crippled without choosing myself as crippled,' writes Sartre. I possess the freedom to choose the way in which I see my disability: unbearable, humiliating, to be hidden, to be revealed, used as an excuse or to show what I can do in adversity. 'Facticities' fix my situation, but for a 'being-for-itself' there is always the question of what to make of those facticities; there is transcendence.

Of course, we may resist Sartre's line of thinking here. Perhaps the truth is that the mishmash of my neurology, upbringing, environment, causes me to see things this way rather than that – to see myself as victim or proud warrior. Even if I am within that proposed causally deterministic world, or, for that matter, a world of randomness, Sartre may rightly reply that I still have to choose what to do or choose how I view things. A causally deterministic world does not justify my collapsing back, saying 'nothing to do with me'. As I quip, I may still need to choose whether to wear the red dress or the blue; any deterministic world does not free me from making such choices.

Our freedom generates the anguish and terror, typically associated with existentialism. Self-deception is a common means of evasion. Sartre beautifully and tellingly describes how someone may try to turn himself into a thing, no longer with freedom, no longer with responsibility for choices. Here is the much-discussed tale of a waiter. Sartre could well have been writing this while in his haunts with Beauvoir, the bars, *Les Deux Magots* and *Café de Flore*, in Saint-Germain, Paris:

> His movement is quick and forward, a little too precise, a little too rapid. He comes toward the customers with a step a little too quick. He bends forward a little too eagerly; his voice, his eyes express an interest a little too solicitous for the order of the client.

Sartre sees this as bad faith, *mauvaise foi*, though we may wonder whatever can justify Sartre in that valuation of 'badness'. The for-itself is trying to secure himself as a being-in-itself, as a café-waiter-object, his being determined by its function.

> Finally there he returns, trying to imitate in his walk the inflexible stiffness of some kind of automaton while carrying his tray with the recklessness of a tightrope-walker by putting it in a perpetually unstable, perpetually broken equilibrium which he perpetually re-establishes by a light movement of the arm and hand.

It is, Sartre continues, as if there is no free choice involved in his rising at dawn, no free choice in his conferring value on the rights and duties of a waiter. Of course, the man is a waiter in the sense that he certainly is not then a diplomat or farmer. In Sartre's paradoxical terminology: he is not a waiter in the mode of a being-in-itself, but is a waiter in the mode of what he is not. 'We are what we are not and are not what we are.'

As observers of the waiter, we, the public, may see his behaviour as a game, and we usually connive and are complicit. In bad faith, we reify ourselves as diners and him as waiter. Sartre mentions many other social roles, where we are in self-deception, evading the anxiety of facing our free choices. There is the dance of the grocer, of the tailor, of the auctioneer, by which they endeavour to persuade their clientele that they are nothing but a grocer, an auctioneer, a tailor. Indeed, a grocer who dreams is offensive to the buyer, says Sartre, because such a grocer is not then wholly a grocer.

We may connect Sartre's concern here with Karl Marx's, despite Marx having the Aristotelian-type interest in human beings as possessed of a species-essence. Marx was keen for people to be free, as we saw, 'to hunt in the morning and criticise after dinner, without ever becoming hunter or critic'. Sartre's waiter, of course, need not even be acting in bad faith. He could be consciously seeing his actions as a game, as a play, and we could be consciously playing at being diners. He and we may be behaving ironically.

In *Nausea*, Antoine cannot help but be intrigued by the bad faith around him. He watches, for example, the rituals of the idiotic hat raising and idle chatter of people to pass the time on a Sunday morning along the exclusive Rue Tournebride.

> I see hats, a sea of hats. Most of them are black and hard. Now and then you see one fly off at the end of an arm, revealing the soft gleam of a skull … 'Good morning, Monsieur. Good morning, my dear sir, how are you keeping? Do put your hat on again, Monsieur, you'll catch cold …'

An intriguing arena for Sartre is our interaction with others, 'being for others' (*être-pour-autrui*), as opposed to with chestnut trees; recall Antoine above in *Nausea*. Sartre has some wonderful perceptive observations on how we can suddenly be aware of 'the look' of another. The look possesses me, making me self-conscious, maybe shaming me, if, for example, I am peering through a keyhole. I am a being-for-others, and 'the Other holds a secret – the secret of what I am'. I need to possess your subjectivity to understand my own, yet in doing so, I am absorbing you, treating you as an object for my subject; and I am being treated as an object by your attempt to understand your subjectivity. Conflict is inevitable. 'Hell is other people.'

Quite how we should understand that conflict is pretty obscure, but Sartre makes it vivid when turning to the fleshy matter of sexual relations. Unlike most philosophers before him, he is not squeamish:

> I make myself flesh so as to fascinate the Other by my nakedness and to provoke in her the desire for my flesh – exactly because this desire will be nothing else in the Other but an incarnation similar to mine. Thus desire is an invitation to desire. It is my flesh alone which knows how to find the road to the Other's flesh, and I lay my flesh next to her flesh so as to awaken her to the meaning of flesh … At this moment the communion of desire is realized; each consciousness by incarnating itself has realized the incarnation of the other; each one's disturbance has caused disturbance to be born in the Other and is thereby so much enriched.

Sexual desire, as Sartre sees it, has a paradoxical nature. My desire is for the other freely to desire me, yet I am making her (or him) an object to be possessed by me, an object lacking freedom.

Sartre gave a popular lecture, with a large audience, soon after publication of *Being and Nothingness*, linking existentialism to humanism. He stressed how we must choose our values, our meaning. He told of a student in 1940s Paris under German occupation. The student anguished between escape to England to join the Free French Forces and remaining in Paris, looking after his mother. The mother was in despair, her elder son having been killed. The student felt for his mother, yet wanted to avenge his brother's death. Advisers may give conflicting advice, but even if unanimous, the student would still need to choose what to do. Sartre's comment was: 'You are free, therefore choose – that is to say, invent.'

The student's choice may come by spinning a coin; yet that would make the matter appear trivial, the choice capricious. The emphasis on 'just choose' may suggest no scope for reason; yet reflection on options helps to highlight consequences and to view actions in new lights. The student, after reflection, discussion and consulting his heart, may suddenly see himself as a coward if staying with his mother, a coward fearing the jeers of his friends. Yet he may lift himself and meet such accusations with courage. Sartre, as with Kierkegaard and Nietzsche before him, is forcing us to confront ourselves with the anxiety of how to see ourselves, how, indeed, to make ourselves. Recall Kierkegaard, relating the story of Abraham 'hearing' the voice of an angel, telling him to sacrifice his son. Sartre points out how we may choose to resist: we may question the voice's angelic credentials or, if accepting them, we may choose to stand up against God.

Once we have grasped that values depend upon our choices, then, in that 'state of forsakenness', he argues, we can will only one thing, and that is freedom as the foundation of all values: From that position, Sartre curiously concludes that I value freedom for *all* of mankind. Sartre's universalizing, as he later saw, does sit uneasily with the rest of his existentialism. Even if my recognizing the value of my freedom means that I should recognize that others may value their freedom, why should I value reciprocal freedom, honouring that freedom of others?

The role of the Other has ultimate significance. On death, writes Sartre, we become 'prey' for the living; we no longer have the freedom to re-write ourselves. That existentialist misery is one of impotency. At big celebrations in Paris, on the centenary of his birth, Sartre was 'prey' in that photographs of him were retouched, to hide his constant smoking. Death alienates us wholly in our own life to the advantage of the Other.

Sartre has much, much more to say about nothingness. Here, I end on that topic with a splendid touch of humour that may take us back to Chapter 19; there we met Lewis Carroll telling of the White King's 'nobody' and then Wittgenstein and Russell arguing about the lack of hippopotamus in the room.

A waiter approaches Sartre in *Les Deux Magots*.

'Can I get you something to drink, Monsieur Sartre?' he asks.

'Yes, please, a coffee with sugar, but no cream.'

A few minutes later the waiter returns, somewhat concerned.

'I'm terribly sorry, Monsieur, we are all out of cream – how about with no milk?'

———

How to think like Jean-Paul Sartre? *Be dizzy at existence, at nothingness – and confront your freedom and the gaze of the Other.*

25

Simone Weil: Refuser and Would-Be Rescuer

Refuse to be an accomplice.
Don't lie – don't keep your eyes shut.
Simone Weil

Let us start with some praise; this is from Albert Camus, writing in 1951:

> Simone Weil, I maintain this now, is the only great spirit of our times and I hope that those who realize this have enough modesty not to try to appropriate her overwhelming witnessing.

Camus, Nobel Prize winner, famous for his novels, for *The Plague*, for his existentialist 'absurdity', was writing to Simone's mother, adding:

> For my part, I would be satisfied if one could say that in my place, with the humble means at my disposal, I served to make known and disseminate her work whose full impact we have yet to measure.

Simone had died eight years earlier, in her thirties, little known in the world of philosophy. She had been living in London, virtually starving herself to death. She lived her life as she thought one should – with awareness of the vast sufferings of others. Her philosophical thinking is intimately, deeply, entwined with how she lived; here is some background.

Brought up in Paris, in a Jewish family, professional, well-off, atheistic, she developed a love for ancient Greek culture and, in later years, a keen interest in Catholicism. She became a committed Christian, robustly rejecting Judaism and Hebrew culture. George Steiner described her as 'one of the ugliest cases of blindness and intolerance in the vexed history of Jewish self-hatred'. Thus a life can be viewed so differently: Camus or Steiner? That may scuttle us back to Sartre on our being prey to the Other – on how our lives are ultimately at the mercy of interpretations by others.

Undoubtedly, Simone Weil was distinctly odd, suffering phobias, illnesses, physically awkward – and she hated being touched. Her brother, a few years older, was a talented mathematician. Maybe in reaction, maybe because of a parental casual comment, she would sign her letters home as 'your son, Simon'. After university in Paris, she took various manual jobs – farm work, factory assembly – as well as teaching philosophy. She insisted on labouring in physical tasks to understand the suffering and fatigue of her fellow man. Given her sickly nature, poor eyesight and instability, she failed to handle that work well or for long; she would be taken ill or be fired. She lived poorly, ate little, yet apparently expensively. Her family would often be secretly helping her financially.

She joined the anarchists fighting in the 1930s Spanish Civil War. Unsurprisingly, that did not go well. She travelled to Italy, delighted in opera – presumably, that went better – returned to France and later, when things became more oppressive for Jews, reluctantly accompanied her parents, in 1942, to New

York. With various travel requirements satisfied, she then moved to Britain where, in London, she joined the Free French movement. She was driven by the hopeless ambition – hopeless, given the heightened relevance of her Jewishness as well as her poor health and physical incompetence – to fight with the Resistance in occupied France. Did she want to die, to test God? We shall meet Wittgenstein, who asked to be put in the Italian front line, in the First World War, to see whether his destiny was to live. (It was.)

In summary of Weil's life, she wanted so much to be rescuer, yet frequently needed herself to be rescued.

Weil's thinking is found in numerous articles, letters, notes, aphorisms, jottings, most only published some years after her death. Her thinking became more and more imbued with religious commitment, with references to Christianity, God's grace and Jesus Christ. Initially, her intellectual work was within Descartes' dualist tradition, investigating how to grasp the subjective viewpoint of human beings given their objective biological status, but she became more and more concerned about the plight of most human beings, their suffering and loss of freedom, a loss of autonomy, of governing themselves.

Weil made much of a distinction between, on the one hand, physical obstacles and, on the other hand, constraints imposed by other human beings. She rightly noted how when we step aside for passers-by, it is not the same thing as stepping aside to avoid billboards. We show respect for passers-by, not for billboards. Alone in our rooms, we get up, walk about, sit down, quite differently from the way we do when we have visitors. Recall how Kant, despite infirmity, rose to greet his doctor. Other human beings possess powers to refuse what we demand, not as a key that refuses to turn in a lock. We often need consent from others; we seek no consent from locks.

For human freedom, there is a need for people to possess a common purpose. A group of us with a common purpose would be free in relation to each other; we could plan a bank robbery, a tour of Europe or a strike for better conditions. It is difficult for a society to have a purpose, with so many disparate members, all needing to be in agreement; it is easy for a society to give rise to injustices. Grasping justice, properly understood, is one of Weil's key concerns.

Justice, these days, is typically presented in terms of human beings possessing rights, be it within society or across societies, and those rights being respected. Weil advocates a more valuable, deeper concept of justice, one not reducible to respecting rights. Why is she dismissive of that reduction?

A quick answer is: we recognize that the right thing to do can well be *not* to insist on our rights. That thought also occurs in a highly influential 1970s academic paper by American philosopher, Judith Jarvis Thomson. A thought experiment, showing how the morality of abortion is no 'black or white' matter, is presented where:

> a woman in hospital awakes to find a man (he happens to be a violinist) plugged into her blood stream for life support; she had not granted consent. She would be within her rights to unplug him, leading to his death, but that would not be the right thing to do, if, say, he needed her streaming help for just a week. The right thing to do, the morally decent thing, would be to manifest kindness and courage.

Here, Aristotelian virtues – kindness, courage – vie with rights over one's body. One week's inconvenience to save a man's life, yes – but ten years? Suppose the foetus has a right to life: does that trump factors of consent, of distress at continuing with an unwanted pregnancy? The just response, whatever it is, digs deeper than rights.

A longer answer by Weil against justice as nothing but protection of rights is that it reduces justice to contracts and 'trade deals'. In *A Theory of Justice* (1971), John Rawls, a most influential political philosopher of the late twentieth century, paints the picture of rational agents, pursuing their own interests; they recognize the presence of others and hence the likelihood of conflict. Justice here evolves as a negotiated compromise between people's interests. The 'collective animal', as Plato termed it, is created in the negotiated resolution, a recognition of rights; that is much better than reliance on brute force – but is it the best path for human relationships?

Consider the workplace when employees are seeking better pay and conditions from the employers. It is as though

> the devil were bargaining for the soul of some poor wretch and someone, moved by pity, should step in and say to the devil: 'It is a shame for you to bid so low: the commodity is worth at least twice as much.'

Reliance on rights runs the danger of treating people as commodities; yes, Karl Marx was an influence on Weil.

Bargaining devalues a proper understanding of justice. A farmer may refuse to sell his eggs, insisting that he has a 'right' not to sell, unless at a good enough price. 'But,' retorts Weil, 'if a young girl is being forced into a brothel she will not talk about her rights; the word would sound ludicrously inadequate.' Regarding the young girl, there should have been 'a cry of protest from the depth of her heart'; instead, we have a 'shrill nagging of claims and counter-claims'.

Of course, we could dig deeper. Were the farmer to be faced with a desperately hungry girl unable to afford the eggs, we should need room for the thought that the farmer is right not to sell his eggs to her; rather, he should make them a gift for her.

Justice is a 'supernatural virtue', thinks Weil. Valuable relationships do not rest on self-interested negotiations, wants and desires. She makes much of the Greek historian, Thucydides, and his account of some negotiations in the Peloponnesian War. He tells of the powerful Athenian leaders demanding submission from the Melians on the basis that it is a law of nature for the strong to rule. When the Melians resist the Athenian demands, they are crushed, with the men killed and the women and children enslaved. It is a mechanical necessity, a natural necessity, insist the Athenians.

Weil contested that claim: 'a man will forbear out of pure generosity – though it may be rare'. On occasions, we choose not to pursue our projects to their limits. We may say to some people, 'You can't do that' when clearly they can, but know that they ought not to. Justice, it would seem, can generate its own necessities. That point is presented by Weil not as a factor requiring natural explanations, but as recognition of the sacred, the role of true faith, the supernatural. 'The supernatural is the difference between human and animal behaviour.' The difference is something infinitely small. She enigmatically links that to Jesus' comment (Matthew 17:20): 'If you have faith as small as a mustard seed, you can say to this mountain, move from here to there and it will move. Nothing will be impossible for you.'

The supernatural virtue of justice 'consists of behaving exactly as though there were equality when one is stronger in an unequal relationship'. The just action is performed because – well, it is performed, we may say, purely because it is just. Of course, we should doubt whether those points would carry any weight for the ruthless, turning them away from their ruthlessness, or would even help them to glimpse their ruthless self-interest and carelessness over justice.

The lack of empirical explanation for why we should be just in the deep sense tells Weil that something beyond this world is needed to draw us away from projects of self-interest. We need to recognize beauty, truth, the good, as beyond this world, enabling us to see the earthly world afresh: 'earthly things are the criterion of spiritual things'. She urges the thought of 'not wanting to change' when attending to beauty, truth, the good. Attending to the natural beauty of the forest makes many of us see that it really ought not to be cut through for motorways; of course, we may readily overlook our reliance on motorways to reach that natural beauty, motorways that tarnish other arenas of beauty. Attending to truth means not fabricating evidence. Attending to the good means ...? Maybe that attention itself needs to be unchanging – but Weil's thinking is obscure; and more obscurities arise.

> Justice, truth and beauty are the image in our world of the impersonal and divine order of the universe. Nothing inferior to them is worthy to be the inspiration of men who accept the fact of death.

Her promotion of the impersonal aligns with her belief that 'Charity does not discriminate', but it is difficult to see how that relates to values of preferences for friends, lovers, family.

———

Simone de Beauvoir reported how Weil wanted to feed the world. When she (Beauvoir) replied that the goal is for people to find a meaning for their existence, Weil responded, 'It is easy to see that you have never gone hungry.' Iris Murdoch's eventual emphasis on food and shelter harmonizes with this response (Chapter 29).

Weil's thinking and feeling aligned her with many social reforming, 'leftist' and union movements. She wanted to merge with the masses, yet inevitably she stood out. The attempts of this intellectual woman from a well-off family to identify with those on the factory floor or in the fisherman's boat were not always well received. Weil grasped for solidarity throughout her life, a life much shortened because of that attempted grasp.

Weil introduces the concept of 'affliction', of a suffering immensely great, with the thought:

> I may lose at any moment, through the play of circumstances over which I have no control, anything whatsoever that I possess, including those things that are so intimately mine that I consider them as being myself. There is nothing that I might not lose. It could happen at any moment that what I am might be abolished and replaced by anything whatsoever of the filthiest and most contemptible sort.

In affliction, 'a kind of horror submerges the whole soul – physical pain, distress of soul and social degradation, all at the same time'. There is a nail whose point is applied at the very centre of the soul. Weil wants us to understand that suffering can be so great that, as affliction, it is an experience of non-being – of extreme and total humiliation – yet it is the condition for passing into truth. Indeed, in *Waiting for God*, she even loses her certitude of God's love when, as she writes,

> I am in contact with the affliction of other people, those who are indifferent or unknown to me as much as the others, perhaps even more, including those of the most remote ages of antiquity. This contact causes me such atrocious pain and so utterly rends my soul that the love of God becomes almost impossible. It would take very little more to make me say impossible – so much so that I am uneasy about myself.

Weil reassures herself of God's love 'by remembering that Christ wept on foreseeing the horrors of Jerusalem's destruction'. She hopes that God will forgive her for her compassion. Thankfully, compassion cannot be ripped from the soul of Simone Weil:

> Human beings are so made that the ones who do the crushing feel nothing; it is the person crushed who feels what is happening. Unless one has placed oneself on the side of the oppressed, to feel with them, one cannot understand.

Weil, throughout, makes clear her placement. Her thinking, although not structured in carefully formulated arguments, although expressed with a passion, sometimes exaggeration, sometimes opaquely, often with appeals to the scriptures, has considerable value in opening eyes to what is truly valuable, to the correct placement. She tells of a vagrant who has stolen a carrot. He stands before the comfortably seated judge, who has an elegant flow of queries, comments, witticisms – recall the Sophists – whereas he, the vagrant, is unable to stammer a word.

> Truth stands before an intelligence concerned with the elegant manipulation of opinion.

Weil's life and deeply felt concerns should show us that with our thinking we must not be engaged in manipulation of opinion, elegantly so or not. We saw a little earlier in this chapter that justice has demands of necessity on us – as does truth. Another demand on us is to be appreciative of the remarkable thinking and 'great spirit' of Simone Weil – a spirit that brooks no compromise.

How to think like Simone Weil? *Refuse to be an accomplice.*

26

Simone de Beauvoir: Situated, Protester, Feminist

One is not born but becomes (a) woman.

Beauvoir

Must we burn Sade? That curious question, if raised at all, would not be readily associated with Simone de Beauvoir. It is, though, the title of her essay that examines the writings and experiences of the Marquis de Sade – his sexual peccadilloes, sadism and imprisonment. She would not burn; she would learn. That learning rests on her approach to philosophical thinking, an approach grounded in the examination of the particular situations of human beings – of how flesh-and-blood conscious beings exist within a society. Those situations affect their grasp, and our grasp, of their freedom, desires and what gives meaning to life.

Beauvoir's approach is 'phenomenological'; it focuses on the phenomena, the experiences we undergo, with the world impinging upon us. To understand Beauvoir, we need to note her own 'situatedness'. Use of that term, rather than 'situation', is an alert to the significance for her of the time and place of a person's lived experience.

From a well-off Catholic family of early twentieth-century France, Beauvoir experienced repressive conventions applying to sexual activity and women. Later, in the 1940s, she was to undergo the dangers, fears and dilemmas of living in a Paris occupied by the Nazis. Situated thus, she did not succumb to the oppressions, but, conscious of her freedom, sought to protest.

In her early teens, she had declared herself an atheist, secured entrance to the Sorbonne, studied the most difficult philosophers, unofficially attended classes at the prestigious and elite École Normale Supérieure, and became involved with Sartre, three years her senior, the one and only man she ever felt her intellectual superior. In France's highly competitive and highly rated *agrégation* examinations in philosophy, the examiners after much anguishing gave Beauvoir second place to Sartre's first – mainly and curiously, it seems, because it was Sartre's second attempt at the examinations, Beauvoir's first.

In the English-speaking world, Beauvoir, if much considered at all, is not usually considered a philosopher, but an impressive novelist and, indeed, intimate friend, lover and follower of Sartre. Some may know her as primarily an early feminist who, in *The Second Sex* (1949), cast a light on society's unjustified acceptance of male domination. Those understandings stand in need of some caveats.

True, Beauvoir and Sartre were lovers in an open relationship – very much 'open'. It is true that she followed Sartre in that her first attraction was to his group of 'bad boys', but it is misleading to see her as a follower intellectually. Some key thoughts in Sartre's *Being and Nothingness* (1943) are to be found in Beauvoir's novel *She Came To Stay*, completed earlier. Who knows who influenced whom? In philosophical discussion, ideas may emerge without any stamp of first ownership; they may be all the better for that.

Throughout their lives, Beauvoir and Sartre remained very close, intellectually, emotionally, politically. Private letters show the extent to which they discussed in detail their sexual relations with others, even, in one case, transferring a younger woman from one to the other. Their activities would not go down well in today's official Anglo-American attitudes towards sexual relationships, power and influence. Sexual relations, of course, were (and are) a fascination, even philosophically; they raise questions of how our conscious embodiment can, in some way, 'possess' the conscious embodiment of another – or of others. Thus it is that Sade can intrigue.

With regard to writings, Beauvoir won the prestigious Prix Goncourt for *The Mandarins* (1954). She engaged in journalism, travel writing and political protest, very much on the side of the oppressed. Despite a few philosophical essays to her credit, she insisted that she was no philosopher. True, she was not a creator of abstract metaphysical systems in the way of Spinoza and Leibniz, even Sartre. She was, though, a philosopher in that she engaged in considerable philosophical thinking, grasping and understanding human lives in particular lived situations, be they real or those of fictional characters.

As for Beauvoir's 'feminism', initially she resisted embracing the term, maybe because her focus was as much on the human condition of both men and women (hence her interest in Sade's sexual libertinism) as on the unfair treatment of women. None the less, *The Second Sex*, with its detailed challenges to the conditioned injustices against women, to which many were then blind, has been highly influential in feminism, though both it and feminism have been understood in different ways at different times. Witness the confrontations that now exist for some between feminism and the trans communities. That points to the situatedness.

The Second Sex delves into the nature of sex and sexual relationships, drawing directly on women's experiences as well as on the writings of, for example, Mary Wollstonecraft and Virginia Woolf. For decades in English-speaking universities, Beauvoir's *The Second Sex* was ignored as an instance of philosophy, perhaps because writers of the typical syllabus were male, embarrassed by descriptions of bodily functions. Beauvoir did not hold back in those descriptions.

'Situatedness', as said, is key to Beauvoir's philosophical approach. Rather than abstract discourses, we need the concrete cases of human beings, situated in particular social conditions. We should resist the seeming Cartesian trap whereby a sharp mind/body distinction is maintained. Beauvoir resists; she emphasizes our fleshy embodiment filled with desires and turmoil. Further, her existentialism means that her novel's characters – and you and I – cannot evade responsibility for how we live and the meaning with which we cloak our lives. It has repeatedly been said – and already mentioned in relation to Nietzsche – that if there is no God, everything is permitted. If that is read as showing that therefore we lack responsibility for our actions, then Beauvoir, as with Nietzsche, is strongly opposed. We have to choose how to live; in so doing, we are declaring commitment to certain values.

In a short essay *Pyrrhus and Cinéas*, Beauvoir considers Plutarch's presentation of the ancient Greek statesman, King Pyrrhus. The King is having his actions questioned by his adviser Cinéas: what is the point of forever striving? The recommended aim, it seems, is passivity; it may remind us of Chapter 1's *Tao*. Beauvoir rejects that aim; it is illusory, denying human reality. In the 'lived experiences', there inevitably are desires, hopes and goals – our situatedness – determining what we see ourselves as being free to do. Of course, the freedom is constrained, but, insists Beauvoir, we always possess the freedom to oppose the constraints. Freedoms that at one time seem out of the question can come into question; people can choose to oppose what was once just accepted. Witness the many protest movements that have led to change. Witness, indeed, how Beauvoir's *The Second Sex* helped women to see and challenge their condition.

Apart from freedom, other notable concepts that she draws upon include 'ambiguity', 'appeal', 'the Other'.

Over the use of 'ambiguity', I cannot help but quip that it is ambiguous (in the standard meaning). For Beauvoir, it seems that we experience ambiguity in that we are aware of ourselves as separate individuals yet also as intermeshed with others. Sometimes, the phenomenon of ambiguity is present in that I grasp myself as a subject, an agent, with a freedom to make choices, yet also as a physical object pushed around by others, but an object that others also typically grasp as a subject. The Other can be a threat to my freedom. In the political sense, 'the Other' specifies those who lack the power. Thus, 'women' are the Other because (it seems) they are dominated by men. Palestinians in Israel are the Other because they lack certain basic rights possessed by Israeli Jews.

What are we to make of Beauvoir's concept of freedom? We have already seen with Sartre that it is accepted that freedom is obviously limited by conditions. Human that I am, I am not free to turn into an elephant. Given my XY chromosomes, I cannot freely choose to be impregnated. Our situatedness also limits our understandings of our mental capabilities, of everything that we know, feel possible and experience about ourselves.

According to Beauvoir, however constrained we may be in the above type of ways, we still possess a subjective freedom. That freedom holds even if I am a slave or tortured or treated as a sex object. We should, though, question the value Beauvoir places on *that* freedom. It may be of little comfort to the tortured to be reminded that they still possess the subjective freedom to ... What exactly? To see the torturing as demeaning the torturer? To imagine oneself as untortured?

'Appeal' is another of Beauvoir's key concepts. Although I am free, I recognize that I need to appeal to others in my projects – to appeal to them as embodied free agents. That brings to the fore the ambiguity (another sense?) of my condition. I am isolated as a free conscious individual, as are others, yet there do exist those others who may help or hinder. Writes Beauvoir:

> A man alone in the world would be paralyzed by … the vanity of all of his goals. But man is not alone in the world.

We need to live as a community with shared 'freely chosen' values, but I cannot force my values upon others, though I may appeal. In my appeal, I may need to struggle against those who seek to silence me; and, of course, my appeal requires there to be others who can respond to my call. Their situatedness may restrict their response; they may lack the resources – the time, the health, the security, the awareness of the injustice. Thus, I may need to enable them to join with me.

There is danger, I note, of a paradox lurking here, one reminiscent of 'pulling oneself up with one's boot straps'. Putting it simply, before there is much chance of success in my appeal to the enslaved to support calls to end slavery, the enslaved need to be sufficiently un-enslaved to hear those calls, acknowledge their enslaved position and be free to march in support of those calls – in solidarity.

Beauvoir was conscious of the problem. When she challenged injustices, be they to do with inequalities concerning gender, age or between white Americans and African American, Palestinian Israeli and Jewish Israeli, she recognized that many in the oppressed groups were not in practice free to protest, to take the risk of imprisonment, to have the time off work and so forth. Some would not even have seen themselves as oppressed; they may have understood their situation as divinely commanded or justified by nature. In some cases, perhaps that was self-deception; in some cases it was maybe a rational response to get by in supremely adverse conditions.

Today, controversy rages over gender, sex and transgender matters, with a plethora of acronyms, from CIS to ENBY to

TERF. Putting those controversies to one side, yes, Beauvoir does draw a distinction between sex and gender. There are clear and obvious biological sexual differences between people by nature, but the 'gendered reality' is dependent, in part, on the socio-political conditions. There is no biological reality of the 'feminine', she insists, but there are the generated socio-political differences. Let us note, though, that it is most odd to believe that the socio-political, the cultures, the customs, lack any grounding in human biology and environment. Let us further note that, however derived, socio-political sources for a state of affairs do not thereby establish undesirability. Some sources have led to beneficial outcomes; some have not. Some have led to fairer treatments; others have restricted important freedoms.

Consider: 'women are the weaker sex'. Biologically on average women are smaller with less body power, but it is a cultural assumption that those qualities should be the criteria for assessing strength. After all, on average women live longer and can give birth; are they not signs of strength? Further, Beauvoir recognizes differences in bodily experiences between the sexes. 'Woman, like man, is her body; but her body is something other than herself.' The pregnant woman, for example, is at once herself, yet also other than herself.

Successful calls for equality between the sexes and genders run the risk, as Beauvoir emphasized, of erasing gender differences; thus the male stance could, unreasonably so, be promoted as the standard to be achieved:

> The price of women's admission to this privileged class is that they must train and live like men. Thus the discriminatory sexual difference remains in play. Only men or those who emulate them may rule.

Insistence on equality should not be an insistence on sameness. The liberated woman must free herself from the idea that to be independent she must be like men, just as she must free herself from thinking that she must be 'feminine'. Let me emphasize the freedom is from the 'must'. Women – and men – if they so choose should be free, for example, to be 'feminine'.

And so, we must return to the Marquis. 'To know oneself, one needs to know Sade,' wrote Beauvoir.

Beauvoir valued Sade for rejecting apathy, for asserting his freedom and for not following the Quietism recommended by Cinéas. Sade lived during the 'Reign of Terror' (1793–4); he was offered a position of authority that would have enabled him to torture and kill with impunity, yet he declined. He was, in fact, appalled at how society authorized itself to murder. Sade took on the responsibility for his sadistic actions.

Sade's sadism highlights the paradox of the Other, and of oneself, as flesh and freedom. That, according to Beauvoir, is what disturbs us about Sade. Of course, we may add that what deeply disturbs us is the infliction of unwanted immense sufferings on others and, indeed, the immense sufferings.

Sade could easily have got away with his secret activities, yet he brought them to public view – and oddly was surprised when the authorities deemed him criminal. Beauvoir writes:

His surprise resembles that of a child who strikes a vase until it breaks. Playing with danger, he still believed himself sovereign, but society was watching; it refused any sharing and claimed each individual entirely.

Once again, we see Beauvoir returning to the Other, be it that of society or of the individual. The goal of liberation, according to Beauvoir, needs our mutual recognition of each other as free and as, indeed, Other. That recognition (sometimes) exists in intimate erotic encounters, where the dimension of the Other can lack hostility; lovers experience themselves and each other ambiguously, as both subjects and objects of erotic desire. That ambiguity is also found in Sartre's approach to sexual relations, though, with Sartre, there exists a bleakness, a feeling of inevitable failure.

Beauvoir presents Sade as revealing how individuals know that they are victims less of human wickedness than of humanity's good conscience, of a terrifying optimism. What does that mean? Well, she writes:

> If the totality of men who people the earth were present to everyone, the air would become unbreathable. At any given instant thousands of people suffer and die, in vain, unjustly, and we are not affected: our existence is possible only at this price.

Once again, Beauvoir focuses on our situatedness – and situated thus, how can we live with ourselves? We encountered that challenge from Nietzsche, a challenge that merits serious attention and no shrug of shoulders, no turning away.

———————

How to think like Simone de Beauvoir? *Take account of the situatedness of others and of yourself – and rise above in solidarity.*

27

Ludwig Wittgenstein: Therapist

Philosophy is a battle against the bewitchment
of our intelligence by means of language.

Wittgenstein

With Ludwig Wittgenstein, we have, so to speak, two philosophers for the price of one – and the second provides a revolution in a way of philosophical thinking. Here are some observations on the nature of philosophy from his later work, published posthumously in 1953, *Philosophical Investigations*:

123. A philosophical problem has the form: 'I don't know my way about.'
124. Philosophy leaves everything as it is.
309. What is your aim in philosophy? – To shew the fly the way out of the fly-bottle.

Wittgenstein possessed the character and behaviour of a tormented genius in appearance and was a tormented genius in reality: the anguished, haunted philosopher, serious, self-obsessed, awkward, refusing to chit-chat, consumed with getting things right. Philosophy, as for Kierkegaard, was a personal matter, not a career move.

At Cambridge's distinguished Moral Sciences Club, he would dominate discussions, so much so that at times his attendance was strongly discouraged. At one meeting held in King's College, the guest speaker was Karl Popper, also a philosopher with a sense of self-importance, sceptical of Wittgenstein's work, envious no doubt of his high standing. There occurred the Poker Incident, a famous incident by philosophy's standards. Wittgenstein, apparently angry at something Popper argued, grabbed the poker, to … Reports diverge. To hit Popper? To threaten Popper? To poke the fire? To demonstrate a point? Without thinking? – and so on. The poker remains at King's.

Wittgenstein serves such a wealth of ideas that many of us deem him the greatest philosopher of the twentieth century, despite that accolade often being granted to Heidegger. Both philosophers sought to root philosophy in the activities of human life, but while Heidegger delighted in obscurity and hyphenated made-up (!) fancy terms, the later Wittgenstein gave us thoughtful reflections, remarks and enticing aphorisms in everyday words, even though they have invited conflicted interpretations and controversy.

The importance of human activity and human life – the form of life – in understanding and 'dissolving' philosophical problems is expressed by Wittgenstein in remarks such as:

If a lion could talk, we would not understand him.

That is an example of a Wittgensteinian comment that merits reflection and discussion. Think how astonished we should be if the lion in the zoo cage suddenly came out, in English, with the words, 'This is terribly unfair, locking me away like this, with my being stared at by tourists.' What sense can be made of the lion having concepts such as unfairness, locks and tourists? If lions in the wild could talk, in 'lionese', however could what they say be translated? The lives of lions are so radically different in so many ways from those of human beings. Of course, that does not mean that there are no similarities at all.

Let us go on a whistle-stop tour of Wittgenstein's life. The tour inevitably needs additions, caveats, nuances, but it provides a flavour of the surroundings of his thinking.

With a successful Bohemian-Jewish industrialist as father, and an Austrian Catholic well-connected mother, Ludwig was born, 1889, in Vienna, one of nine children (some were to commit suicide), into one of Europe's wealthiest most talented families, a cultural centre. The Wittgenstein Palace attracted famous artists of the day: musicians, painters, writers – Klimt, Brahms and Mahler.

Ludwig avoided the industrialist life planned for him, studied engineering at the University of Manchester, became intrigued by the philosophy of mathematics, was recommended by Gottlob Frege to see Bertrand Russell and, with the arrogance of wealth and upbringing, knocked on Russell's door in Cambridge, without warning, where Russell quickly judged him to be no crank, but a genius.

Wittgenstein worked on the philosophy of logic. With the coming of the First World War, he joined the Austro-Hungarian Army, chose front-line duties – was he destined to live or die? – spent time in an Italian prisoner-of-war camp and completed his work on logic. It was published in 1922 with the title *Tractatus Logico-Philosophicus*. Here is a teeny extract to show its formal structure:

WITTGENSTEIN'S *TRACTATUS* – A SAMPLE

1	The world is everything that is the case.
1.1	The world is the totality of facts, not of things.
1.11	The world is determined by the facts, and by these being all the facts.
1.12	For the totality of facts determines both what is the case, and also all that is not the case.
1.13	The facts in logical space are the world. [...]
4.0312	The possibility of propositions is based upon the principle of the representation of objects by signs. My fundamental thought is that the logical constants do not represent. That the logic of the facts cannot be represented.
4.032	The proposition is a picture of its state of affairs [...]

The *Tractatus* having 'solved' the problems of philosophy – it was much praised by the Vienna Circle – Wittgenstein returned to Austria and worked as a primary school teacher, though a scandal arose over his striking a boy. He lived poorly, refusing all financial help (he had given away his vast inheritance), but was persuaded to return to Cambridge by John Maynard Keynes and the young F. P. Ramsey. He returned in 1929. Keynes wrote in a letter, 'Well, God has arrived. I met him on the 5.15 train.'

Back in Cambridge, Wittgenstein's *Tractatus* was awarded a Cambridge PhD (Moore wrote that it was a work of genius, but still deserved the Cambridge PhD), enabling him to be paid as a lecturer and subsequently as professor. His lectures consisted of many anguished silences and struggled thoughts, given to a small band of selected students, held in his college room of austerity. Wittgenstein handed out two sets of notes; they were published posthumously as the *Blue and Brown Books*.

He commented later to the effect that as his students probably left his lectures with nothing in their heads, at least they had something in their hands.

Stimulated by Ramsey's criticisms and by a Neapolitan gesture from Sraffa (an economist brought to Cambridge by Keynes), he rejected his *Tractatus* picture theory of language, though not the idea behind the *Tractatus* that philosophy proper is an activity rather than a set of propositions. He realized that to work through philosophical problems, to dissolve them indeed, he needed to recognize language's mishmash of different uses as different actions, with different aims – some akin, for example, to Neapolitan snubs. His *Investigations* in form and content gave expression to those ways, deploying aphorisms, interjections, short dialogues.

> 11. Think of the tools in a tool-box: there is a hammer, pliers, a saw, a screw-driver, a rule, a glue-pot, glue, nails and screws.
> – The functions of words are as diverse as the functions of these objects. (And in both cases there are similarities.)

Wittgenstein saw his earlier thinking as mistaken because he had tried to regiment language into propositions that *pictured* reality; the mistake was a 'craving for generality'. Some understand his later philosophy not merely as anti-theory, but as a presentation of philosophy as a form of therapy:

> 255. The philosopher's treatment of a question is like the treatment of an illness.
> 593. A main cause of philosophical disease – a one-sided diet: one nourishes one's thinking with only one kind of example.

John Wisdom – a few years later he held Wittgenstein's chair – was a keen admirer and follower of Wittgenstein, but when he suggested the 'therapy reading' to the world, it seemed not to go down well – well, not with Wittgenstein.

Here is an example of Wittgenstein's revolutionary way of looking at philosophical perplexities related to the mind.

I can know what someone else is thinking, not what I am thinking. It is correct to say 'I know what you are thinking,' and wrong to say 'I know what I am thinking.' (A whole cloud of philosophy condensed into a drop of grammar.)

Contrary to that, save for odd circumstances of dreamlike delirium, most philosophers, students of philosophy and people in the local tavern hold that surely I can and do know what I am thinking and that I am thinking. As for wondering what we know about others, it is easy for all of us to fall for the temptation that we cannot *really* know what others are thinking. We may easily be tempted into insisting that we only ever witness the behaviour of others, never their experiences – if they, indeed, have any experiences at all. How do I know that 'other minds' exist? – a worry met earlier with Descartes.

Wittgenstein tries to dissolve such worries. How did we come to learn words? How did I acquire the word 'pain' or the expression 'I'm thinking'? As a child, I shriek out when hitting my thumb with a hammer. 'That must be painful; it must hurt,' says the parent, rushing to rub the thumb better. That does not mean that there are no hammer-wielders who pretend to be in pain when not; it does not mean that there are no stoics who manage to hide their pains. How we have acquired the concept of pain, use of the word 'pain', allows room for such cases.

Knowledge, argues Wittgenstein, requires the possibility of error, of doubt. When I am in pain, I cannot start wondering whether I am making a mistake, though I may wonder about the cause of the pain. Of course, I may say 'I know I am in pain' for emphasis when doctors insist they can find nothing physically wrong. I may say 'I know I am in pain' as a joke, accepts Wittgenstein – so much, you may surmise, for philosophers' humour. 'I know I am in pain' is though a bit of nonsense, says Wittgenstein, but with the qualification 'if "I know" is being used in its normal sense' – and adding: 'How else are we to use it?'

That question needs serious dwelling; why ever think that we philosophers have special superior access to the 'true meaning' of a word? As Wittgenstein and John Wisdom emphasized: 'don't ask for the meaning, ask for the use'. Recall Humpty Dumpty's silliness presented by Lewis Carroll.

Wittgenstein suggests that 'I am in pain' is akin to shrieking '*Ouch*', not a case of stating a fact – and, of course, it is linguistic nonsense to say, 'I know *ouch*'.

Moore, in a talk, pointed out that 'I believe he has gone out, but he has not' is an absurd thing for someone seriously to say, yet it could well be true: he has not gone out, yet I believe that he has. Wittgenstein seized on this, Moore's Paradox as it became known, treating it as highly revealing for the proper treatment of the expression of certain psychological states. 'My own relation to my words is wholly different from other people's.'

When, in response to some people's query, I say, 'I think the bus will be on time', that is not a descriptive assertion about my state of mind, but an assertion, with a degree of hesitancy, that the bus will be on time. When the bus fails to turn up and those people suggest that sadly I was wrong, it would be at best a weak and unwelcomed joke to reply, 'No, I was perfectly right. I was only describing my psychological state; I did *think* the bus would be on time.'

In many ways, Wittgenstein challenged our easy and misleading assumptions about the nature of mind and mental states. For example, what is it to have correctly grasped the meaning of a word, to have learnt to 'go on in the same way' with the use of a term? Maybe we feel, wrongly so, he suggests, that there are rails stretching out into future uses, to keep us true to the meanings – and to enable us to recognize when we have gone off the rails, into some new meanings. Yet such rails do not exist.

Wittgenstein's later approach to philosophy led Russell, a great admirer of Wittgenstein's early work, to complain that Wittgenstein's philosophy became 'at best, a slight help to lexicographers and, at worse, an idle tea-table amusement'. Now, that condemnation might well have applied to some Oxford 'ordinary language' philosophy, such as J. L. Austin's (noted in Chapter 22 as contrasting with Moore's), but not to Wittgenstein's. Wittgenstein, throughout his philosophical labours, grappled with the deep puzzles of how mind, reality and the limits of language, can be understood.

During the Second World War, Wittgenstein could not bear thinking he was still lecturing in philosophy while others were dying in the trenches. He worked as a porter in Guy's Hospital, London, and elsewhere. Russell maintained that Wittgenstein's experiences of fighting in the First World War had changed him; he had become more ascetic, anxious about the meaning of life; and, of course, there were the traumas of sex. Throughout his life, at various times in his life, he valued certain close homosexual relationships. Let us remember, homosexual activity was then illegal in Britain. That seemed not to worry all that much the likes of Keynes, E. M. Forster and others of the Bloomsbury Group, yet that repressive law led to the suicide of Alan Turing, another alumnus of King's, Cambridge, and a nervousness among many in the public eye, such as Benjamin Britten.

Wittgenstein, both the early and the later, anguished about the meaning of life and what constituted a good life. He knew he fell short. Although the *Tractatus* was espoused by the Vienna Circle's members – Ramsey had introduced it to them – Wittgenstein despaired at their failure to attend to its final propositions. We met some in Chapter 1. For Wittgenstein, they are of the greatest significance.

6.4312   […] Is a riddle solved by the fact that I survive for ever? Is this eternal life not as enigmatic as our present one? The solution of the riddle of life in space and time lies *outside* space and time.

6.521   The solution of the problem of life is seen in the vanishing of this problem. (Is not this the reason why those who have found after a long doubt that the sense of life became clear to them have then been unable to say what constituted that sense?)

6.522   There is indeed the inexpressible. This *shows* itself; it is the mystical.

And there is the famous, final proposition, Proposition 7:

7.   Whereof one cannot speak, thereof one must be silent.

Nearing his death (from cancer), Wittgenstein quipped on his birthday, 'No more happy returns.' His last few months were at his doctor's home in Cambridge; he was cared for by the doctor's wife. His last words were that he had had a wonderful life. Philosophers wonder what he meant by 'wonderful'.

———

How to think like Wittgenstein? *Resist the craving for generality – and always remember: if a lion could talk, we would not understand him.*

28

Hannah Arendt: Controversialist,
Journalist?

*The more successful a liar is, the more likely it is
that he will fall prey to his own fabrications.*
Hannah Arendt

Hannah Arendt was a philosopher, though she said she was
not. Sometimes she was distressed, it seems, that others
failed to treat her as a philosopher or at least as a serious
political theorist, but more as 'just a journalist'. A former
journalist, briefly UK prime minister at the beginning of the
2020s, then returned journalist, observed that no one puts
up statues to journalists. Of course, few philosophers acquire
the statue status and it is unlikely that Arendt sought such
status. Maybe she saw her dismissal as a proper philosopher
to be grounded in a then prejudice against the thinking of
women. In fact, over the years, her thinking has received
increasing reflective support; yet some continues to generate
horror.

Although she was a talented student of philosophy, the events
and experiences of antisemitism in her 1930s Germany drove
her subsequent thinking; it is that experienced eventfulness
that brings some intrigue when looking at her work. The
work has no encompassing theme, but contains reflections on
politics, society and being human. Her philosophical thinking,

she would emphasize, is from her *lived experience* – as should be all our philosophical thinking.

In the educated public world, Arendt became notorious for her five-part article in the *New York Times*, reporting on the Israeli trial of Adolf Eichmann. It was her expression, 'the banality of evil', when assessing Eichmann that got her into trouble. Maybe things were not helped by her reports of Nazi horrors being surrounded by glossy advertisements for cushioned chairs, colour televisions and Cartier diamond hairclips. Before turning to that notoriety, let us take a look at her life's experiences, so important to her thinking.

Niccolò Machiavelli, famous for his early sixteenth-century work *The Prince*, comes to mind when reflecting on Arendt. She had an express interest in his republicanism and the need for participatory democracy. There are two additional ways in which we may see Machiavelli arising in her life.

First, she recognized that, compared to most Jews in Germany, she was saved by Fortuna, by good fortune. Machiavelli emphasized how the success or otherwise of political lives in part rested on Fortuna. Miss Fortuna, as I term her, is the major factor, I add, in all our lives. Who we are, our talents and circumstances, result from good or bad fortune.

Second, Machiavelli recognized the so-called 'reality' for leaders, for princes; to rule successfully, they needed to engage in deceit and worse. They needed 'not to be good'. Arendt wrote of that reality and sought a society that would change that reality.

Machiavelli, I suggest, recommended a two-tier morality: one for the citizens who should follow the rules and one for leaders who are 'above' the rules. That 'aboveness', permitting 'dirty hands', is justified as needed for the security and prosperity of the citizens of, in Machiavelli's case, Florence, leading to the glory of the leaders. Great Britain and the United States have not been immune to leaders embracing deceit and thinking they are above the law – and not even for the benefit of their people, but with the primary motive of maintaining political power, self-interest and personal aggrandizement – well, so it seems. Arendt in her times, both in Germany and in the States, directly experienced the deceit in politics – and loathed it.

Returning to Miss Fortuna, let us see her in operation in Arendt's life.

Arendt was brought up in a secular family, German-Jewish. She studied under significant philosophers: first under Heidegger, then Husserl, then Karl Jaspers. She had a committed romantic affair with Heidegger and even when that ended, even when his antisemitism became obvious, even when both participants were married to others, she remained in contact, visiting him much later in life.

With the Nazis in power in the 1930s, hope of an academic placement vanished and, becoming more aware of the growth of antisemitism, Arendt actively involved herself in Jewish and Zionist movements. As a result she was arrested by the Gestapo in 1933, interrogated for eight days, but, as Fortuna would have it, was released, whereas others in similar circumstances were found in dingy basements, murdered.

She managed to flee to Paris, being received as an 'illegal exile'. Some paid employment came her way with Jewish/ Zionist organizations, despite (or probably because of the reasons for) her illegal, stateless and homeless conditions. Fortuna again was at work. The French authorities, just before the German occupation, sent all 'illegal aliens' to internment camps near the Spanish border. With Fortuna in operation, she managed to escape, met up with her husband and mother and, courtesy of yet more luck, travelled to Portugal, eventually securing the desired end in 1941 of arrival in New York. Despite initial adversities – little money, little English language – she progressed to holding academic positions, becoming more than 'just a journalist'.

Arendt's experiences led her to write about the horrors of being stateless, of being excluded. In Germany, as a Jew, she was excluded; in France, as an illegal immigrant, she was excluded. Enemies, she noted, send their foes to concentration camps; friends send them to internment camps. In Nazi Germany, she, as a Jew, was an outcast, a pariah. The term 'pariah' derives from Tamil, a use applying to the lower caste. That led her to speak of how some Jews would settle for their position and, working within, would assimilate as a 'parvenu', a social climber – for some, a form of self-deception. Arendt argued that one ought not to connive in collaboration; one should make a political commitment as a conscious pariah. Indeed, her works are concerned with how to improve political discourse, not least to benefit the excluded; she did, though, lack the political activism in the US of a Russell, Sartre or Beauvoir that leads to arrest.

She drew on her experiences to make vivid what it is like to be expelled from the human community, to lose, as she put it, *the right to have rights*. To be state-less is to be right-less. Such individuals are not equal before the law, are not even unequal before the law; they are outside of the law. The ultimate expression of that expulsion was manifested in the Nazi concentration camps, where individuals, unlike even slaves, were no longer treated as human beings. The ideology, the logos of concentration camps, was that inmates lacked personality, lacked personhood, and were just parts of the camp's mechanism; there was no more sense of attending to their thinking or privacy than there would be of attending to the thinking or privacy of a tractor or dustbin. Treating human beings as no longer human has occurred, of course, in genocides and wars more recently.

Heading in the direction of human beings losing the right to have rights is the treatment of refugees and desperate migrants crossing the US–Mexico border or arriving on the shores of Great Britain after horrendous journeys from afar, ending with perilous crossings of the English Channel. Despite international conventions, those arriving in Britain are readily deemed 'illegal immigrants', to be shipped elsewhere almost as human cargo. Indeed, in Britain, people of the 'Windrush generation', many African-Caribbean individuals who legally entered Britain in 1948 on the HMT *Empire Windrush*, suffered from government policies and legislation in the 2010s, promoting the 'hostile environment'. Lacking required paperwork, they were treated almost as if they had no right to have rights, save to be sent back. They were not 'true' British.

In Arendt's influential 1951 work *The Origins of Totalitarianism*, related matters are explored, linked to antisemitism, racism and imperialism. Her writings at times can be used to mislead, as if only in totalitarian states can one be an outcast, but, as she makes clear, people can also be outcasts within liberal democracies, within capitalist states. One can certainly be condemned for thinking the wrong thoughts – and she was.

As a result of a 1954 US Supreme Court ruling, troops enforced racial integration in a school in Little Rock, Arkansas. Two years later, Arendt's paper 'Reflections on Little Rock' objected to that desegregation; it caused outrage. How could Arendt – 'Lady Arrogant' as some called her – a great opponent of antisemitism, opponent of racial discrimination, support segregation?

The answer is that she relied on her distinction between the political and the social. She was fond of categorizations. Each time we leave home and enter the public world, we enter the social arena, she says, not thereby the political, and so not thereby one that demands equality of treatment.

If as a Jew I wish to spend my vacations only in the company of Jews, I cannot see how anyone can reasonably prevent my doing so; just as I see no reason why other resorts should not cater to a clientele that wishes not to see Jews while on a holiday. There cannot be a 'right to go into any hotel or recreation area or place of amusement,' because many of these are in the realm of the purely social where the right to free association, and therefore to discrimination, has greater validity than the principle of equality.

She opposed discrimination in public services, buses, trains, where everyone needs them to pursue their lives, yet curiously failed to include public education in those services.

Her stance made her a pariah, an outcast, in the eyes of many, especially African Americans. Arendt seems to have forgotten the importance of taking the standpoint of others and becoming conscious of their lived experience, an importance that she usually highlighted. The controversy, though, has merit; it reminds us that there is a dilemma regarding where to draw lines and when not to discriminate. We may ask: on what basis does she judge that free association in the cases she cites has 'greater validity' than equality in educational access?

To extend the dilemmas of line-drawing, what can justify the procedures for access to the courts and hence to justice that are discriminatory? Many people cannot afford to gain access whereas the wealthy can. Similar discriminations are accepted that disadvantage the already disadvantaged with regard to health, necessities for living, even the ability to vote in elections. Voter-identification laws have been introduced in certain US states and in Britain that, it is shown, adversely affect the poorest.

It was in 1963, with the publication of *Eichmann in Jerusalem: A Report on the Banality of Evil*, that Arendt's thinking led to more heated controversy. Her reference to the 'banality of evil' was justified by Eichmann's demeanour at the 1961 Israeli trial; he was a man without imagination, dutifully carrying out orders, yet murdering thousands; he would never have acted illegally, killing his superior, for example. He was mechanical, with a bureaucratic justification for his horrendous deeds. There was a thoughtlessness about it all. He showed no deep feelings; he came over as boring, superficial, banal, his one motive being to advance his personal career. That was a simple fact.

Again, Arendt became something of a pariah, now especially for the Jewish communities. They felt that she was being flippant, trivializing the brutality of the concentration camps and the horrors of antisemitism. Of course, that was not her intention. She was not exonerating Eichmann; she even agreed that he should be executed. She was drawing attention to how politics can become trapped in a scientific bureaucratic mindset, allowing no room for genuine public debate, for proper thinking. She speaks of the need for *thinking without a banister*. 'Evil comes from a failure to think.' She is at heart reminding us of the Enlightenment project, of thinking for oneself, as encountered earlier in Hume and Kant.

Creativity in thought, argues Arendt, is undermined by those philosophers whose reason shows how a state should be run and how there is an expertise for rulers to acquire. She had Plato in mind. Of course, her prescription of the need for civil engagement, for a republicanism, is also saying how a state should be run. Putting that paradoxical problem to one side, we should value the fact that she at least does highlight dangers in our liberal societies.

The dangers, she sees, result from the human sciences, economics, sociology, political science, aping the physical by mathematization and use of statistics. There is an assumed conformity in the thinking, namely that the end is wealth accumulation. Even in liberal democracies where ostensibly some political debate takes place, there is much clinging to the banister. By contrast, she valued encountering diverse opinions, having people thinking differently, shielding us from that Godlike certainty that 'reduces social relationships to those of an ant heap'. The political needs spontaneity.

Because she had the courage to speak out – and to bring to the fore disagreeable truths – Arendt had found herself something of a pariah well before the 'Banality' upset. In the dreadful times of 1930s Germany, she was cast asunder by many of the Jewish community. Although initially supporting Zionism, she became appalled at the Zionist project of taking over a portion of Palestine and, in effect, generating a statelessness for millions of Palestinians. She refused to hold fast to the banister of Zionism; she was silenced.

———

In 1940, Bertolt Brecht wrote the poem 'To those born later'. It starts, 'Truly, I live in dark times' – but Arendt hoped for at least a little illumination even in such times. The illumination is:

> less from theories and concepts than from the uncertain, flickering, and often weak light that some men and women, in their lives and works, will kindle under almost all circumstances and shed over the time-span that was given them on earth.

———

How to think like Hannah Arendt? *Attend to people's lived experiences; participate in political discourse – and cling to no banisters.*

29

Iris Murdoch: Attender

*Those who want to be saved should look at the stars
and talk philosophy, not write or go to the theatre.*

Iris Murdoch

Here is Elias Canetti, a Nobel Prize winner in Literature, writing on Iris Murdoch's 1992 work, *Metaphysics as a Guide to Morals*.

> Her book is very badly written, sloppily, like lectures that haven't been revised sufficiently. It wouldn't matter so much if she had something to say, but all she does is quote hundreds of passages and pronouncements of Wittgenstein, in that slavish way of the Wittgenstein cult, particularly in Oxford.

We may cast some doubt on Canetti's objectivity; the couple did 'have a fling' and while Murdoch wrote many admired novels, Canetti was not so prolific. Here is Murdoch, philosophizing, without any slavery to Wittgenstein:

> I am looking out of my window in an anxious and resentful state of mind, oblivious of my surroundings, brooding perhaps on some damage done to my prestige. Then suddenly I observe a hovering kestrel. In a moment everything is altered. The brooding self with its hurt vanity has disappeared.

Murdoch is 'unselfing', a focus of her philosophy. Attending to the kestrel and its beauty clears her mind of selfish concern; she takes herself 'out of her *self*. She writes of the Sovereignty of Good, alluding to Plato's ascent to objective values such as Beauty. Here is her background.

Engaging with philosophy at Oxford in the 1940s were four young women: Philippa Foot, Elizabeth Anscombe, Mary Midgley – and Iris Murdoch. The war affected how these four viewed moral philosophy. The horrors – the Nazi concentration camps; the deliberate targeting of civilians; the atomic bombs dropped on Japan – convinced them of the wrongness of the idea, then fashionable in parts of philosophical academia, that philosophy could only look at the use of moral language; no foothold existed for determining what was objectively right and wrong, good and bad.

How did these philosophically minded friends progress? Well, the distinctly upper-class Foot continued in Oxford's academia, while Midgley moved away, bringing up a family, turning to philosophy some years later in Newcastle upon Tyne – and had a big and continuing spat from 1979 with the scientist Richard Dawkins, author of *The Selfish Gene*. The formidable Anscombe, already encountered in Chapter 19, fell under the spell of Wittgenstein in Cambridge and eventually held his professorial chair.

Murdoch, as already shown through Canetti, was also much affected by Wittgenstein – she moved to Cambridge, yet managed only one brief meeting with him. Apparently, he commented, 'It is as if I have an apple tree in my garden and everyone is carting away the apples and sending them all across the world.' Well, Murdoch did send herself at least across Europe, meeting Sartre, Beauvoir and many others. She was soon writing a short introduction to Sartre's thinking.

Within the philosophy community, Murdoch is recognized as a philosopher; outside, she is primarily a well-regarded

English novelist (true, not all that well regarded by Canetti). Unlike Sartre, she sought to avoid philosophy within her novels. We should doubt whether she achieved what she sought.

'Morality does not hang free,' Murdoch tells us. That is an attack on the Logical Positivists (mentioned in Chapter 13) and on Existentialists; both groups view morality as necessarily independent of the empirical facts.

Existentialism, crudely read, tells us that values, be they moral, political or aesthetic, are freely chosen. They hang free from the empirical world; they hang free from our feelings, from reason, from any sense of duty or conscience. We may deliberate that, for example, whistle-blowing could lead to employees losing their jobs or driverless cars would endanger lives. Those facts, together with our feelings about them and our deliberations, are not enough to tell us what we *ought* to do. That generates the anguish of our freedom; we have to choose. The choosing will is footloose and empty. As an aside, we may then wonder, why bother with fact gathering and deliberation at all, if, in the end, our choices could go in any direction?

Murdoch insists – surely correctly – that, when deciding what to do, we do not typically experience ourselves in that 'random choice' way. In choosing a toothbrush, we may have no good reason or feeling for choosing this one rather than that, the blue rather than the purple, but choosing whether to break a promise, to help someone out or to mislead your electorate, is unlike that dental deliberation.

The above outline of existentialism needs qualification, at least if representing Sartre's version, for he recognized that 'facts' can be value-laden. 'Whistle-blowing' possesses an evaluative element, as does 'endangering' – as do lying, helping, promising. Reflect on the many descriptions we deploy: he is coarse, unkind, impolite; she is generous, loving, anxious; the remark was spiteful; the performance disgusting.

The evaluative expressions just used have become known as of 'thick' moral concepts, opposed to thin ones: 'good', 'bad', 'right', 'wrong'. We may reasonably feel, though, that a thick concept twins a thin evaluation with a description. 'Lovers of the thick' reject that reduction to a duo: a thick concept is meant to be unitary, in some way indivisible. That unitary position is difficult to maintain. Yes, there is thickness in that, for example, people's courage may be manifested by a wide range of actions; but we still need to acknowledge that, in the end, we offer the 'thin' evaluation of praise or blame, 'right' or 'wrong', 'good' or 'bad'. We may sometimes view the actions as foolhardy and not to be praised; we may even accept that the actions are courageous, yet insist that in that context, such courageous actions were wrong.

Whichever way the arguments flow over the thick and thin, the introduction of thick concepts harmonizes with Murdoch's call for us to *attend* – to see that nuances and differences, carrying valuations, are present in the world.

Murdoch's rejection of the footloose will is very clearly a rejection of Logical Positivism – that philosophy much identified with the Vienna Circle of the early twentieth century. The Circle's thinking was brought to prominence in Britain by A. J. (Freddie) Ayer; he regurgitated its conceptual revolution in his famous *Language, Truth and Logic* (1936). Some years later, he acknowledged the book was wrong on more or less every page. That is in contrast, by the way, to Dawkins' assured comment, much challenged by Midgley, on the continuing rightness on every page of his *The Selfish Gene*.

In line with David Hume's empiricism, the Circle claimed that statements to have sense must either be of the empirical world – open to some degree of verification or falsification through experiences – or relations of ideas, truths and falsehoods grounded in conceptual definitions. Anything else – even this Circle's claim? – was nonsense; it should be 'committed to the flames', to quote Hume. There would seem, then, to be no place for claims of morality, such as 'killing is morally wrong' – well, no place other than the flames.

The Circle's approach gave rise to the Emotive Theory: morality is nothing but expressions of 'boo' to some things, 'hurrah' to others, maybe tied with recommendations to do whatever generates the 'hurrah', resist whatever has the 'boo' factor. Disagreements in morals are akin to disagreements in taste: 'I like gin,' says A; 'I dislike gin,' says B. The moral wrongness in torturing people just for fun – or the genocides or modern slavery – surely, though, do not amount to nothing but a distaste for the activities. Attend closely, urges Murdoch; the atrocities are not atrocities just because we think they are. They are atrocities, objectively so, and merit moral outrage.

Murdoch also challenges the belief that morality necessarily is tied to action. It often is – 'by one's deeds, one shall be known' – but her emphasis is on how moral concerns can exist solely in our inner lives. Her rather verbose example, though one considered highly fertile by a few, tells of a mother-in-law (M) and a daughter (D) married to M's son. M behaves beautifully throughout the couple's stay, yet, throughout, M has a low opinion of D.

> M finds D quite a good-hearted girl, but while not exactly common yet certainly unpolished and lacking in dignity and refinement. D is inclined to be pert and familiar, insufficiently ceremonious, brusque, sometimes positively rude, always tiresomely juvenile. M does not like D's accent or the way D dresses.

M is intelligent, well intentioned, capable of self-criticism; and so, she *attends* to her attitude towards D. 'Perhaps I am old-fashioned, snobbish, jealous – my son has been taken from me.' There is a morally significant change in M's mind, though nothing has altered in her behaviour towards D or in D's behaviour. M now sees the daughter to be 'not vulgar but refreshingly simple, not undignified but spontaneous, not tiresomely juvenile but delightfully youthful'.

The mother has been engaged in 'active vision,' says Murdoch. The mother sees the daughter in a new light, yet there have been no behavioural changes. When the mother saw D under the aspect of the noisy and juvenile, her vision was constricted; maybe previously she lacked imagination and sympathy. M cares, though, about getting matters right; it was a question of sincerely attending, not a footloose change of mind.

As noted with Bertrand Russell, Keynes famously said, 'When the facts change, I change my mind; what do you do, sir?' Here, even when the facts do not change, we may change our mind, maybe rightly so – please see the Taj Mahal hat (next chapter). Murdoch, though, does not answer the question of how we can tell when the attention is sufficient or properly applied. Presumably, it is not always the latest attended revision that is right; after all, self-deception may be in play.

Murdoch has not made the moral life easy and has not made easy what she means. She calls for 'a just and loving gaze' and recognition of the need to seek the Good. As well as being taken with ideas from Plato, she sees some kinship with G. E. Moore's position that 'good' is undefinable. Her emphasis, though, is on our capacity to reflect on ourselves and see how we may grow morally through imagination and attention. Morality requires the vision of the artist rather than some scientific analysis or the adoption of a moral theory. In her first published novel, *Under the Net* (1954), the 'net' alludes to Wittgenstein's *Tractatus*; the net is one of generalization and theory that needs to be resisted – as Wittgenstein himself had come to see, thus moving him on from his *Tractatus*. One shoe does not fit all. 'All theorizing is flight.'

Attention is needed to the particulars. Inevitably, though, we shall engage with applying concepts, albeit ones that are cloudy and shifting. There is a mysticism in Murdoch, yet it has a practical utilitarian feature; she has an 'immersion in the real world' of human suffering and human need.

> When I was young I thought that freedom was the thing. Later on I felt that virtue was the thing. Now I begin to suspect that freedom and virtue are concepts which ought to be pinned into place by some more fundamental thinking about a proper quality of human life which begins at the food and shelter level.

Recall Simone Weil's 'you have never gone hungry' – a fine 'put down' to Simone de Beauvoir's priority for giving meaning to one's life (Chapter 25). It is all very well, we may add, to speak glowingly of the glory of freedom, but how does that help the dispossessed who lack the means to enjoy society's so-called freedoms?

The contingency of human needs awkwardly intrudes upon Murdoch's flights of fancy, yet that should not detract from the importance of those flights. She sometimes turns to the erotic – hence, again to Plato – to give a feel for what she has in mind.

As seen in Chapter 5, Plato thought of erotic love as a possible step towards grasping a lofty vision of the Form of Beauty, leading the soul to the Form of the Good. True, continuing in that direction is not at all easy. With erotic love there is often a possessiveness; further, bodily desires for sexual satisfaction may inhibit us from bothering to attend beyond. Murdoch is well aware of those difficulties; she had many affairs. Love can close eyes to the Other as a person rather than encouraging attention; yet when things go well ... It can – as with the kestrel – draw us away from obsession with the self.

What are we to make of Murdoch's philosophical thinking? Its appeal, I suggest, is its uneasy combination of the grubby realities of life with a yearning to grasp something beyond. That yearning, in different ways, occurs in Plato, Kierkegaard and Simone Weil. Although Murdoch writes a lot on the vision of the Good – although she warms to Plato's embrace of eroticism in attaining knowledge – she is well aware of the messy world of being human, of recognizing others and also being Other to those others. Here is Charles Arrowby from *The Sea, the Sea*:

> Then I felt too that I might take this opportunity to tie up a few loose ends, only of course loose ends can never be properly tied, one is always producing new ones. Time, like the sea, unties all knots. Judgements on people are never final, they emerge from summings up which at once suggest the need of a reconsideration. Human arrangements are nothing but loose ends and hazy reckoning, whatever art may otherwise pretend in order to console us.

We may be reminded of Kierkegaard's struggles with identity in living his life forwards; we may recall Sartre's emphasis that in death we are 'prey' to the Other – and we are next to encounter a despairing bleakness cast over all this, courtesy of Samuel Beckett.

How to think like Iris Murdoch? *Attend and unself, with eyes open to the erotic and love, to the Beautiful, the True and the Good.*

30

Samuel Beckett: *Not I*

> *I can't go on. I'll go on.*
> Samuel Beckett

We often hear of people saying that they are passing the time. With his characteristic wisdom and wit, Samuel Beckett's rejoinder is 'Time would have passed anyway.' And time passing is a central theme for Samuel Beckett in novels, plays and poetry – in poignantly portraying what it is to be human for many people, undergoing suffering, boredom and pointlessness. As with the work of any good philosopher, it makes us think. It may even pull up sharp those complacently satisfied with their lives, careless about the plight of others, casual about their own mortality – even with eyes closed to that mortality.

In one of Beckett's earliest short stories, *Dante and the Lobster*, Belacqua collects a lobster for his aunt. Once it is unwrapped, he is suddenly aware that it is alive; it moves – no wonder the fishmonger said it was fresh. The lobster had survived various adversities, a witless cat had clawed at the package, but now the aunt was about to drop it into scalding water.

> She lifted the lobster clear of the table. It had about thirty seconds to live. Well, thought Belacqua, it's a quick death, God help us all. It is not.

How are thirty seconds of being boiled felt for a lobster – and felt for how long from the lobster's perspective? Recall the question of how the bat experiences the world (Chapter 11).

Beckett's novels and plays – and his life – display an acute awareness of suffering. His principal characters are often the destitute, the exploited, the excluded, in sordid conditions, their biological malfunctions sometimes coarsely described. Beckett's philosophy in his art shows us reality through honest portrayal, a reality so different, so distant from, for example, examination of linguistic niceties over a glass of sherry in an ivory tower, even though in his writing, he paid considerable attention to using the right word and rhythm for a sentence.

In his life, distinct from his art, Beckett would help others whenever he could. He was touched, deeply affected indeed, by the suffering of humanity – and also by the suffering of non-human animals. With regard to the latter, he made gestures: he avoided eating meat whenever possible, though, living in France with its gastronomic talents, and with Beckett ever polite as a dining guest, the avoidance would often fail.

The smallness, the experience of loneliness, of helplessness, in a vast universe is found in many of Beckett's works as also in those of Kafka. Beckett exposes and emphasizes our human inadequacies, the fruitlessness of our toils, the ultimate emptiness. In line with Schopenhauer, he sees the mortal sin of Adam not in gaining forbidden knowledge, but in procreation. Beckett had no children, was uneasy in their company and apparently, off the record, had some outrage at those who insisted on having families, despite the likely bleak outcome.

Many of Beckett's characters highlight the disturbances, contingencies, accidents, of coming to be, of birth, as much as those of our eventual demise and non-being. In the 1957

Endgame, Hamm curses his father, though he tends not to think all that badly of his mother:

I know she did all she could not to have me, except of course the one thing, and if she never succeeded in getting me unstuck, it was that fate had earmarked me for less compassionate sewers.

We may think that it is better not to have been born – a thought we found expressed by Sophocles in the chapter on Schopenhauer. That thought becomes conceptually somewhat baffling, if expressed as 'It would have been better *for me* not to have been born.' How 'for me', if I was not then in existence? Could it have been better 'for me' for my birth not to have been successful or for an early painless death in infancy?

What to do, now that we are here, existing, alive, in the 'sewer of life'? Kafka's aphorism may be apposite: 'From a certain point there is no more turning back. That is the point that must be reached.' Unable to turn back, Beckett, it seems, recommends living on as painlessly as possible, ideally with art, wry humour and helping others. Of course, many turn to sex, relying on biology's erotic demands and the inevitable succumbing – Beckett was not immune – but those demands as worthy received Beckett's scepticism.

The narrator in *The Unnamable* describes his sexual encounter with Ruth – or was her name 'Edith'? – where, in his words, 'I toiled and moiled until I discharged or gave up trying or was begged by her to stop … A mug's game in my opinion … But I lent myself to it with a good enough grace, knowing it was love, for she had told me so.'

Beckett's first outstanding success on stage was the two-act *Waiting for Godot* (1953). The central characters, Vladimir and Estragon, tramps, suffer the passing of time, trying to fill it, with no end in view, no business at hand, save waiting for Godot. One critic wrote of it as 'a play in which nothing happens – twice'. Many in the audience found it too successful – in being painfully boring; many still do. Others are overwhelmed with what the play expresses, even if it be twice. Indeed, repetition often plays a part in Beckett's thinking, given his interest in time and change.

———

Beckett was born in 1906, near Dublin. Some commentators assumed he must have suffered a bleak, guilt-ridden Catholic upbringing; in fact his background was secure upper-middle-class Protestant, fitting in well with his becoming a keen cricketer of some status. He read French and Italian at Trinity College Dublin; he could have been destined for high academia but was determined to be a writer and, at first, the nearest he got was as an impoverished writer, one who lived mostly in Paris. Much of his work, including *Waiting*, was written in French, with his own translations into English.

In the 1940s, he remained in Paris, preferring 'France at war to Ireland at peace'. His activities during that time are somewhat shrouded, not least because he was active in the French Resistance, risking his own life. By the 1960s, Beckett was a recognized literary figure; in 1969, he received the Nobel Prize in Literature, a 'catastrophe', casting the international spotlight on him. He gave away all the prize money.

Ambition and the trappings of success had no appeal. He remained true to the bleakness expressed in his works. In the 1960s, the story goes, he was crossing Regent's Park, London; he was off to Lord's – yes, cricket again – and was commenting on the beautiful blue sky, the green trees, the company of his friends. One remarked, 'Yes, on a day like this, it's good to be alive.' Beckett's reply: 'Well, I wouldn't go as far as that.'

Waiting's Vladimir and Estragon, in passing the time, show their humanity; they rely on each other's presence to get by. Some commentators see the play as hinting at the hope of salvation, with Godot being God. Beckett's response is that had Godot been God, he would have named him so. The Deity as Godot to one side, in the play there is discussion of the crucifixion of Christ and the two thieves. 'One of the thieves was saved – It's a reasonable percentage,' comments Vladimir. That 50:50 chance of salvation would probably have had Beckett warming to the quip: 'I can handle the despair; it's the hope that gets to me.'

That there are divergencies of response to what may be drawn from the philosophical display on stage is itself of significance when thinking about philosophical thinking. What is expressed can be seen in different lights, understood in different ways. That may remind us of the drawing that one moment appears as duck, the next moment as rabbit.

John Wisdom, the Wittgensteinian mentioned in Chapter 27, drew attention to how words can suddenly cast a very different light. He tells of a woman trying on a hat, wondering whether it is quite suitable for the occasion. Her friend looks over and exclaims, 'The Taj Mahal'. Those words were sufficient for the woman to realize in a flash that the hat was unsuitable for what was intended.

As well as divergencies in perception, *Waiting* reminds us of the fleshy biological condition that human beings bear, with the chewing and swallowing, the vomiting – 'all oozing' as Estragon notes. In much of Beckett's philosophizing about life, we are faced with not only the dregs of humanity, but also the decay of the flesh, the bodily leakages not typically spoken of in academic philosophical tracts – the disease and disablements, disintegrations, self-disgust, that affect us all, leading to death. In the novel *Molloy*, he has Molloy reflecting on the time of life:

> now I speak of it as of something over, now as of a joke which still goes on, and it is neither, for at the same time it is over and it goes on, and is there any tense for that?

Beckett, instead of using Descartes' *cogito ergo sum*, wrote of *nescio quid ergo sum*: 'I don't know what I am then.' And that applies to many of Beckett's principal characters. In the 1972 monologue *Not I*, performed on a blackened stage, the focus is on a spotlighted Mouth that rapidly oozes words of past events and conflicts, but whose? – '… out … into this world … tiny little thing … before its time …'

Even when we have a person clearly embodied, the mystery, the fluidity, the changes, of personal identity are being highlighted. In the 1958 play *Krapp's Last Tape*, the sole character, Krapp, is about to record his current thinking. It is his sixty-ninth birthday. He goes through spools of tapes, mouthing the sound 'spool', looking for the recording when he was thirty-nine. That tape's playback has Krapp reflecting on himself as the idealistic young man of twenty with 'fire in me', but now 'burning to be gone', yet still with determination to achieve …

Krapp starts to record a new spool for his sixty-ninth, but with irritation, despair, disappointment. He speaks into the microphone how he now 'revelled in the word spool. Spoooool.' What else can he say? That's the best he has.

The mysteries of identity, of memories, of repeating them, are also in Beckett's BBC television 1965 play *Eh Joe*. Joe feels he is safe in a room, yet then a woman's voice comes to him – his voice? – challenging him, recalling his past, mocking him for trying to protect himself, as he sits there with the light on … And so on.

The above are bafflements to do with our consciousness and bring home how, once we reflect, once we think philosophically, we are at a loss to make sense of ourselves – of the persistence of the 'I' through time. David Hume told us that in formal prose, Marcel Proust's artistry showed us memory and its trigger points with fine literary style and detail – Beckett makes us feel the bafflement as painful, as a horror.

Beckett's portrayal of life contrasts with that of other philosophers. Try F. P. Ramsey, met earlier with Wittgenstein:

> I don't feel the least humble before the vastness of the heavens. The stars may be large, but they cannot think or love; and these are qualities which impress me far more than size does. I take no credit for weighing nearly seventeen stone ... In time the world will cool and everything will die; but that is a long time off still, and its present value at compound discount is almost nothing. Nor is the present less valuable because the future will be blank. Humanity, which fills the foreground of my picture, I find interesting and on the whole admirable.

That is from the privileged perspective, in 1925, of a much-admired young Cambridge don, Fellow of King's College, considered a genius with a great future ahead. He died five years later – in hospital with jaundice – at the age of twenty-six.

Contrasting with Ramsey's attitude, Beckett's is more aligned to that expressed by Schubert in both music and words – well, as expressed by Schubert when increasingly ill with syphilis, with no cure. Schubert died in 1828, aged thirty-one. In a letter, he had written:

> I feel myself to be the most unhappy and wretched creature in the world. Imagine a man whose health will never be right again, and who in sheer despair over this ever makes things worse and worse, instead of better ...

Schubert adds 'For each night, on retiring to bed, I hope I may not wake again; each morning but recalls yesterday's grief.'

In Beckett's 1980 monologue *Rockaby*, the focus is on a woman in a rocking chair with her recorded voice, rocking the words. It commences: till in the end / the day came / in the end came / close of long day… / time she stopped …

Some seek to see Beckett's thinking as a commitment to Quietism, a feeling associated with Taoism (Chapter 1). In the 1951 novel *Malone Dies*, the narrator speaks of 'beyond this tumult there is a great calm, and a great indifference, never really to be troubled by anything again'. Beckett's characters, though, nearly always have a bleakness or a bewilderment present rather than quiet contentment. Like Beckett, they tend to be stoical. In the novella *The End*, the final words are 'without the courage to end, nor the strength to go on'; in *Endgame*, we have:

Clov: Do you believe in the life to come?
Hamm: Mine was always like that.

Tony Hancock, a depressed, yet one-time highly successful British comedian in the 1960s, spoke of his gravestone having inscribed the words:

He came.
He went.
In between –
Nothing

With Beckett's 1969 play *Breath*, about twenty-five seconds long, there are no words, just the sound of a breath. And so …

And so, we circle back round to Chapter 1, harmonizing Beckett here with a suggestion for how to think like Lao Tzu: best, ultimately, to say nothing.

———

How to think like Beckett? *Reduce to bare bones, to a minimum; reduce to breath – reduce to nothing.*

EPILOGUE

Day by day she would weave at the great web,
but by night would unravel it.

Homer

Having strolled through thirty philosophers, their competing claims, magnificent musings and ways of living, did we come this far to come only this far? I think not. Leibniz spoke of a whole new world opening before him when he delved into the single concept of substance. Here, with concepts a many, puzzles and questions aplenty, many wonderful worlds are revealed; they merit musing and mulling – and, for some, eventual rejecting.

Musing and mulling, yes, rejecting even, yes, though also with some smiling. My comment above, 'I think not', reminds me of the scenario of Descartes, in a bar, being asked whether he would like a drink. His reply was, 'I think not' – and so, not thinking, he went out of existence in a flash.

Humour can often shine a light on bizarre features of a philosophical thesis or bring to prominence an underlying puzzle. The above quip about Descartes reminds us that with his understanding of the nature of the self as essentially thinking, he is committed to believing that even when we are fast asleep, if we are to exist, we must be having thoughts, experiences, though no doubt typically forgotten on waking. Is that an acceptable philosophical conclusion or is it paradoxical, suggesting something has gone wrong with his reasoning?

The motto that heads this Epilogue derives from Homer's *Odyssey*. Penelope is Queen of Ithaca, faithful wife of Odysseus. With Odysseus absent year after year, maybe dead from battle, many suitors seek to entice her into marriage. Playing for time, she insists that she cannot marry until she has finished weaving a shroud for Odysseus's deceased father; hence, she weaves by day, but by night secretly unravels the day's weaving.

Penelope shows herself to be a shrewd thinker. Her weaving and unravelling may remind us of repetitions and revisions over time. For this work, the Penelope tale can illustrate how one philosopher weaves a philosophy that is then unwoven by another later, yet then another re-weaves in the manner of the first, though with different patterns. In that way, philosophy differs from the apparent progression through scientific investigations. In philosophy, there perhaps is no clear linear development, whatever Hegel and Marx may argue. Philosophers present reality, morality and knowledge in different lights. Seeing things differently, with different perspectives both in time and space, can sometimes have considerable value. Think how different a staircase may be from the perspective of a servant and from that of lord of the manor.

———

At universities, philosophy tutorials can amount to a spotting game: spot where this or that great philosopher has gone wrong. The twentieth-century poet Stephen Spender described his Oxford philosophy tutorials as akin to obstacle races, with logical traps that students must get round. Philosophy seminars are sometimes locations for point scoring, as if good philosophical thinking must be competitive. In that spirit, some are keen to win by quickly declaring a fallacy, ideally with an awe-inspiring Latin name, in an opponent's argument. Of course, no fallacy may have been committed, but even when one has, generosity of spirit and desire for truth should lead to reflecting whether there is a good underlying point that could be expressed without fallacy, with or without Latin tag.

In this book, I have lapsed a little into (to my mind) discreditable ways of point scoring against one or other great deceased philosopher by way of demonstrating how, for example, a conclusion fails to follow or a position is self-contradictory. I have an excuse; after all, this book is meant to show how philosophers think and live. In general, though, I urge an openness to views and arguments; I also urge some humility, if one sincerely is seeking to understand. Unable to resist, I must add that sometimes a philosopher's reasoning is like bird seed that is far too hard for even the most strenuous pecking. How? What? Well, the reasoning is 'impeccable'.

All thirty figures of the chapters – well, more than thirty – are individuals of some renown, whether they be recognized as philosophers or not, whether they be generally praised or not. There is, for example, a Blue Plaque for Karl Marx round the corner here in Soho, where I am writing these words; he lived there in a small flat during the early 1850s. Tourists have it pointed out, even though the building now houses an expensive restaurant. By way of contrast to greatness, let me draw on a reflection by the novelist E. M. Forster.

Forster was associated with the Bloomsbury Group. He was also a member of Cambridge's well-known secret society, the

Apostles; other members included Bertrand Russell, Maynard Keynes, Rupert Brooke, F. P. Ramsey. Some of the group would occasionally meet round another corner here, in Kettner's, a restaurant, which, at that time, had an interesting reputation for certain encounters.

Forster wrote a biography of Goldie (Goldsworthy Lowes Dickinson), a don also of King's, Cambridge, and one of the Apostles, also indeed with a Blue Plaque, this one in Kensington, London. Forster pointed out that Goldie was neither a great philosopher nor a talented writer nor a successful reformer – he was 'never shipwrecked or in peril, never starved or penniless, never went to prison for his opinions' – yet

> his beloved, affectionate, unselfish, intelligent, witty, charming qualities ... were fused into him, making him a rare being, leaving people who met him more hopeful about other men because he had lived.

When carried away with the great thoughts of the great philosophers in these thirty chapters, that reflection on Goldie should help to put into perspective what is important in living, in a human life. What is also important is to be free from many taboos. At the time of writing, Forster could not make public the traumas Goldie suffered in trying to handle his frustrated homo-erotic desires connected with leather boots. Goldie candidly described them in his autobiography, yet it was felt unwise to publish it until forty years after his death, when a more liberated attitude to sex was within the public domain.

In some quarters, 'What's the point?' is deployed as a quick dismissal of philosophy. One point of philosophy, we may respond, is to bring out how certain activities are valuable, even if without point. What's the point of gazing at a sunrise, hiking round the Grand Canyon, attending live concerts or talking the sun down with friends, wine and gossip? A final answer may be the pleasure of the experiences, yet then we should respond, 'Well, if that is so, you'd presumably be keen on simply being injected with a drug to give you the pleasures.' To use an example derived from Plato: if pleasurable satisfactions are all that are ultimately valuable, buy some itching powder, apply the powder and then scratch, receiving that scratching satisfaction – and repeat.

Our philosophical thinking can bring home to us that there is more to life than experiences. It should also make us at least question the programmes of some philosophers and neurologists who seek to understand human life through artificial intelligence or more detailed knowledge of human neurology. Let us reflect a little.

Is the idea that our every thought, every twinkle of the eye, every doubt, every stroke of the keyboard, every visual impression of these words, every reference to Cavafy's 'Ithaka', are all to be fully explained by reference to neurological changes within? If so, then are we not betting on Miss Fortuna – good luck – being radically on our side? After all, what are the chances of whimsical-like electrical impulses and chemical signals being so patterned that, when we engage with shapes on paper and sounds from mouths, we encounter things that 'make sense' – assertions that are true, deductions that are valid, reasoning that is good? Of course, this questioning would also be at the mercy of Miss Fortuna.

Our thirty philosophers all sought the truth, but some saw the way forward more as a scientific enterprise, more formal, whereas others were more impressionistic. Some sought an objective 'God's-eye' view; others settled for what was from 'within'. An expressive example of a related divergence comes again from Wittgenstein. Here, in 1930, he is talking to Maurice O'Connor Drury, close friend, one-time student – Drury became resident psychiatrist in a Dublin hospital:

> I was walking about in Cambridge and passed a bookshop, and in the window were portraits of Russell, Freud and Einstein. A little further on, in a music shop, I saw portraits of Beethoven, Schubert and Chopin. Comparing these portraits I felt intensely the terrible degeneration that had come over the human spirit in the course of only a hundred years.

An extension of our philosophical appreciation can occur through music, through song, through opera – and through the other arts. To put it paradoxically, philosophical thinking need not be confined to thinking. In Schubert's *Winterreise*, the music and words describe the hurdy-gurdy man who, in the snow, plays as best he can. Maybe with a Quietism, maybe with Beckett's resignation, maybe in accord with Tao, he lets 'everything go on as it will, although no one wants to listen; his hurdy-gurdy never stops'.

In the Prologue, Cavafy's 'Ithaka' enjoins us always to keep Ithaka in mind. Later on, the poem urges 'do not hurry the voyage at all / It is better to let it last for many years'. In our philosophizing, Ithaka may remain elusive – yet throughout our voyaging, whatever we are doing, thinking, questing, from the mundane to the magnificent, merits philosophizing for, to return to that ancient saw linked to Nietzsche (Chapter 20), certainly where philosophy is concerned:

All things conspire.

DATES OF THE PHILOSOPHERS

including some additional –
those with noteworthy mentions

Lao Tzu	c.6th century (?) BC
Sappho	c.630–570 BC
Parmenides	c.515–460 BC
Zeno of Elea	c.495–430 BC
Socrates	c.469–399 BC
Plato	c.427–347 BC
Aristotle	384–322 BC
Epicurus	341–270 BC
Lucretius	c.99–55 BC
Avicenna	980–1037
René Descartes	1596–1650
Elisabeth, Princess of Bohemia	1618–80
Christina, Queen of Sweden	1626–89
Baruch Spinoza	1632–77
Nicolas Malebranche	1638–1715
Gottfried Wilhelm Leibniz	1646–1716
George Berkeley	1685–1753
David Hume	1711–76
Immanuel Kant	1724–1804
Georg Wilhelm Friedrich Hegel	1770–1831
Arthur Schopenhauer	1788–1860
John Stuart Mill	1806–73
Søren Kierkegaard	1813–55
Karl Marx	1818–83

Lewis Carroll	1832–98
Friedrich Nietzsche	1844–1900
Bertrand Russell	1872–1970
G. E. Moore	1873–1958
Martin Heidegger	1889–1976
Jean-Paul Sartre	1905–80
Simone Weil	1909–43
Simone de Beauvoir	1908–86
Ludwig Wittgenstein	1889–1951
Hannah Arendt	1906–75
Iris Murdoch	1919–99
Samuel Beckett	1906–89

NOTES, REFERENCES AND READINGS

Many of the philosophers' key works are now freely available online. Most of the quotations used above can be found through internet searches. For each philosopher, I offer a few suggestions for encountering their lives, thinking and critical commentaries. Because the information is readily available, I have not cluttered the pages with unnecessary details of publishers, page references and the like, so beloved of academia in recent decades.

PROLOGUE

For a collection of important writings from many of the philosophers, there is John Cottingham, ed., *Western Philosophy: An Anthology*, 2nd edn (2007). For film, the BBC television series with Bryan Magee in discussion with the then current philosophers is well worth watching. It is available on YouTube and in print as *The Great Philosophers* (1987). Distinctive takes on certain philosophers can be found in Raymond Geuss, *Changing the Subject: Philosophy from Socrates to Adorno* (2017) and Jonathan Reé, *Philosophical Tales* (1987).

1. LAO TZU

I particularly recommend an enjoyable and quirky introduction by a logician, Raymond M. Smullyan, *The Tao is Silent* (1977). A more standard introduction is Chung-yuan Chang, *Creativity and Taoism* (1963). The *Tao Te Ching* is available in different translations, new and old, e.g., by Paul Carus (1913) – fertile ground for diverse interpretations.

2. SAPPHO

Various creative translations are available, some by poets, keen to build on Sappho's fragments, some by classicists keen to secure putative original meanings. Anne Carson highlighted the 'bittersweet' and has a distinctive and much-admired translation of Sappho in her *If Not, Winter: Fragments of Sappho* (2002).

3. ZENO OF ELEA WITH PARMENIDES

A definitive collection of Presocratic writings is G. S. Kirk, J. E. Raven, M. Schofield, eds, *The Presocratic Philosophers: A Critical History with a Selection of Texts*, 2nd edn (1983). For papers on the paradoxes, see Wesley Salmon, ed., *Zeno's Paradoxes* (1970). For paradoxes more generally, there is my *This Sentence is False: An Introduction to Philosophical Paradoxes* (2010).

4. SOCRATES

Dialogues that provide a good introduction together with Socrates' *Apology* are *Euthyphro, Crito, Phaedo*, combined under titles such as *The Last Days of Socrates*, e.g., Penguin Classic (2003). For Socrates' life, try Armand D'Angour's approach in *Socrates in Love: The Making of a Philosopher* (2020).

5. PLATO

A single volume is John M. Cooper, ed., *The Complete Works of Plato* (1997). Plato's *Symposium* (see Frisbee Sheffield and M. C. Howatson edition, 2008) may be a good way into his thinking. A major work is Plato's *Republic*, e.g., translated by H. D. Lee, introduced by Melissa Lane, Penguin Classic (2007).

Bernard Williams has a short introduction, *Plato: The Invention of Philosophy* (1998), also in his *The Sense of the Past* (2006).

6. ARISTOTLE

There are two hefty hard-going volumes, edited by Jonathan Barnes, *The Complete Works of Aristotle* (1984). Probably the best entrance to Aristotle directly is his ethics; try Robert C. Bartlett and Susan D. Collins, *The Nicomachean Ethics* (2011). An introduction orientated to 'how to live' is Edith Hall, *Aristotle's Way: How Ancient Wisdom Can Change Your Life* (2018). For 'lè': Michael Nylan, *The Chinese Pleasure Book* (2018).

7. EPICURUS WITH LUCRETIUS

Epicurus sets out his philosophy in his *Letter to Menoeceus* and Lucretius in his *On the Nature of Things*. For comparisons and contrasts regarding Epicureanism, Stoicism and others, try A. G. Long, *Death and Immortality in Ancient Philosophy* (2019) and the very detailed work by Martha Nussbaum, *The Therapy of Desire, Theory and Practice in Hellenistic Ethics* (1996).

8. AVICENNA

Avicenna's *Compendium on the Soul* is readily available in various translations, though many of his works in English translation are still not easy to find at reasonable prices. For a clear introductory survey, see Jon McGinnis (2010). A very good collection on Avicenna's life and works is Peter Adamson, ed., *Interpreting Avicenna* (2013).

9. RENÉ DESCARTES

A 'must-read' is his *Meditations on First Philosophy*. I recommend the John Cottingham 2016 translation and edition; it contains Descartes' replies to some then objections. For a speculative work on Descartes' life as spy, there is A. C. Grayling, *Descartes, the Biography* (2005). For a careful analysis of Descartes' philosophy, try Bernard Williams, *Descartes: The Project of Pure Enquiry* (1978).

10. BARUCH SPINOZA

The works by Steven Nadler provide excellent introductions: *Think Least of Death: Spinoza on How to Live and How to Die* (2020) and *Spinoza's Heresy* (2000). For Spinoza direct, try Edwin Curley, ed., *A Spinoza Reader: The Ethics and Other Works* (1994). Please see below regarding a link with Leibniz. An excellent work, setting Spinoza in context, is Susan James, *Spinoza on Philosophy, Religion, and Politics: The Theologico-Political Treatise* (2012).

11. GOTTFRIED WILHELM LEIBNIZ

For selections, including *Monadology*, see G. H. R. Parkinson, ed., *Leibniz's Philosophical Writings* (1973). For a difference in lifestyles, the following is enjoyable: Matthew Stewart, *The Courtier and the Heretic: Leibniz, Spinoza, and the Fate of God in the Modern World* (2006). An introduction to Leibniz's philosophy is Richard T. W. Arthur, *Leibniz* (2014). Thomas Nagel made prominent 'bat-like' questions. The important work regarding possible worlds by Saul Kripke is his 1970s lectures series, published as *Naming and Necessity* (1980) and highly readable.

12. GEORGE BERKELEY

Berkeley's *Three Dialogues* is a good beginning; it is in the collection edited, with notes, by Desmond M. Clarke, *Berkeley: Philosophical Writings* (2009). Regarding Berkeley's life, there is Tom Jones, *George Berkeley: A Philosophical Life* (2021). John Locke's work to which Berkeley and others responded is his *An Essay Concerning Human Understanding*, e.g., Roger Woolhouse edition (1997).

13. DAVID HUME

Most readable by Hume are his essays, such as 'On Suicide', 'On Miracles', 'Of Tragedy'. See also Hume's very brief and touching autobiography *My Own Life*. Hume's attempt to make his *Treatise* more accessible is his *An Enquiry Concerning Human Understanding* – e.g, the edition by Stephen Buckle (2007). The classic biography, updated in 1980, is E. C. Mossner, *The Life of David Hume*. An interesting read is Dennis Rasmussen, *The Infidel and the Professor: David Hume, Adam Smith, and the Friendship that Shaped Modern Thought* (2017). For the Vienna Circle, please see David Edmunds with his enjoyable *The Murder of Professor Schlick: The Rise and Fall of the Vienna Circle* (2020).

14. IMMANUEL KANT

The Critiques are very hard going, but need to be faced. Try the Cambridge editions: Guyer and Wood, *Critique of Pure Reason* (1998) and, for the ethics, Christine Korsgaard's, *Kant: Groundwork of the Metaphysics of Morals* (2012). Roger Scruton's introduction to Kant is very readable; it has been republished in *German Philosophers: Kant, Hegel, Schopenhauer, Nietzsche* (2001).

15. ARTHUR SCHOPENHAUER

Schopenhauer's more popular essays are found in his *Parerga and Paralipomena: Short Philosophical Essays II* – see the

Cambridge edition (2016), edited by Christopher Janaway – and try Janaway's introduction to Schopenhauer in the *German Philosophers* collection, cited in Kant above. A more sustained work is Bryan Magee's expanded, *The Philosophy of Schopenhauer* (1997).

16. JOHN STUART MILL

To gain a measure of the man, see his *Autobiography*. That apart, his *On Liberty*, *Utilitarianism* and *The Subjection of Women*, are the obvious first readings, found in various collections. For his life in context, there is Richard Reeves, *John Stuart Mill: Victorian Firebrand* (2015) and for his socialism, Helen McCabe, *John Stuart Mill: Socialist* (2021).

17. SØREN KIERKEGAARD

For works, C. Stephen Evans, ed., *Fear and Trembling* (2006), with Evans' introduction, is a good place to start. A good biography, though written in something of a speculative style – 'Kierkegaard's fellow passengers look as wretched as he feels' – is by Clare Carlisle, *Philosopher of the Heart: The Restless Life of Søren Kierkegaard* (2020).

18. KARL MARX WITH GEORG WILHELM FRIEDRICH HEGEL

Francis Wheen, *Karl Marx* (1999), is a good accessible starting point. For digging more directly, try first Peter Lamb, *Marx and Engels' Communist Manifesto: A Reader's Guide* (2015) with the *Manifesto* that Lamb uses (Yale 2012). For Hegel, Peter Singer's introduction is a good start in the collection on *German Philosophers* cited in Kant above. Singer also introduces Marx in his *Marx: A Very Short Introduction*, 2nd edn (2018).

19. LEWIS CARROLL (CHARLES DODGSON)

The best collection of the two Alice books, with commentary regarding philosophy and historical figures, is Martin Gardner, ed., *The Annotated Alice: The Definitive Edition* (2000). For Carroll's life, try Donald Thomas, *Lewis Carroll: A Portrait with Background* (1996). I recommend also the 2016 BBC documentary, *The Secret Life of Lewis Carroll*, now available on YouTube.

20. FRIEDRICH NIETZSCHE

To step into Nietzsche, try his *Beyond Good and Evil: Prelude to a Philosophy of the Future* via the Rolf-Peter Horstmann edition (2002). Dipping into any of his works can give a good flavour of his style and many provocations worthy of reflection. For overall review, see Michael Tanner in *German Philosophers*, noted in Kant above. For closer detail, there is Maudemarie Clark, *Nietzsche on Truth and Philosophy* (1990).

21. BERTRAND RUSSELL

A classic is Russell's *The Problems of Philosophy* (1912). To appreciate the wide breadth of Russell's work, from the popular to the scholarly, there is Egner and Denonn, eds, *The Basic Writings of Bertrand Russell* (2009). Ray Monk has a two-volume detailed biography: *Bertrand Russell: The Spirit of Solitude 1872–1921* and *Bertrand Russell: 1921–1970, the Ghost of Madness* (1996). It is worth watching the elderly Russell in the BBC *Bertrand Russell, Face to Face* interview with John Freeman, now available on YouTube.

22. G. E. MOORE

For Moore's papers, there is Thomas Baldwin, *G. E. Moore: Selected Writings* (1993). Moore's *Principia Ethica* (1903) is readily available online. For the influence on Bloomsbury, see John Maynard

Keynes, 'My Early Beliefs' in *Two Memoirs* (1949) and Paul Levy, *G. E. Moore and the Cambridge Apostles* (1979). Those times as background appear in various documentaries, now on YouTube, such as those on E. M. Forster and Virginia Woolf; for example, *E. M. Forster*, BBC Obituary Programme (1970).

23. MARTIN HEIDEGGER

It is probably better to read an introduction to Heidegger before going to the original; hence, Paul Gorner, *Heidegger's Being and Time* (2007), or, more generally, Mark Wrathall, *How to Read Heidegger* (2005). The standard translation of *Being and Time* is by John Macquarrie and Edward Robinson (1962). Hubert L. Dreyfus makes Heidegger intelligible in his *Being in the World: Commentary on Heidegger's Being and Time, Division 1* (1991). The speculation about the Hitler/Wittgenstein interaction when they were schoolboys is in Kimberley Cornish, *The Jew of Linz* (1998).

24. JEAN-PAUL SARTRE

Sartre's existentialism comes over well in his novel *La Nausée* (1938) translated by Robert Baldick in Penguin's edition, *Nausea* (1963). His *Existentialism and Humanism* is short and readable, available in various editions, though, in part, subsequently repudiated. His major work, *Being and Nothingness*, was first translated by Hazel E. Barnes; a recent translation is Sarah Richmond's (2020). Iris Murdoch's first book – and the first book in English on Sartre – is *Sartre: Romantic Rationalist* (1953).

25. SIMONE WEIL

A good collection of her writings is served by Siân Miles, *Simone Weil, An Anthology* (1986). A light introduction is Robert Zaretsky, *The Subversive Simone Weil* (2021). A deeper and more difficult work is Peter Winch, *Simone Weil, The Just*

Balance (2008). The chapter refers to John Rawls, *A Theory of Justice* (1971); a very different, influential and provocative approach from that of Rawls and of Weil is Robert Nozick, *Anarchy, State and Utopia* (1974).

26. SIMONE DE BEAUVOIR

A novel that reflects Beauvoir's relationship with Sartre and their thinking is *She Came To Stay* (1949). Beauvoir's famous non-fiction work is *The Second Sex* (1949), but many subsequent works are valuable; for example, her *Old Age* (1972). For a review of her work, please see Karen Vintges, *Philosophy as Passion: The Thinking of Simone de Beauvoir* (1996). For her life, there is Kate Kirkpatrick, *Becoming Beauvoir: A Life* (2020).

27. LUDWIG WITTGENSTEIN

As introduction to the later Wittgenstein is his *The Blue and Brown Books* (1960). For greater flavour and breadth, do at least dip into *Philosophical Investigations* (1953) and try Arif Ahmed's guide (2010) that relates it to the *Tractatus*. For notes on life and meaning, try *Culture and Value* (1984); 'How small a thought it takes to fill a whole life!', from those notes, is used in Steve Reich's speech melody *Proverb* (1995). For Wittgenstein's life, there is the award-winning Ray Monk, *Ludwig Wittgenstein: The Duty of Genius* (1990) and the BBC Horizon film, *Wittgenstein: A Wonderful Life* (1989), now available on YouTube, as is *Wittgenstein's Poker: Lost and Found in Cambridge* (2009). There is a comprehensive and readable survey of Ramsey's works and life in Cheryl Misak's *Frank Ramsey: A Sheer Excess of Powers* (2020).

28. HANNAH ARENDT

A good collection is Peter Baehr, ed., *The Portable Hannah Arendt* (2000). Also readily available is Arendt's *Eichmann in Jerusalem: A Report on the Banality of Evil* (1958). For articles discussing her work, please see D. R. Villa, ed., *The Cambridge Companion to Hannah Arendt* (2000) and Patrick Hayden, ed., *Hannah Arendt: Key Concepts* (2014). For Machiavelli, see Quentin Skinner's short introduction, 2nd edn (2019).

29. IRIS MURDOCH

For the four women philosophers, lives and impact, try Cumhaill and Wiseman, *Metaphysical Animals: How Four Women Brought Philosophy Back to Life* (2022). For Murdoch directly, try *The Sovereignty of Good* (1970). Her *The Sea, the Sea* (1978) won the Booker Prize and shows her as novelist and philosopher. Peter Conradi has a biography of her and is impressed by her philosophy in *Iris Murdoch: A Life* (2001). For essays examining her work, please see Justin Broackes, ed., *Iris Murdoch: Philosopher* (2012).

30. SAMUEL BECKETT

If unfamiliar with Beckett, try first the short plays such as *Play* (1963) and *Rockaby* (1980), both available on YouTube, and a novella such as *Company* (1980). For Ramsey's contrasting view on life, see Cheryl Misak, cited in the Wittgenstein notes above. John Calder was Beckett's publisher and friend; I recommend his *The Philosophy of Beckett* (2001). An enjoyable review of Beckett, with photographs of him and some of his performances, is Enoch Brater, *Why Beckett* (1989). Elements from Beckett's *The Unnamable* are used in the intriguing third movement of Luciano Berio's *Sinfonia* (1969).

EPILOGUE

For Goldie, there is E. M. Forster, *Goldsworthy Lowes Dickinson* (1934). Dennis Proctor is editor of *The Autobiography of G. Lowes Dickinson* (1973). The Drury papers on Wittgenstein are in Rush

Rhees, ed., *Ludwig Wittgenstein: Personal Recollections* (1981). For papers on philosophy and humour, please see Laurence Goldstein, ed., 'Humor', *The Monist*, Vol. 88.1 (2005). For debates on understanding the mind as nothing but neurology, see M. Bennett, D. Dennett and P. Hacker, *Neuroscience and Philosophy: Brain, Mind, and Language* (2007). I promised to thank Nick Smedley for transmission of the 'impeccable' quip.

ACKNOWLEDGEMENTS

With so many years in the philosophy world, the list would be exceptionally long of all who have influenced me, for better, for worse. Of course, I am particularly indebted to all those whom I have read on the above – my apologies to them all for not naming the numerous names, well, for not naming the numerous authors. I can rightly mention institutions – much fewer in number – that have been so important philosophically for me, from the BBC – when it dared to have 'Brains Trust' talks and erudition on its main (and then only) television channel and on its radio's Third Programme – to University College London, King's College, Cambridge and The Open University, the latter being especially valuable because of its wonderfully comprehensive online library.

On that practical level, considerable help has been courtesy of the Athenaeum Library and staff, particularly Laura Doran and her setting off to and fro the London Library. Many thanks, too, to Tomasz Hoskins, Jonathan Pegg, Nick Fawcett and Sarah Jones for getting this book a-going and improving.

Over many years, a philosopher and friend has been distinctively influential: Ardon Lyon. He has had nothing directly to do with this work, but I dare say that all my many mistakes can, unfairly, be traced back to dear lovable, philosophical Ardon and his 'Oh, really?'s (recall Keynes on Moore, Chapter 22). Of course, what one dares to say does not guarantee truth.

IN MEMORY

In the midst of writing this book, there occurred the state funeral of Queen Elizabeth II, with millions of people apparently grieving, certainly millions declaring gratitude for how she reigned and, it seems, approving of her highly privileged life courtesy of sheer luck and associated gross inequalities. Hundreds of thousands queued for many hours so that they could walk by the draped coffin in the Great Hall of the Palace of Westminster. I neither grieved, nor was particularly grateful, nor queued, though I recognized the historical relevance and personal distress for her family.

In the midst of writing this book, around the same time as the Queen's demise, there occurred the death of Roger Coe, an uncle, and Andrew Harvey, a brother-in-law. Their lives and deaths hit no headlines. They were mourned by those who knew them.

The lives of Andrew and Roger were far removed from the lives of the well-off in Britain, though, of course, they suffered neither the desperation of starvation nor the fear of bombardments that haunt millions of people throughout the world. Andrew lived with a phenomenal memory, with books at home, with books in town at Carlisle's wonderful Bookcase shop. Ever ready to discuss matters politico-religious – especially Trotsky – he stimulated my thinking as he did readers of his newspaper contributions. Roger, in contrast, was not bookish, but stimulating through common sense and rural appreciations – 'the salt of the earth' comes to mind. He worked on Northamptonshire boot-and-shoe factory lines; his enjoyments were those of village life: the fields, the lakes, the local; cricket, football, gardening,

Although with very different interests, Andrew and Roger were both concerned about others, always ready to help out, to do their best. Their lives are as worthy of celebration as Queen Elizabeth's radically easier life of international fame and prestige. Indeed, their lives are, I suggest, worthy of far greater respect – as are the lives of millions and millions of others who never hit the headlines.

NAME INDEX

Chapter entries are in **bold**.

SUBJECT INDEX

Chapter entries, in **bold**, are given when the subject arises *passim*.